Kate M. Cleary

Susanne K. George

Kate M. Cleary:

A Literary Biography with Selected Works

University of Nebraska Press
Lincoln & London

♾ The paper in this book meets the minimum
requirements of American National Standard for
Information Sciences—Permanence of Paper for
Printed Library Materials, ANSI Z39.48-1984.

Library of Congress Cataloging-in-Publication Data

George, Susanne K. (Susanne Kathryn), 1947–
Kate M. Cleary: a literary biography with selected
works / Susanne K. George.
p.   cm.
Includes bibliographical references (p.   ) and
index.
ISBN 0-8032-2164-9 (cl: alk. paper)
1. Cleary, Kate M. 2. Women and literature—
United States—History—19th century.
3. Authors, American—19th century—Biography.
4. West (U.S.)—Literary collections.
5. Nebraska—Literary collections. 6. Women—
Nebraska—Biography. I. Cleary, Kate M.
II. Title.
PS1299.C87Z68   1997
818′.409
[B]—DC20   96-41034
                                            CIP

Text set in New Caledonia. Designed by
Stephen Canine.

Contents

Illustrations

Preface

Much has been written about the impact of literature in shaping the attitudes about America of the American public and of the people of the world. The theories of Frederick Turner and Michel-Guillaume-Jean de Crèvecoeur as well as the novels of James Fenimore Cooper, Willa Cather, Owen Wister, O. E. Rolvaag, and Hamlin Garland have succeeded in establishing or perpetuating the myths of the American West as either a new Eden or a hostile environment where pioneers struggled wearily and bitterly to survive, often losing their homesteads, their family members, and their belief in mankind or in God. Interest in women's diaries, journals, and letters has caused us to reevaluate such myths and to reconsider women's roles in American history. These writings are important documents in helping scholars re-view our heritage from a more balanced perspective. This book recovers more texts, both personal and fictional, that continue this reevaluation of American history and rethinking of the American literary canon.

Reclaiming Kate McPhelim Cleary's life and works for this book has involved personal intuition, intensive primary and secondary research, and a little Irish luck. While perusing the 1891 volume of *St. Nicholas* magazines, I came across "Lost in a Cornfield," a children's story by Cleary set in Bubble, Nebraska. That led me to *The Nebraska of Kate McPhelim Cleary*, edited by Cleary's son James, which in turn put me in contact with her grandchildren. The family offered to share with me their collections of original photographs, letters, story clippings, scrapbooks, and unpublished manuscripts—if I was interested. Eureka!

Throughout Cleary's life, her husband, Michael, collected clippings of her published works, book reviews, and memorabilia in a series of scrapbooks, recorded their daily lives in photographs, and saved letters. These materials, important cultural history in themselves, have provided the backbone for this book. Yet, as valuable as these sources were to me, they posed several problems. Few of the letters are dated, nor are the dates or publishers of the clippings noted, and although the family had a general sense of Cleary's life, many important gaps in their knowledge existed. To fill in these biographical and bibliographical voids, I reviewed literally hundreds of microfilms of newspapers and magazines, searched historical archives in Nebraska and Illinois, examined county, court, and institution records, and consulted the writings of turn-of-the-century experts as well as modern scholars to come up with what I consider an accurate view not only of Cleary's life but of her times.

In compiling this biography of and selected works by Cleary, I had to make several choices. Believing that Cleary's life and her works inextricably complement one another, I decided not to simply write a biography or collect her works with a brief biographical and critical preface—although a volume could have been compiled using either option. Because Cleary is basically unknown and the biographical and bibliographical material are virtually inaccessible, I believed that each part was crucial to the work as a whole. Without her writings, Cleary would be simply another nineteenth-century woman, albeit a compelling one. And without the literary biography, the historical, cultural, and autobiographical elements of her writings would not be available to ensure a full reading of her texts. In addition, the biography offered me a good opportunity to incorporate selections from those of her writings that have more autobiographical, historical, or cultural claims than literary merit, leaving the selected works section to highlight some of the best examples of her writing. Cleary's life exemplifies the struggle of the nineteenth-century woman to stand strong against all personal, physical, and social odds, while her writings add valuable new works to the American literary canon. Although this is a rather unorthodox combination, I believe the balance works.

Editing choices, too, had to be made. First, I decided to excerpt portions of letters and writings in the biography rather than include the complete texts there because of the quantity of material from which I had to choose. Next, I had to arrange the predominantly undated letters into a coherent sequence so that I could incorporate them into their appropriate locations in the biography. Fortunately, Cleary's excellent writing skills made editing unnecessary. Except for a few silently corrected typographical errors, excerpts from Cleary's letters, some of which were handwritten, others typed, and a few transcribed from the original by family members, are published as she wrote them. Several of the stories were collected for reprinting by Cleary's son James, who did some minor editing; whenever possible, I have reprinted the originally published versions, and I have made only minor corrections, such as supplying missing periods and quotation marks.

Documenting my sources became cumbersome. Because each historical, literary, and biographical fact is supported by primary or secondary research, often one sentence would bear three or four citations. The notes became intrusive and grew almost as long as the main text. To remedy this, I decided to incorporate only essential sources and to consign the rest to the works cited section and to general explanations in the notes.

My bibliography of Cleary's works created the greatest challenge for me and consumed the most time. I believe it is one of the most important aspects of this project, for it will make her works accessible to the public for the first time. Cleary wrote voluminously for popular magazines and newspapers throughout her life, using various pseudonyms, but I chose to begin her bibliography in 1884, the year she married, because that is when her most important works began to appear. I also decided to attempt to document predominantly her prose because of the sheer volume of her poetry. Then I painstakingly combed the *Chicago Tribune,* the *Chicago Daily News,* the *Omaha World-Herald,* the *Nebraska State Journal,* and about two dozen periodicals from 1884 to 1906 to document the publishers and dates of her writings. While doing so, I found several dozen Cleary works that were unknown to her family. I arranged the writings in chronological order by year, adding as much data as I could find. Some entries are incomplete, with publishers, dates, page numbers, or all information except the name of the story missing. Often I had to use my best judgment in assigning approximate dates by comparing works to others written during a time period.

Such research requires assistance, and I have been generously supported by many institutions and individuals. The Nebraska Humanities Council, the Center for Great Plains Studies, the University of Nebraska at Kearney, and the UNK Research Services Council have provided grants and fellowships to fund assistantships, travel expenses, and microfilm and copying costs, as well as funds to allow me time during the summer to concentrate on my research.

I am indebted to many friends, both old and new. Jean Keezer-Clayton and Nancy Johnson, who spent months reading microfilm to discover stories about the West and then meticulously copied and triple indexed them, continued their interest in my work through its many stages. Their scholarly and emotional support never flagged, even after we realized the enormity of the task. Alta Fread, the intrepid force behind the UNK Inter-Library Loan Office, managed to keep track of the constant stream of microfilms coming and going from a myriad of sources and also ferreted out obscure books and magazines for me. And my neighbor, Karen Nixon, who "held down the fort" for me during my various absences, encouraged me when she knew I'd rather be riding my horses. Without the help of these friends, this book could not have been written.

Collecting primary data to reconstruct Cleary's life involved much collaboration. Kathryn Harris of the Illinois State Historical Society; Phil Costello of the Cook County Court; Arlene Porter, Roma Posey, Frances Stradley, and other residents of Hubbell, Nebraska; Jackie Williamson and Virginia Priefert of the Thayer County Historical Society; and John Thomas, Joan Falcone, Mark and Alice Peattie, and Noel Peattie—all came to my aid in valuable ways.

Kenneth Nikels, Charles Peek, Robert Luscher, Michael Herbison, and Wayne Briner, all colleagues at the University of Nebraska at Kearney, also provided assistance. Thanks, too, go to my loving and ever supportive family and friends, who have endured five years of my constant preoccupation with "Kate" and Hubbell, Nebraska.

But it is to the grandchildren of Kate and Michael Cleary that I owe my deepest and sincerest gratitude. They openly and enthusiastically shared family treasures with me, copying pages and pages of materials when I could not travel to their homes. Marguerite Cleary Remien of Chicago and Aileen Bullard Droege of Plymouth, Massachusetts, spent a week in Nebraska bringing me additional documents and pilgrimaging with me to Hubbell. Marguerite invited me to her home for a week, and she and her sisters, Jeanne Cleary Goessling and Mary Evelyn Cleary Sundlof, shuttled me to libraries and historical societies, helped me search *more* microfilm for their grandmother's works, gave me the grand tour of historical Chicago, and took me to hear the Chicago Symphony. In addition, they patiently read drafts of the biography, untangling family relationships, providing crucial insights, and offering sound editing advice. One of my favorite memories is of the four of us lined up on microfilm readers at a Chicago archive, laughing and sharing our finds (in an otherwise empty room), to the chagrin of an attendant used to his solitude. I experienced firsthand the Cleary sense of humor and joie de vivre. No writer could ask for a more cooperative or compassionate "family."

Biography of
Kate McPhelim Cleary

1

From New Brunswick to Nebraska: 1863–1891

A soft evening breeze sifted through the lace curtains of the south window by Kate's writing desk in the parlor of her two-story Victorian home. The leaves of the houseplant on the end table in front of the window and the pages of the newspapers randomly piled on the desk beside her typewriter rustled soothingly as she tilted back in her chair, closed her eyes, and escaped to the imaginary world of her fiction. Most people in the newly established frontier town of Hubbell, Nebraska, were in bed, but the light in the Cleary house burned on into the night, and the sound of Kate's typewriter drifted out to the board sidewalk in front of her home. Kate M. Cleary, wife, mother, and writer, was at work. It was a familiar task, for throughout her life she had helped support her loved ones through her writing.

Born in Richibucto, New Brunswick, on 22 August 1863, Kate Theressa McPhelim, blue-eyed and black-haired, enjoyed a comfortable early childhood. Kate's mother, Margaret Kelly McPhelim, was born in Ireland but moved to Canada with her mother when her father, a physician, died. There, Margaret met Kate's father, James McPhelim, an immigrant Irishman educated at the University of Louvaine. A prominent pioneer in the Canadian timber and shipping business and high sheriff of Kent County, McPhelim was known for his courage and wit.[1] They married in 1856, and Margaret bore four children, Edward Joseph, Catherine Chrystal (who died in infancy), Kate Theressa, and Francis Albert.

Cleary later described the cold beauty of her Canadian childhood home in her essay "Midnight Mass under Three Flags." The St. Lawrence River, she recalled, "frozen in its winter bondage," served as a broad highway for travelers, with bonfires signaling where the ice was unsafe. "The sleighs—their number continually increased by fresh arrivals from solitary farms at either side of the river—made a long procession." Cleary, especially intrigued by the skaters, remembered "a girl hand in hand with her lover," "an Indian woman with her papoose strapped to her back," and "sinewy Indians, scarlet-sashed Canadians, trappers, hunters, lumbermen from camps up the river, men of the sea" flashing by. Fantastic images, "the occasional howl of a wild beast," "snatches of songs in French and English," and "the steady ring of steel" stirred in her memory, too.[2]

James McPhelim died suddenly in 1865 at age forty-six. The family remained in Canada, with Kate attending the Sacred Heart Convent in St. John, where she studied the classics and learned the arts of writing and painting. Sometime in the 1860s or 1870s, financial difficulties forced Kate's mother to return temporarily to Ireland with her three children to live with relatives at Ivy Lodge and at The Mall, Templemore. Kate climbed the crumbling ruins of Castle Fogarty, the ancestral home nearby.

Eventually, dwindling resources forced Mrs. McPhelim and her children to emigrate to America, settling in the late 1870s in Philadelphia, where the family struggled to survive. Somehow, despite the family's financial difficulties, Kate's brother Edward graduated with honors in 1879 from St. Joseph's College near Memramcook, New Brunswick, and for a time considered entering the priesthood but ultimately chose journalism instead. Fourteen when she published her first poems, Kate began selling them by the dozen to supplement the family income. The rhymes and rhythms of poetry came naturally to Kate; her mother, using the pen names Daisy or Mrs. M. M. M., wrote regularly, often giving poems to her children as gifts during their unsettled times. On Kate's fourteenth birthday, her mother presented her with a poem that lovingly explained,

> *Accept this little ring, dear,*
> *I've worn it many years;*

Some that were bright and sunny
And others dimm'd with tears.
'Twill tell you how your mother
Loves her own darling pet
And thus we'll love each other
Until life's sun shall set.[3]

Kate's early poetry, with its lilting iambic trimeter and tetrameter rhythms and its variable rhyme schemes, reflects her mother's influence. These poems, many of them published in *Saturday Night*, a weekly family literary periodical, are sentimental poems of love and loss, and nearly all of them contain rich descriptions of nature.

For a while, Kate quit writing because profits from her paintings and sketches brought better income to the family. But her hiatus must have been a short one because in 1878, when she was fifteen, *Saturday Night* published her first short story, "Only Jerry." Using the pseudonym K. Temple More, after the name of her mother's home in Ireland, Kate turned her full attention to fiction and poetry. Typical of the popular literature of the time, Kate's early stories are conventionally sentimental with romantic themes and plots; however, a developing sense of irony runs through them all.

In "Only Jerry," Kenneth Earle, thirty-five, wealthy, and decidedly "the catch of many seasons," falls in love with seventeen-year-old Geraldine "Jerry" Carden, the companion of the rich Clarissa Earle, the distant cousin whom all assumed he would marry. Jerry's innocence, her "clear, ringing laugh, good to hear," and her "dimpled, wild-rose face" win Kenneth over, and sincerity triumphs over wealth, simplicity over beauty, and quaintness over stately manners.

The style of "Only Jerry" is surprisingly mature and rich in sensory detail for a fifteen-year-old author. Kate set the pastoral scene of the story with pictorial clarity: "For under a great, leafy oak-tree, a girl sits, clad in a simple calico dress and snowy apron, unconsciously making, in the flickering sunlight, a quaint, pretty picture. Her broad-brimmed hat of coarse straw lies on the grass beside her, and she is busily engaged in the unromantic, rapid, finger-staining occupation of topping strawberries." Kate handled the inevitable moment of amorous awakening deftly, rhythmically: "For a moment brown eyes meet blue—for a moment her hand rests on his; then she turns and flits up the wide, oaken staircase to her own room." "Only Jerry" is informative, too, because of what it suggests about the young writer, who, like many a girl of her day, might have fantasized about a rich Prince Charming who would overlook her poverty and escort her to a world of carriages and glass slippers.

In 1880 Mrs. McPhelim moved her family to Chicago, where Kate attended the St. Xavier's Convent school. All four members of the family continued writing to bring in money, especially articles, stories, and poems for the *Chicago Tribune* and for Philadelphia's *Saturday Night*. Kate continued to use pen names, usually K. Temple More, Kate Ashley, or Kate Chrystal, in honor of her deceased sister.

Cleary later described the family's early Chicago years in a strongly autobiographical short story entitled "Why We Didn't Hear Nilsson," published in the *Chicago Tribune* on 19 March 1899. In it she lamented, "We were poor. We were disgustingly poor. We were absurdly poor. Not that our poverty distressed us. We generally got what we wanted—on credit. To our credit be it said we always paid—when we had the money." She recalled that her mother economized on family expenses, always believing that something would turn up. "She was a reliable prophet. Something generally did turn up, and if it didn't [Edward] and I burned the midnight kerosene in the production of what we fondly considered literature and which the family story papers—this was long before the blessed day of 10-cent magazines—bought from us at rates which we considered munificent."

The story explains that the family had income from an "Irish estate," but it also mentions that the rent was infrequently paid. Undaunted, the family members rationalized that although they were financially poor, "intellectually we were wealthy. We were quite a brilliant family. When our poverty reached its lowest ebb—the stage where it ceased to continue lamentable and became ridiculous—we were prompt to see its vulnerable points, and we hurled at these, between a sob and a laugh, sharp lances of wit." The story also describes the family's home in tones of amused nostalgia: "We had a flat. It wasn't a bad flat when you reached it. Flats in Chicago in the early '80s were called French flats. Now we dub anything similar 'apartment houses.' Almost all of the French flats then were converted—or perverted—residences. Once we tried to rent a whole house and sublet it. The attempt proved such a disastrous failure that even we were discouraged."

In the story, Cleary humorously and lovingly remembered her family in those early days. She described Edward as "a tall, thin, saintly faced young student with brains too big for his lank body, a devotion to the drama, and poetical aspirations. He wrote poems at the rate of twelve a week. The rate at which these were paid for by the story papers was $36 a dozen." The younger Frank "was a chubby chap of 12, with an aspiring nose, a dense crop of freckles, and a lot of curly, fair hair." The family wanted him to be an artist but decided he was better fit for a lawyer when he "exchanged with [his brother] a silk handkerchief for a silk cravat, and then put on the cravat and appropriated the handkerchief."

Cleary portrayed herself in the story as "slim and angular as 16 is apt to be, loving beauty the more for having been allotted but a scant share of it, and striving to do glorious things with a square of academy board, half a dozen tubes of paint, an all-over apron, and a couple of bristol brushes." She termed herself "the housekeeper of the flat. I had [Edward's] tastes, but lacked [Edward's] ability. I wrote nice, little stories that brought nice, little prices, and was properly appreciative of my brother." Cleary also humorously recalled her storytelling heritage, influenced by her creative but absentminded mother, who would begin a tale and then expect her daughter to finish it. Margaret McPhelim, "neither unread nor uncultured," had a memory with "a wholly unaccountable trick of vanishing when most needed."

Although the family lived precariously, they found time to laugh and to love. While in Chicago, Kate found her prince, an "older man" like Kenneth Earle in her story "Only Jerry," and they may even have fallen in love at a ball. Among Kate's memorabilia is a dance card for a ball hosted by the Irish-American Club at the Palmer House during the 1882–83 social season, with the name Cleary boldly written in for the third dance, the "Langiers."

Michael Timothy Cleary, born in Clonmel, Ireland, in 1855, was a charming and handsome man. A member of Company B of the First

Regular Infantry of the Illinois National Guard, he had served his country during the Chicago riots of July and August 1877. Although dashing in his uniform, he was far from wealthy. "Sonnie" or "Timmie," as he was affectionately nicknamed by his family, was working with his father to bring the rest of his family from Ireland to Chicago. But the damp, cold Lake Michigan winds caused him health problems, and by the time he met Kate, he was considering resettling in the West.

Influenced by his brother-in-law John Templeton, Michael decided to relocate in Nebraska, where the weather was drier and better for his health. Templeton, already well established in the lumber business in Superior, Nebraska, had expanded into the neighboring communities of Guide Rock, Endicott, and Reynolds. In the fall of 1883, Michael boarded a train for the West to seek his fortune so that he and Kate could marry.

Hubbell, Nebraska, was by 1883 a mushrooming community. Three years earlier, the Burlington and Missouri River Railroad had constructed the Republican branch of the line through land belonging to Hubbell H. Johnson, a pioneer from Illinois who had homesteaded in 1869 on 160 acres north of the Nebraska-Kansas border. In 1880, he deeded 120 acres to the Lincoln Land Company to establish a town, and they platted and named the streets and sold lots for one hundred dollars each. According to the *Belleville Telescope* of 28 December 1880, the site changed from a cornfield to a town boasting of one hundred buildings in just ninety days. The new prairie settlement was called Hubbell, which was Johnson's Christian name and his wife's maiden name. The resettlement there of most of the residents of Ida, located just four and one-half miles south of the border in Kansas, stimulated the boom. An 1880 article about Hubbell's future predicted, "In this country and being in the best sections of the agricultural country of the West and possessing as it does the advantage of splendid water power afforded by Rose Creek, it is destined at no distant day to be one of the leading cities of the West."[4] Like much of the frontier rhetoric designed to draw settlers, this grand prediction did not come true, but Hubbell did grow into a respectable town. Soon both a waterpowered gristmill and a sawmill provided necessities for the inhabitants.

Three limestone quarries aided Hubbell's growth. One of the first businesses in town was a drugstore, located in a building made of limestone quarried from nearby hills. Next, townspeople built another drugstore, two livery stables, and a hardware store, which also served as the post office. Saloons and pool halls flourished. Since Kansas was a "dry" state and since the border town had no early closing laws, Hubbell became a magnet for Kansas trade. As in any typical western town, the Hubbell marshal had difficulty handling the frequent disturbances in the saloons, and at least one death resulted from a drunken brawl. However, a Presbyterian minister soon began holding meetings in private homes, and within a year the Presbyterians had erected a church and selected a minister. Hubbell was born again.

By 1881, four passenger trains were stopping daily in Hubbell, and the population soon blossomed to six hundred. A grain elevator, a lumberyard, two hotels, two cafes, two drugstores, two doctors, two banks, a creamery, a jewelry store, a harness shop, a hardware store, two grocery stores, two general stores, and two churches, the Presbyterian and the Methodist, catered to the new settlers. Civilization gained an even stronger hold when citizens borrowed three thousand dollars and built a four-room school, one of the largest in the county. Four teachers, one man and three women, began conducting classes from first through eighth grade. More lots for the town became necessary, and an addition to the north, called the Coon Addition, increased the city limits.

Michael spent several months in Nebraska analyzing his prospects and writing daily to "My Own Dear Kittie" in Chicago. Although Hubbell held much economic promise, Michael realized its cultural limitations when he wrote to Kate on 10 November 1883, "I'm glad you are getting lots of passes to the theaters for it may be you will have very few chances to go hereafter." By 27 December, he was lonesome for Kate, and he chided her for not accompanying him to the West: "If you had come out you would not have gone back in a hurry, I can assure you and I would never need something a little more substantial than pictures to console me. I have three of them before me and they don't console me worth a darn." He also voiced concern about her health, begging, "Seriously Kittie you must take care of yourself. I won't have you do anything that hurts your health whether writing or anything else. I would like to prescribe for you the quiet evenings you can at any time find in Hubbell with your own fond Michael."

For the next several weeks, Michael "took stock" at all the Templeton Brothers' lumberyards. He noted proprietorially in a 24 January 1884 letter that, at Endicott, "we did better than we expected although not as well as at Reynolds or Guide Rock. In fact to more than pay expenses is to do well at Endicott." His personal financial status was more uncertain, though, for he added, "My Father did not send me money, he sent me his note due in June for Five Hundred Dollars. I have no way of using notes and in any case I would not like to discount it, so I will just file it away until he feels like paying it." His worry about beginning a new business and his longing for Kate apparently even kept him awake nights; he commented, "I am very sleepy did not rest well for the last few nights and have worked hard on the books every day." Ultimately, he overcame his hesitation, for a lumber business in such a booming town promised to be lucrative. By the end of January, Michael had rented a house, and on the last day of the month he wrote Kate, "I took Will up and showed him the house I rented. I had a party offer me half as much more as I paid and to pay for a year in advance. Money can't rent a house in town."

Meanwhile, writing was again consuming Kate McPhelim's life. She was working on a novel, *The Lady of Lynhurst,* using the pen name Kate Chrystal. Street and Smith published it in 1884 as number eight in their "Leading Novel" series.[5]

Michael resolved his money problems, opened Cleary Lumber and Coal, and was able to return to Chicago to marry Kate. On 26 February 1884, at five in the afternoon at St. Malachi's Church, the Reverend Father Hodnett pronounced them husband and wife. After the ceremony, Kate's mother hosted the reception in their home. Michael was twenty-eight and Kate, twenty. The *Chicago Citizen,* in the typical journalistic exuberance of the times, described the couple: "The happy groom, who is a handsome young scion of a historic family, resides in Hubbell, Neb., one of the prominent merchants of this city, and with the generous and jovial characteristics of his nationality. The bride is more than worthy of him. She is one of the brightest and most intellectual young ladies of all the land." The editors also lauded Cleary's writing talents, predicting that "she has but to cultivate the brilliant gifts with which nature has endowed her and she will win for herself a niche in the temple of literary fame which will do honor to her name and her race."

That evening after the reception, the couple left for a two-week wedding tour to St. Louis, where several of Michael's relatives resided. When the newlyweds returned to Chicago, they received friends and then packed their wedding gifts and Kate's mother's belongings for the move. Mrs. McPhelim would be residing with them in Nebraska. A few days later, the family stepped off the train at the Burlington depot in Hubbell to begin their new life in the West.

Busily establishing herself in her home and happily settling into marriage, Cleary began work on another novel, *Vella Vernel*. Her publishers, Street and Smith, sent a Western Union telegram on 5 September 1884 exclaiming, "The first installment is great just what we want. If you can keep up excitement make it double the length at double price." Two months later, on 18 November, they urged, "If you can on receipt of this without inconvenience forward me more of 'Vella' you will oblige us by doing so." They went on to comment about the "superior" quality of her previous work, *The Lady of Lynhurst*, encouragement indeed for a twenty-one-year-old author.

However, since Cleary no longer needed to write for family survival, she set aside her novel-in-progress, looked around at the assortment of people settling the West, and began to write humorous local-color essays recounting her experiences as a bride in the West. In "Fresh Laid Eggs," an unpublished manuscript, Cleary laughed at the incompetencies of a "city bride" who purchases forty chickens so she can have farm-fresh eggs in her own backyard. Once installed in their lavish and picturesque chicken coop, the birds refuse to lay eggs. Frustrated, the bride consults her neighbor, who discovers the problem: thirty-nine of the chickens are roosters! One of the few works that Cleary is known to have published during this time is the essay "A Nebraska Hired Girl," printed in the 27 December 1887 *Chicago Tribune*. This essay humorously describes her difficulties finding competent domestic help on the plains. The young author left the unfinished *Vella Vernel* in a drawer of her desk for a later day.

Cleary's ability to smile at life and find humor in its "vulnerable points" served her well in Hubbell, a typical little frontier town with aspirations to culture, plunked down in the middle of a cornfield. In a 22 January 1888 sketch in the *Chicago Tribune* titled "Mrs. Cleary's Visitors: The Neighborly and Entertaining Ladies of Bubble, Neb.," later reprinted with the title "Visitors," Cleary described her welcome to the close-knit rural community. She adopted the name Bubble for her literary town, perhaps to preserve the real one's anonymity, perhaps because of her love of rhyme and wordplay, or perhaps because she could see the tenuousness of the little community's existence on the harsh expanse of the prairie. The sketch begins, "Visitors! How kindly, much too kindly, curiously, and persistently at first they came. Now, our door-bell, the first, by the way, of the three Bubble at present boasts, but rarely rouses our protesting dismay."

The most humorous visitor is Mrs. McLelland, the undertaker's wife who reappears in many of Cleary's stories and novels. This sketch may have been the genesis of this character, who is one of Cleary's most memorable: Mrs. McLelland "is not easily overlooked. She is six feet two and exceedingly stout. She wears a black alpaca flounced, a net fichu, gold-rimmed glasses which cost $8, as she repeatedly informs you, and a set of bewitchingly exact and snowy store teeth. She called on me when I came here as a bride—frequently since. Indeed she insists on being neighborly, and presents herself at the kitchen door whenever the desire to 'run over' takes possession of her."

In this sketch, Mrs. McLelland, excited over her husband's purchase of the local undertaker's business, bursts into the kitchen exclaiming, " '[Pa] allus had a hankerin' for that business. Home in Illinoy, where we come from, there wasn't a berryin' within twenty miles pa hadn't a hand in. And now—*now*,' complacently she folded her fat hands on her fat stomach, triumphantly she regarded me, 'now he can see corpsus all the time!' " Although this sketch may have been fictionalized, Cleary must certainly have met a similar personality upon her arrival in Hubbell as a newlywed.

The first few years of Cleary's married life centered around her husband and home, and she published only a few stories. In 1886, she returned to Chicago briefly to consult with a doctor about her inability to conceive, and on 19 January 1887, James Mansfield "Jim" Cleary was born. That spring, Cleary decided to complete her novel, and in October 1887, Street and Smith published *Vella Vernel, or An Amazing Marriage* in their Select Series, using Mrs. Sumner Hayden for Cleary's pseudonym.[6] The sentimental plot, advertised by the publisher as being based on actual events that occurred in a major western American city, presumably Chicago, follows the tradition of the eighteenth-century comedy of manners, with a complex scheme of star-crossed lovers, mistaken identities, fortuitous meetings, financial scandals, and murder.

The protagonists, seventeen-year-old twins Vella and Voyle Vernel, were taken in by a rich uncle after their father died ten years earlier. Conflict arises when the uncle tries to force Vella to marry the old, rich, and ugly Jonas Claflin. Twists and turns abound in the young twins' lives. Voyle is jailed, and Vella steals in and trades places with him so he can go through the ceremony in her place, nullifying the marriage. Of course, everyone links up with the right person in the end, and the twins even discover that they are independently wealthy because their uncle stole their father's money.

However, Cleary's intellectual background, her wily sense of humor, her subtle wit, and her keen eye added spice to the potboiler. She prefaced each chapter with an applicable quote from literature, predominantly Shakespeare, Tennyson, Elizabeth Barrett Browning, and Robert Burns, but she began one chapter with a poem by K. Cleary and another with a stanza by E. J. McPhelim. Even though Cleary would not be publicly recognized as the author, she managed to leave clues as to her ownership of the text.

Local-color descriptions of Chicago's palatial estates, the hustle of State Street, and the city's annual Interstate Industrial Exposition add substance to *Vella Vernel*. In a complex one-half-page sentence that would do justice to her contemporary Henry James, Cleary detailed with sensory precision the scene in the impressive great hall of the Chicago Exposition Building: ". . . in the center of the building a gigantic fountain, which, from its loftiness, pours down again into the enormous basin below its broad and roaring torrent; the crashing blare of a great band—nocturne, opera, waltz; add to all this thousands of people, the main floor dense with them, the galleries black with them, the stairs a-swarm with them, and all surging, admiring, jostling, sauntering, purchasing, expatiating, comparing, criticizing—all adding to the thunder of the waterfall and brazen music of the band, to the clamor of traffic and the rattle of machinery" (75).

Cleary also began to record her son Jim's childhood in verse. In 1888, the prestigious family magazine *St. Nicholas* published four of her poems, paying what was for her an unprecedented ten dollars apiece. "All a-Blowing" and "A Rhyme for Little Folks" celebrate her delight in her new baby. "All a-Blowing" describes a child who "lies on the grass where the shadows pass / With thoughts too deep for knowing." Cleary symbolized the passing of time with blowing leaves and grasses as the parents visualize "A boy who can walk and a boy who can talk, / Instead of a bit of a baby." The other rhyme was probably composed as Cleary rocked little Jim to sleep. It begins:

> *Oh, I'll tell you a story that nobody knows,*
> *Of ten little fingers and ten little toes,*
> *Of two pretty eyes and one little nose,*
> *And of where they all went one day.*

On 18 January 1889, a daughter, Marguerite M., joined the family, followed by Gerald Vernon, born on 8 September 1890. Only her brother Frank's sudden death from pneumonia on 14 April 1889 in Chicago at age twenty-four marred Cleary's tranquil life.

Marriage and motherhood delighted Cleary, and the writings she produced during this period reflect her consuming passion for her family and home. "An Old Fashioned Mother and Wife," an essay written around 1890 shortly after Gerald was born and published posthumously in *Extension* in September 1912, gives us a glimpse into a typical day for Cleary in Hubbell and emphasizes her domestic contentment. As the mother croons the baby to sleep in her arms, she luxuriates in the evening's tranquillity: "Outside the dew-wet flower stalks are wands of ivory in the lustre of the moonlight. She drinks the air blowing in at the open window with a pleasure in its purity and perfume so intense as to be almost pain. In the town-hall the band is practicing. Mellowed and magicized by distance, the music floats to her. Fireflies—those lantern-bearers of the fairies—go flashing by, their flame, like love, most luminous in the shadows."

Cleary's full life expanded even more with the addition of a new friendship. Shortly after her third child was born in 1890, she and Elia Wilkinson Peattie, a former Chicagoan and fellow Nebraska writer, became close friends. Peattie, a year older than Cleary, had married Robert Peattie, a journalist for the *Chicago Tribune*, in 1883. In 1884, Peattie's first child, Edward, was born, followed by Barbara the next year. The Peatties spent their evenings writing stories together to supplement Robert's sporadic newspaper income. Then the *Chicago Tribune* asked Elia, "who knew nothing about society or art," to become the art and society editor for the paper. She acknowledged that although she may not have been the best society editor in Chicago's history, she gained an enduring love for and knowledge of art and made lasting friendships with Chicago artists. Peattie's modest columns led to larger fields, and she soon became the second "girl reporter" in Chicago, covering visiting royalty and exposing fraudulent spiritualists. Among her friends was Edward J. McPhelim, legendary Chicago newspaperman and brother of Kate McPhelim Cleary.

The Peatties moved to Omaha in 1888 when Robert became managing editor of the *Omaha World-Herald*. The newspaper hired Elia, too, and she wrote bylined editorials, edited the women's page, and contributed a weekly column for the Sunday edition. It was in this column that her feature on Cleary, "A Bohemian in Nebraska," appeared on 23 April 1893. After Roderick, Peattie's third child, was born and her husband's frail health necessitated frequent absences from work as well as from Omaha, Peattie wrote even more prolifically for publication, providing the majority of her family's financial resources.[7]

When Cleary and Peattie's friendship began is unknown; they may have already been acquainted before Cleary left Chicago through their publishing with the *Chicago Tribune* or through Cleary's brother Edward. Regardless of the genesis of their relationship, similarities in their childbearing and child-raising experiences, the health and financial problems both their husbands suffered, their love of writing, and their shared sense of isolation from the strong writing community in Chicago must have cemented their emotional ties during their Nebraska years.

Peattie's first known visit to Hubbell occurred shortly after Cleary's son Gerald was born in 1890. Upon her return to Omaha, Peattie consulted her own doctor about a prescription for quinine chocolates to soothe the baby's irritated stomach and mailed the medicine to Cleary in Hubbell. Peattie wrote in the undated letter she sent with the medicine, "My dear girl, I had a beautiful time with you, and it was with an actual feeling of reluctance that I put our pleasant week aside and resumed the responsibilities of my own life."

The emotional support shared by Peattie and Cleary became even more important in the next few years, as the health and financial burdens placed on the two women grew heavier. Although both maintained a brave front for their respective families, with each other they could be more honest. Their bond was so close that often they had only to allude to a problem in their letters, knowing that the other would instantly understand.

On one hot summer day, 28 July, presumably in 1891, after the 1890 visit, Peattie wrote a reply to one of Cleary's letters, which apparently related her frustrations with child care; Jim was four, Marguerite, two, and Gerald, ten months old: "I have been thinking of you since the curse of the hot winds came on you and wondering if Hubbell was blistered and burned with them. The summer is a hard one for you—perhaps it is the most difficult in some ways that you will ever have. Next summer both of your little ones will be out of your arms." Peattie shared her own dark feelings, too: "The Black Shadow is always about me, and will not let me win out to the sunshine. But I have not the impertinence to complain of the inevitable." She added by way of support: "You are a wonderful woman and I'm glad I know you. You know I always was an impatient letter writer and never inclined to put anything I feel on paper. But if I were to see you I would have some things to tell you, and some thoughts to exchange for your own. Meantime, you are to think of me as a fellow burden bearer and your loving friend."

The "Black Shadow" to which Peattie referred was probably her upcoming labor and delivery. In the late nineteenth century, women's letters, diaries, and journals refer repeatedly to the pain of labor and delivery and to the fear of death, a fear that was universal and well grounded. Medical guides, especially those written by women physicians, acknowledged this fear. In 1888 in her volume *Maternity: A Book for Every Wife and Mother*, Dr. P. B. Saur acknowledged that "undefined fear of pending evil, anxiety about the future, and fear of dying, forebodings and gloom, even to despair, often overtake" the pregnant woman (102). In urban centers as well as rural areas, obstetrical practices remained primitive, with high mortality rates for both mothers and infants. Women died during or after childbirth in alarming numbers, especially from puerperal fever, or "childbed fever." Even into the twentieth century, childbirth was the leading cause of death among women of childbearing age; as many as forty in a thousand died in private practice, and stillborn infants and deaths of babies within the first month claimed one child in twenty.[8] Women like Cleary and Peattie were expected to sublimate their fears and uncertainties, expected *not* to "complain of the inevitable."

In addition, a woman's duty was to sustain not only the physical well-being of her children but the emotional stability of her whole family. Society reinforced this idea from the pulpit, from the home, and from a myriad of articles and books. Dr. Saur advised, "A wife's life is made up of little pleasures, of little tasks, of little cares, and little duties, but which, when added together, make a grand total of human happiness; she is not expected to do any grand work; her province lies in a contrary direction, in gentleness, in cheerfulness, in contentment, in housewifery, in care and management of her children, in sweetening her husband's cup of life" (15).

Cleary's writing may have helped her bear these idealized societal expectations and cope with her own fears and frustrations as she realistically portrayed women and childbirth in her poems and stories. For the nineteenth-century woman, pregnancy was a perpetual condition and birth control an unreliable option. Dr. Mary Melendy, in *Perfect Womanhood for Maidens, Wives, and Mothers: A Complete Medical Guide for Women* (1903), mistakenly advised women that conception takes place "at about the time of menstrual flow" (264). Even as late as 1911, Professor T. W. Shannon, in his best-seller *Perfect Manhood: How Inherited, Attained, and Maintained; How Wrecked and Regained,* preached mostly self-restraint and abstinence as birth-control methods, believing that "if before marriage they could both live continent lives there is no reason why they should not in married life." He conceded, however, that if this was not possible, the ideal method of birth control "would be for these relations to take place ten days before or after the menstrual periods" (126).

It is no wonder, with women being urged to have marital relations with their husbands at their most fertile times to *avoid* conception, that Cleary's four-stanza poem "Another Baby" would have had a wide and understanding audience:

> *When the wild winter winds did blow,*
> *The bitter winds of January,*
> *That swept with sparkling swirls of snow,*
> *The wastes of Western prairie;*
> *A little child came to my arms,*
> *To bring me joy—or sorrows maybe,*
> *And so, beset by vague alarms,*
> *I sighed "Another baby."* [9]

As the poem continues, the mother not only worries about her ability to feed and care for "another baby" but dreads more the sorrow that will come if the child should die, as many did. By the end of the poem, though, the mother is reconciled through her religion to accept the child, however unplanned, as a gift of God. Cleary was a devout Catholic, and her faith helped her to accept the inevitable. Members of the Sacred Heart Catholic Church of Hebron, Nebraska, the Clearys offered their home to the priest to say Mass when he was in Hubbell.

In one short story, "Feet of Clay," Cleary depicted the state of childbirth practices on the plains. Margaret, a wealthy eastern young girl, moves west with her new husband, a Kansas farmer, to live with him and his mother. When her time to deliver arrives, only her mother-in-law is there to attend her:

> Then the baby came. That was a day of horror never to be blotted out. Barret was in the pasture, not a quarter of a mile off, and his mother refused to send for him.

"He's gettin' in the last of that late hay," she grimly responded to every agonized appeal. "He can't be put about for whimsies."

So the supreme crisis of a woman's life found Margaret exiled and practically alone.[10]

In her fiction, Cleary could work through her own fears and pain as well as confront the callous attitude of many people toward the whole childbearing experience.

Even with a doctor to assist in childbirth, problems still arose. With the displacement of midwives by male physicians trained in "scientific" delivery, the use of drugs and forceps increased. So did the incidence of "childbed fever" and "milk fever," as doctors carried germs on their instruments from one delivery to the next.[11] This new reliance on instrumental delivery added to the potential problems for both mother and child. In another story, "The Road That Didn't Lead Anywhere," Cleary protested the inadequacies of rural physicians. As Elsie Miller, a frail, sixteen-year-old pioneer wife, begins labor, her husband rides to town for the doctor. Elsie says that when the two men arrived her husband " 'was not like he should be. And the doctor was worse. He was dead drunk. I begged him to go away, but he thought he could help. He didn't know what he was doing. He had things in his bag— steel things. . . . He was not careful. He—' She pointed to a deep depression in which you might have rolled a marble at one side of the baby's head. 'He did that. It didn't kill the baby. I,' she broke down sobbing, 'I wish sometimes it had!' " The baby had suffered brain damage from the hands of an incompetent doctor: "There was nothing attractive about the baby. Its face was round and full, but of a sickly white, and there was a startling look of vacancy in the staring eyes."[12] Cleary was certainly aware of the problem births in her community, and writing afforded her the opportunity to put her frustrations onto paper and bring them out into the daylight for the scrutiny of society. However, with an eye always to publication, she made certain that her stories had happy endings. In this case, a passing stranger gives the young woman some money to pay for surgery to correct the child's defect.

Supported by societal images of the frail, Victorian "Angel of the House," nineteenth-century women not only viewed pregnancy and confinement with fear but looked upon it as an "illness"; women were encouraged to remain in bed for weeks after delivery, which added to their concern about childbirth. Peattie and Cleary both subscribed to these ideas. In a 21 August 1891 letter, Peattie wrote to Cleary that "the only complication during my illness came from [an] old trouble with my breast and resolved into drying up my milk." Because of this universal attitude toward pregnancy and childbirth as an "illness" with the need for prolonged recuperation, as well as the real need for domestic help with the other children and with the heavy and tedious everyday household tasks, women worried, too, about finding "hired girls." To many young mothers, this concern superseded even that of finding a competent doctor.[13]

The sparse population of frontier towns compounded the difficulty of finding domestic help. Although Cleary's mother was still living with her in Hubbell, Cleary needed more assistance for her growing family. Peattie and Cleary often took the train between Hubbell and Omaha to visit each other after a child was born, for both physical and moral support. In September of 1891, Cleary appealed to Peattie for help, hoping an Omaha girl would be interested in a position in the Cleary home. Peattie's 19 September response was negative: "How ridiculous that girls should have such an aversion to living out of the city—as if there was anything in this dull town to invite any living creature! A desert could not be more stupid, while it might have more repose." After her first child was born, Cleary's sense of humor came to her aid, and she was able to pen a sketch entitled "A Nebraska Hired Girl," in which she laughed at the domestic crisis in her Garden of Eden: "Out here in Nebraska, where the boundless prairies billow under the bluest of skies; here, where the passage of time is only told by the birth of flowers—the violets of April, the daisies of May, the wild roses of June, and the sunflowers of July; here, where the meadow-lark's regular triple note, the pipe of the quail, and the whistle of the plover are sounds familiar and sweet—here surely should reign the peace of paradise. But, alas! there was a serpent in Eden—we employed a hired girl in

Nebraska."[14] The sketch caricatures a variety of Cleary's domestic "helpers," who often created more problems than they alleviated.

With domestic help difficult to find in the small frontier towns, even in such a "modern" home as hers, Cleary spent many hours caring for her family and house. Because of the scarcity of housing in Hubbell and the availability of lumber through Michael's business, the newlyweds soon built a new, two-story home on the lot directly north of Hubbell Johnson's elaborate house. Included in it were many extras. Besides the sunny bay window to the south, the doorbell, and the luxurious zinc-lined bathtub—the only one in Hubbell, one that even drained out into the backyard—Cleary may have appreciated her kitchen most of all. The house featured a sizable pantry with a three-foot-deep storage cupboard on the outside of the house but accessible from the pantry, where Cleary could put her meat to freeze in the winter and her pies to cool in the summer. Beneath this windowlike opening in the pantry was a broad board that folded into the wall and that when let down could be used to roll out pie dough. In the kitchen, Cleary also had a cupboard built under the chimney where she could store her large skillets, irons, and grease cans. A gathered curtain in front hid the equipment from view. In a small basement room under the kitchen nestled a laundry that held the cistern and pump where Cleary could do her washing without having to clutter the kitchen with piles of dirty and wet clothing.[15]

Impressed with Cleary's homemaking skills, especially her cooking, Peattie boasted of it in her article on her friend, "A Bohemian in Nebraska." She commented that "when Mrs. Cleary found herself stranded, as it were, in mid-plains, and confronted by the deplorably small bill of fare of a country town, that she set about making a scientific cuisine. In all the arts of salad making, roasting, deviling, baking, preserving and mixing, she is a connoisseur—and more, she is original." Being careful not to offend her rural readers, Peattie added, "It would be absurd to commend all of her methods to the busy farm woman who has neither time nor money for making fine dishes, but I am sure the isolated life out on the plains would take to itself a little more charm if other women would do as Mrs. Cleary has, and make a study of how to use cream and eggs, poultry and pork, vegetables and the native fruit. It's a great art; and it takes brains of a good sort—so no one need scorn it because of the idea that it is not intellectual."[16]

Much of Cleary's writing now centered around the domestic arts, and her contributions appeared regularly in women's periodicals including *Good Housekeeping* and the *Housewife*. Articles such as "For the Housewife: Trifles That Make Perfection," "The Storeroom: Its Convenience and Contents," "A Bunch of Bananas, and Fifteen Ways of Serving Them," "Angel Food with Variations," "Ten Tongues: And How to Cure Them, How to Cook Them, and How to Serve Them," and "Cooking Quail: With Fifteen Tested and Reliable Recipes" attest to her culinary creativity. In Hubbell, which was located far from a reliable and diverse food market, she learned the importance not only of foresight but of "making do."

Both Cleary and her husband enjoyed hunting, and Cleary's article on quail shows how readily she adapted to the frontier cuisine. She suggested, "Epicures have widely decided that game, the meat of which is dark—prairie chicken for instance—shall be kept as long as possible before cooking. The reverse rule applies to quail, the meat of which is white. I have eaten quail within an hour after being shot, and it was more flavorous, more juicy, more altogether delectable, than when held for a few weeks, and that under the most favorable conditions of temperature."[17]

Cleary's older brother, Edward McPhelim, now the literary and drama critic for the *Chicago Tribune,* mailed her the latest novels to enjoy and to review for the paper. He advised her in an 1885 letter that "the only object of reviewing is to say something clever or bright—in praise or dispraise, it doesn't matter which, as long as it will read well. Will send you other novels by express afterward, all of which you can keep." Cleary's reviews, such as the ones on *Irish Idylls,* by Jane Barlow, and *Janis the Sang-Digger,* by Amelie Rives, were usually printed without her byline. Another critique known to be by her examined Bret Harte's *Maruja* in 1885. For her critical efforts, Cleary was able to read the newest authors and keep abreast of the latest publishing trends. Moreover, the *Chicago Tribune* considered her their "correspondent" and sent her regular payments. What more could she ask for?

The first eight years of Kate's married life flowed smoothly along. Michael recorded their happiness with the camera he purchased around 1890 in photographs that are quite candid for the times. In one Michael sneaks a kiss from Kate; in another she cuddles in his arms in a chair; and in several Kate unabashedly displays her pregnant condition. Others show Kate and her mother standing proudly on the boardwalk of downtown Hubbell with a baby bundled up in a wicker carriage; Michael, his beard neatly trimmed, his watch chain glinting in the sun, and his hands stuffed into his pockets, looking the dignified businessman; a group of boys playing baseball on the main street of town; and the family in a buggy pulled by horses named Minnie and Charlie.

Photographs of the children prevail, of course, as do views of the exterior and interior of the house, of which the couple was obviously proud. Lace curtains graced the south bay windows in the parlor, where Cleary's houseplants drank in the prairie sunlight. Armchairs and footstools upholstered in dark velvet rested upon oriental-figured carpets, and paintings and family portraits framed with thick gilt borders crowded the walls. A shiny isinglass heater warmed the parlor. But Cleary was most pleased with her "library." Six shelves of books, many of them leather-bound sets, lined the walls on either side of the dining-room doorway. A bookcase stood near Cleary's writing desk, a large mahogany piece with lots of drawers, plenty of space for piles of magazines and newspapers, and room leftover for her typewriter. A swivel chair allowed her to turn from her work when a son needed his shoe tied or a daughter required a hug. A rattan rocker stood beside it for her reading or sewing or for singing lullabies while rocking babies. These years were, indeed, fulfilling for Cleary—as a wife, a mother, and a writer.

2

The Difficult Years:
1892–1897

Until the birth of her second daughter, Rosemarie Catherine, on 19
May 1892, her fourth baby in six years, Cleary's pregnancies, childbirths, and child-raising experiences proceeded happily. Concentrating
on her family, she published works chiefly in *Good Housekeeping* and
Puck, a humorous periodical of caricature.[1] Unfortunately, shortly after
Rosemarie's birth, the baby contracted a poliolike paralysis, and soon
catastrophes began to snowball. Cleary's life during the next six years
became a series of emotional highs undercut by devastating lows.

In 1892 it seemed that Cleary's literary skills would finally be recognized. Because of her growing reputation, editors Frances E. Willard
and Mary A. Livermore included Cleary in their 1892 collection *A
Woman of the Century,* published by Charles Wells Moulton of Buffalo, New York. The editors declared in their preface that "among all
cyclopaedias and books about famous women, this is intended to be
unique and to supply a vacant niche in the reference library. The nineteenth century is a woman's century. Since time began, no other era
has witnessed so many and so great changes in the development of her
character and gifts and in the multiplication of opportunities for their
application." Cleary's entry included a photograph and a short biography. Michael, proud of his wife's achievements, purchased one of the
leather-bound editions to present to Kate on their ninth wedding anniversary, inscribing on the front pages, "To Kate with my Love, Michael T. Cleary. Hubbell, Nebr. Febr. 26, 1893."

The Chicago World's Fair of 1893 also bolstered Cleary's spirits, for her poetry was featured at the opening of the newly erected Nebraska Building, built in the classical Corinthian style and boasting of twelve thousand square feet of floor space and a double staircase.[2] Cleary traveled to Chicago in June to attend the Nebraska Day ceremonies, opened by Buffalo Bill Cody leading the United States Cavalry on his white charger. Reluctant as always to speak before crowds, she decided to let someone else read her poems at the ceremony; she stood nearby as Mrs. Henry Fiske of Chicago read two of her poems in the impressive reception hall.

In the first lyric, "The Corn," Cleary emphasized the then accepted belief that the West was a Garden of Eden, and she employed the metaphor of rows of corn as an army conquering the plains, a typical visualization of the myth of Manifest Destiny. The six-stanza poem begins in the spring and concludes in September as the corn ripens for harvest. It opens:

> *When the merry April morn*
> *Laughed the mad March winds to scorn,*
> *In the swirl of sun and showers*
> *Were a million legions born;*
> *Ranked in rippled rows of green,*
> *With a dusky ridge between,*
> *O'er the western world was seen,*
> *The great army of the corn.*[3]

Fiske read a second poem by Cleary to close the program. Entitled "Nebraska," this narrative poem of eighteen stanzas written in vernacular dialect, a popular literary device of the period, depicts the darker side of the homesteading experience for the first Nebraska settlers "twenty years ago." The poem begins:

> *Ten of us living there, sir,*
> *In a sod house on the bluff,*
> *All the world outside, sir,*
> *Inside cramped enough;*

An' another baby comin'
We thought wus kind o' rough.

The poem continues to discuss the hardships of the mother and the family, but the new baby's happy nature becomes the bright spot in the family's life. However, the baby dies, and the mother continues to rock the cradle, the same one in which all of her children have slept, covered by a blanket made from the mother's wedding gown. The family feels that God has paid them back "straight and square" for thinking that the family was too large already. In the irony and pathos of the ending, Cleary emphasized the cost in human lives and suffering that the civilization of the West necessitated:

Twenty years! but it hurts like
'Twas only yistiday,
Seems if the pictur's clearer
Further it gits away—
Of mother rockin' the cradle
Where the little dead baby lay.[4]

Perhaps stimulated by her Chicago journey, Cleary published a wide assortment of writings in 1893. *Puck* printed over a dozen of her humorous poems and sketches, most of them in their special World's Fair editions, and the *Housewife* printed three articles on cooking. Most important, though, was the publication of "Feet of Clay" in *Belford's Monthly*. A naturalistic view of the pioneer experience, "Feet of Clay," a tale much like those of Hamlin Garland's in *Main-Travelled Roads* published two years earlier, emphasizes the negative effects of the environment, of isolation, and of physical labor on women. Although many frontier women thrived, others could not cope, and some went insane. Snapshots in the Cleary albums of sod houses and log cabins near Hubbell, one of them with a woman peering out of the doorway, confirm that such lives did exist in Cleary's own backyard.

Later that summer, Cleary's mother died unexpectedly of pneumonia. Because of the great love between Cleary and her mother, amplified by Mrs. McPhelim's closeness to the children while residing with them in Hubbell, this must surely have been traumatic for the whole family. The death was even more tragic because Mrs. McPhelim was in Chicago at the time, probably visiting her son Edward, and Cleary was not able to be with her. Margaret McPhelim was only fifty-nine when she died. Her obituary explained the loss that the family endured: "Absolutely without guile and incapable of anything but tenderest thoughts and self-sacrificing endeavors, she kept 'the whiteness of her soul' to the last hour of her loving and lovable life." The editor added, perhaps by way of condolence, "The genius of her mother—and in an added degree—has descended to the daughter, and Mrs. Cleary has become widely known as a writer of fiction, bright sketches and poems. Mrs. McPhelim herself, while her children were young and dependent upon her, did much literary work, first in St. John's and afterwards for the newspapers and magazines of Philadelphia and New York."[5]

The following year, 1894, Vera Valentine was born to the Clearys on 14 February. The Hubbell newspaper printed this gossipy item under the headline "A Little Valentine": "Wednesday morning M. T. Cleary came down town with his head up in the air and stepping prouder than a little boy with his first pair of red topped boots. On being questioned as to the cause of his strange actions, he answered, it's a girl. Mother and child are doing well, and the physician feels hopeful that Mike will get along all right."

Vera was a strong and healthy child, unlike the frail Rosemarie. Cleary, however, was *not* doing well after the delivery, and her husband telegraphed the Peatties in Omaha to send a nurse immediately. They complied, and Elia Peattie penned this short, undated note to a worried Michael: "Miss Randall has the reputation of being one of the finest nurses in Omaha, and she is, also, I hear, a very sensible and good woman. I hope and believe she may meet your needs. Telegraph me for anything you want." Peattie evidenced her own fears when she added, "If you would feel safer to have me come out I will come immediately. My children are almost well, and can be left in my sister's care. Mr. Peattie has been doing my work since they were sick, and would willingly continue to do it. If you want me to take the baby or any of the children I will come and get them." The letter ended with words of encouragement: "Do not be too much alarmed. Kate has wonderful recuperative ability. Remember, ask for any service—no matter how slight or large—and if it is in our power we will perform it."

Cleary had contracted the dreaded puerperal fever, or childbed fever, which is caused by infection during delivery. On 24 February, a concerned Peattie wrote to her, "Your thoughtful husband has written me at least every other day, and the letter I got this morning tells me that you are still suffering from fever, and that bad nursing was the cause. I can imagine the gruesome particulars. But do not fret. Miss Randall will fix you up. Mr. Cleary has a genius for keeping an eye on the children and you will have to take things as quietly and resignedly as possible. If you are not too sick, you can perhaps enjoy your rest." Peattie advised her to "be a quiet sensible girl, do everything you are told, and let the world wag. You'll be all right presently, though the present time must seem hard and trying indeed. Dear girl, I love you, and always shall, and the thought that you might be in danger tortured me more than you could think."

Medical books of the period list many symptoms of childbed fever, among them elevated temperature, inflammation, vomiting, shivering fits, severe pains in the head, and sometimes delirium. Their authors believed the major cause to be "instrumental or difficult labor" or "other animal poisons [bacteria] . . . as conveyed by the persons and dresses of the attendants of the patients, even after the exercise of great caution." Recommended treatment included hourly medications of tincture of aconite for fever, hops and vinegar for the bowels, hop-yeast and charcoal for inflammation, a mustard poultice for the stomach, and vaginal injections of carbolic acid.[6] Antibiotics were not available in the late 1900s, and all of the remedies doctors did have were either inappropriate or misdirected; several, such as the carbolic acid applications, caused more harm to delicate tissues than good.

Cleary's case was serious and her recovery slow. By the end of March, she was still dangerously ill and continued to require the services of the professional nurse. Peattie wrote frequently, and her comments revealed her concern. On 27 March she wrote, evidently in reply to Cleary's first letter since the childbirth: "This is only a line to say that I viewed your mark with feelings of very mixed pleasure, and

would much rather have seen your bold and defiant signature there."
She continued, using humor to revive her friend's spirits: "So you think
you're so sick you couldn't talk to me. I don't believe it. You may be
sick—but not that sick. When in heaven's name are you going to get
out of bed? When will your poor side stop aching? I'm 'joshing' you,
perhaps, but really, joshing aside, I'd give anything I possess to know
you were up again and happy and strong." Complications from this
illness would continue to plague Cleary throughout her life.

That November, Marguerite, age five, came down with typhoid fever, which was often caused by the contaminated water common in
the developing communities of the West. Cleary, still weak from her
own illness, shared her worries with Peattie, who hurried to Hubbell
to support her friend in her crisis. Upon her return to Omaha, Peattie
wrote in an undated letter: "I have just got your letter, and am glad to
hear that Marguerite is no worse. It would not be reasonable to expect
her to be better yet. But I firmly believe that she will get through if
no new and unexpected symptoms arise. It did me good to see and
hear you, even if your spirits were burdened with many cares and
anxieties."

Despite all that Cleary, her husband, and the doctor could do, Marguerite did not get well. She died on Sunday morning, 2 December, a
month before her sixth birthday. Cleary penned Marguerite's obituary
herself: "Though only six years of age, she was an unusually bright and
interesting child. To hear her relate the interesting and beautiful Bible
stories, which she delighted in so much, with the enthusiasm of an
older person, would touch the hardest heart. These beautiful stories
were taught her by her devoted grandmother, who has preceded her
a short time." Marguerite, whom Cleary had always dressed in white,
was interred in Calvary Cemetery in Chicago beside her grandmother.

Cleary also composed a black-edged funeral card bearing Marguerite's photograph, the dates of her birth and death, and this short
lyric:

> *Dear, the meanings of thy name*
> *Flower and jewel are;*
> *May the fragrance and the shine*

Of that sweet, short life of thine,
Prove a guidance for our feet,
Little, loved, lost
Marguerite.

As 1895 began, Michael's health problems recurred. Still physically weak from her own illness and grieving the loss of her daughter, Cleary shouldered the family responsibilities—the care of the household tasks and of Jim, seven; Gerald, four; Rosemarie, two; and Vera, nine months. To complicate matters, the economy of Hubbell had begun to decline.

In 1886, a competitor of the Burlington and Missouri River Railroad, the Rock Island, had established lines north and south of Hubbell, cutting off the lucrative country trade by giving settlers alternative shipping points. Hubbell had managed to adjust modestly to the economic decline and stymied growth until the general depression of the early nineties, when property sales and the building of new homes and businesses plummeted, and many enterprises boarded their doors. The little community began to wither like the sunflowers and goldenrods lining the dusty roads of Thayer County in October.

The decrease in Hubbell's development had a disastrous effect on Michael's lumber business, although his sideline of selling coal lessened the impact; cold winters in Nebraska were never a variable. In addition to the Clearys' financial difficulties, Michael's lung problems flared up, and he felt that a change of climate could, perhaps, help both his physical and economic problems. He left for Chicago in February and remained there nearly six months, seriously considering staying permanently to help run his father's wholesale liquor business.

Cleary must have accompanied her husband as far as Lincoln when he departed for Chicago, for Peattie referred in a February 1895 letter to Cleary's sadness at having to return to Hubbell alone: "Your homecoming haunted me! Poor girl! The black sorrows have been closing in around you of late. But you have some dear children left—think if Marguerite had been the only one! I am sure the house which has been such a home in the best sense of the word must seem strange and bereft now with your husband gone. I hope he may be able to live in Chicago. But it seems doubtful, and I hope you will not be very much disappointed if he has to give it up. He could, probably live in Omaha, or any other place besides—Denver, or Tucson or Santa Barbara." Peattie added her concerns about her own husband's health: "Robert keeps astonishingly well all things considered. But he does not venture out at night, and has to be exceedingly careful of himself." Closing with her usual note of support, she consoled: "I shall come to see you by and bye. It may not be until March. But I must come sometime then, since you cannot come here. You know if I had my way I would come at once. My heart aches for your sorrow. But it is a sweet, pure sorrow, after all. You can make it beautiful and blessed. So many sorrows are hideous with shame and sin and the unspeakable. God bless you my dear, and give you courage and show you light."

Michael Cleary evidently stopped briefly at the Peatties' in Omaha on his way to Chicago, revealing to Peattie problems even Cleary had not mentioned to her. When he left, Peattie penned this letter, dated February '95, to Cleary: "Your Michael has just been here and talked with me for an hour. There have been so many things you have not told me about—Gerald's continued illness, your injured hand—your struggle alone without a nurse girl. Dear girl, it is hard for you to be left there alone, and I can see it almost broke your husband's heart to leave. And, by the way Kate, this is a good place to pause to remark that while as good a man as Michael loves you the way he does, all can not be sad. He's a lovely fellow, and my heart melts toward him. I never knew a man whose sweetness appealed to me more."

Recognizing Cleary's physical isolation, Peattie consoled her: "He tells me it is cold and horrid out on the prairie, and did not especially urge me to come. But all the same I am coming presently. I shall bring Rod, and we will take care of babies together for a few days. I suppose it seems to you now as if the babies would never get out of your arms. I must admit that Rosemarie will be a trial for a long time to come. But the other little girl will be shooting up before you know it. You've a dear household, Kate, and the sweetness of it will comfort and console you, I know."

Peattie alluded to the health of both of their husbands: "Robert wants to go—to the West Indies. I tried to get Michael to go. He didn't think it would be much better than Hubbell. And perhaps it wouldn't." Although no mention is made by either the Peatties or the Clearys of tuberculosis, or "consumption" as it was commonly termed, Robert's and Michael's symptoms and their attempted cures indicate that this may have been the problem. Consumption was a dreaded disease at the turn of the century. The *Encyclopedia of Health and Home: A Domestic Guide to Health, Wealth, and Happiness,* edited by I. N. Reed and published in 1882, lists the disease's chief symptoms as impaired digestion, debility, difficulty breathing upon the slightest exertion, hoarseness or weakness of voice, irregular pains in the chest, a persistent cough, and bleeding of the lungs (134–36). In their letters, Cleary and Peattie often remarked about their husbands having such symptoms.

The encyclopedia notes that consumption was curable and refers to "numerous cases in which persons, after suffering one or more attacks of bleeding of the lungs, regain their health completely" (135). Recovery, though, could only be produced by "pursuing a rational and judicious course of treatment" (136). The book advises sufferers to do the following: "You require the purest and dryest atmosphere. Therefore, go North, rather than South. Then travel, hunt, fish, and eat freely of the game. Take a friend with you, for society, or to lean upon in your troubles. . . . Do not wait to leave home, until after you have vainly tried everything else and are just ready for the grave . . . but start out as soon as you become aware that the disease has fastened upon your lungs; and then you may not unreasonably expect a cure" (139).

Physicians disagreed on whether a southern or northern climate relieved consumptives more, but all agreed that travel produced the most significant cure: "In many instances, the greatest benefits derived from traveling, either north or south, consist in the exercise involved, the agreeable sensation produced by the motion of the cars and steamboats, the ever-varying change of sights and sounds—these are what open anew the springs of life" (144–45). Both Michael and Robert traveled often and extensively, forever looking for climates that would "cure" them.

A month after her husband left for Chicago, in March of 1895, Cleary endured yet another loss—Rosemarie, age three.[7] Michael

Cleary was ill, evidently, and unable to return to Hubbell for the funeral, so Cleary had to gather whatever strength she had left and confront the tragedy on her own. Her courage is impressive, for with no hint of disappointment or anger over her husband's absence at this mournful time, she described the arrangements she made to him in a letter: "My Dearest: Don't expect me to write much now. I can't just yet. We only decided at 10:30 yesterday to have the funeral yesterday afternoon. Our darling was pretty in life—she was smiling and BEAUTIFUL in death. The services were simple but so nice. I arranged them. First we all sang the 'Our Father' together. Then the children sang. Then Mrs. Conklin read 'Only a Girl' by Mrs. Browning. Then I said 'A Song for the Girl I Loved.' The children sang again. Miss Felty read a poem by Adelaide Proctor 'Our Dead.' "

Cleary refused to have her daughter's body transported to the Hubbell cemetery in a hearse, so she and Michael's sister, Annie Cleary, from Superior, Nebraska, held the coffin in their laps while John Templeton, their brother-in-law, drove the carriage with the other children in front. "Everyone here has been very kind," Cleary told her husband. "Mr. Kissick [a Hubbell friend] could not have done more. As far as it was possible he took your place. I am keeping brave for you and the THREE." Admitting that "it has been harder for you, Tim [Michael] darling, than for me," Cleary quietly expressed her own sorrow: "She did not suffer much. She was such a quiet little girl, but now that she is away the house seems full of that 'loud lonesomeness.' And to have only ONE little head laid down on my knee, and ONE baby to trot after me seems hard to bear. But I am thankful for you and the boys and V. V."[8]

The deaths of Marguerite and Rosemarie precipitated an outpouring of writing from Cleary as she memorialized her beloved daughters in stories and poems. An autobiographical narrative eulogizing Rosemarie, "On Hubbell Hill," which she most certainly shared with the family as a part of the healing process, may have helped to soothe Cleary's sorrow.

Cleary began the narrative with a description of Rosemarie: "She had the most beautiful eyes that ever looked love into a mother's face. They were hazel eyes, white lidded, dark lashed, liquidly brilliant, too, although their expression was one of gentleness." The story describes the close relationship between Jim and Rosemarie, especially Jim's devotion to his sister, his pride in her "pluck and endurance," and his sorrow upon losing her. The peaceful setting of the tiny hilltop cemetery comforts him: "There were but few slabs or monuments on the hill. From its eminence one looked down on the commonplace town below, with its school, its church, its square dwellings, all set out, even to the cows, for all the world like a Noah's ark arranged by a child on a green tablecloth. And around to the south and east and west the prairies billowed—vast surges of yellow and brown and green."[9]

In another sketch, "An Incident of the Prairie: A Board, a Saw, a Few Nails, and a Mother's Hot Tears," probably published in the *Chicago Tribune* the same year, Cleary empathized with a pioneer mother's sorrow over the loss of her child while traveling westward. Perhaps based on a true incident that Michael experienced in his lumber business when a man came to him for lumber and tools to build a coffin, the story reveals Cleary's difficulty in letting go of the pain, just as the mother in the narrative can not hand over her dead child to her husband for burial: "A pale woman seated on the ground cries at the sight of him and strains more tightly to her bosom the little form in her arms. She rocks to and fro while he nails the rough boards into a box. He goes toward her. 'Wait!' she quavers savagely."

The husband digs the grave, lines the handmade coffin with cottonwood leaves, gently takes the baby from the mother, and buries it. Then the family continues on: "The sun has set. It is still chokingly hot. The horses toil westward. They reach the top of a bluff. The woman looks back towards the creek. Then the wagon jolts down the draw."[10]

Cleary exposed her latent feelings of anger in a sketch entitled "About Cradles and Coffins." The story features Mrs. McLelland, the undertaker's wife, bemoaning the fact that her husband's business has slowed lately but gloating over the knowledge that "the water's gittin' pretty low in the wells." She remarks, "you know what that means mostly," alluding with "dreamy and delicious anticipation" to the numerous children's deaths from typhoid fever that would ensue. Pa had ordered "a nest of children's coffings [*sic*] . . . the little ones inside the others," as well as several cradles, so he could catch them both "coming and going."

Hubbell's main well, one of the two from which the schoolchildren bucketed their water daily to the stone jar in their classroom, was dug in 1880 and was only eighteen feet deep. Although the Clearys had their own windmill and cistern in their backyard, their children shared water, and probably the same tin cup, with their schoolmates. The most bitter piece Cleary ever penned, this manuscript, with the word "True" penciled upon it, was never published, but it must have served as a cathartic outlet for the despairing young mother.

Cleary wrote prodigiously in 1895, as if the clatter of her typewriter keys could drown out her grief. In addition, the publication of her stories and poems helped alleviate her financial worries in Michael's absence. Many of her best stories depicting the harsh life of pioneers on the plains were published during this year, most of them in the Sunday edition of the *Chicago Tribune,* including "The Camper," "A Man Out of Work," "A Race Horse to the Plow," "The Judas Tree," "A Western Wooing," and "A Dust Storm in Nebraska." Deterministic in tone, these tales, for the most part, document the struggles of early settlers, especially women, trapped in an indifferent wilderness or held hostage by unremitting biological forces.

Although Cleary was influenced by the contemporary trends of realism and naturalism, she also applied themes and styles that suited her purpose and mood. Like the realists, she believed in the mimetic theory, convinced that if she accurately represented the surface of life, she would reflect it truthfully. Thus, most of her western stories written during this period excel in local-color descriptions of the people, the communities, the land, and nature. Although some Nebraskans resented her verisimilitude, she perceptively and accurately portrayed the positive and negative features of life in the New West. The men and women who people her stories represent all facets of the pioneering experience.

Many of Cleary's stories from this period also reflect a naturalistic attitude toward life, one made popular in American periodicals by writers reacting against romanticism, such as Hamlin Garland, Frank Norris, and Jack London. Guided by what was being published as well as by her own personal despair and disillusionment, Cleary often depicted people as having little opportunity for choice. For many of her protagonists, life is a vicious trap, a cruel game. Her women are rigidly bound by their gender, struggling to survive multiple childbirths and to maintain their sanity in the restricted role ordained for them by society, a role difficult to accept in a democratic West where men and women toil side by side to survive. Powerless in their battle against socioeconomic restrictions, victimized by environmental forces, and isolated from a supportive network of other women, these pioneer characters are often from the lower classes—poor, uneducated, or unsophisticated—yet they comprehend the incompleteness of life and suffer powerfully. Occasionally, Cleary's female western protagonists, usually young brides from the East, come from upper-class backgrounds and are dropped into sod houses or homestead shanties, rarely surviving the shock. Such things, Cleary knew, did happen in real life.

Sentimentalism sometimes flaws the realism of Cleary's texts. These two concepts opposed each other in the mainstream American literature of the day, argues Charles Fanning in *The Irish Voice in America,* and writing like Cleary's "mirrors the uneasy, transitional, ambivalent culture that produced it" (156). This realism flawed by sentimentalism is especially pervasive, according to Fanning, among late-nineteenth-century, third-generation Irish-American writers, who were unable "to decide between respectable romance and rebellious realism" (157). Such writers often lapsed into "a familiar pattern consisting of realistic settings, characterizations, and incidents marred by concessions to sentimental romance in the form of implausible resolutions of plot" (178). Fanning believes, however, that "Cleary's Nebraska stories are an effective antidote to the anti-urban romantic pastoralism" of the period, which promoted the belief that "moving to the country would solve all Irish-American ills" (180).

Ironically, Cleary also wrote some of her most romantically pastoral poems and humorous sketches at this time. Years later, when Cleary's children published *Poems,* a collection of their mother's, uncle's, and grandmother's poetry, her son Jim declared, "All the good things that the plains yielded during the hard years there are found in her poems. Her stories pictured the grinding struggles of the pioneers—the harsher aspects of the new Kansas-Nebraska border country. When the prairie smiled it inspired a poem."[11] This stanza from Cleary's playful poem "Spring Is Coming" exhibits both her love of nature and her delight in the sounds and rhythms of words:

> *Spring is coming, with silver rains rustling—*
> *With swallows a-twittering under the eaves—*
> *With brooklets a-darkling, and dimpling, and sparkling,*
> *Rippling in time to the leaves.*[12]

Other lighthearted verses, such as "How Many?," published in *Puck*, and "Leslie's Lucky Sixpence," a children's story published in *Youth's Companion*, attest to Cleary's ability to see both the dark and light sides of life. Focusing on the beauties of nature or the joys of childhood brought sunlight into her life.

Her writing could not help Cleary completely conquer her grief; in a short lyric poem she revealed the irony she discovered in her loss of three loved ones within a year and a half. Although she had been able to write consoling poetry for others, when tragic losses overwhelmed her, words would not come for her own relief. "The Singer" lyrically reflects this realization:

> *The poet's song of sorrow*
> *That sweetly soothed the smart*
> *Of sorrow's sting, came ringing*
> *Out from a happy heart.*
> *But rose no song of solace*
> *From stricken lips and dumb*
> *When to that heart had sorrow*
> *Supreme and bitter come.*[13]

The summer of 1895 was a difficult one for Cleary, for not only did she have to deal with the recent deaths of her two daughters, but she had to do it alone. One wonders how such a "lovely fellow" as Michael, even with his own health problems, could leave his wife in the "cold and horrid" prairie two months after the death of a child, especially when both she and their son were ill, and then not return for the funeral of a second child. However, neither Cleary nor Peattie berated him.

Sensing her friend's depression, Peattie wrote an undated letter urging Cleary to visit her in Omaha: "How is the deserted matron of the Nebraska Sahara? . . . Dear girl, come and bring your babies as soon as you like. We will have a jolly time. You need not even wait for our house cleaning, because I do not care if the house is dirty. We will not have time to look at it anyway. . . . I hope you are all well, and that only good news comes from your lonesome Tim [Michael]." Cleary did not need much persuading; a month after Rosemarie's funeral, she took the children to Omaha to spend two weeks with the Peatties.

Peattie's daughter, Barbara, returned with Cleary and her family and spent the month of June enjoying the freedom that the large yards and wide, dusty streets of Hubbell provided; her mother came for her and returned the visit. In her memoirs, Peattie recalled evening buggy rides across the prairie: "The little 'ponies' would be hitched to the family carryall, the Clearys would pile in and a loose rein laid on the backs of the strong, gay little beasts, who would race up and down the hills of the rolling plain, gathering sufficient impetus as they went down one hill to dash up another. It was a mad sort of sport, and what would have happened if a wheel came off I shudder to think. But it did not."[14]

Even with the added novelty of company, Cleary still felt despondent. Peattie kindly offered her own daughter as a sort of replacement for the two daughters Cleary had just lost: "So you are trying not to love Bab! You'll have hard work of it. And I really don't see why you should make the effort. She is yours to love all the rest of her life and yours, and I'll share her with you any time you please." She sympathized in the undated letter, "One of your last letters was as blue as a company of little devils. I can say nothing to comfort you. I know of no balm in Gilead. Devotions of one sort and another, forgetfulness of self—these are the only things I know of." Then she added intimately: "Robert is urging me to go to Chicago—this is confidential—take the children, and get out of this accursed country. I hardly dare. It seems so easy to get hungry nowadays. And Rod—fancy if Rod should get hungry! I'm in the grasp of the develines [sic] too, but for different reasons than you, and I have summoned them, perhaps."

Although couched in vagaries and personal allusions, the conclusion of Peattie's undated letter reveals the support system between the two young mothers: "Upon my soul I'm sick of certain things! You think I am making for myself imaginary sorrows? Well—but I will not bore you. You've quite enough troubles of your own. And I swear I would not even have said to any one else that there was a trouble."

Constrained by social mores, both Peattie and Cleary struggled to keep their problems to themselves and to present to their respective families and communities a positive front. By July, a series of "heart attacks," probably angina episodes, and a case of dysentery added physical problems to an already troubled Cleary. She unburdened herself to Peattie, who replied to her friend on 3 July 1895: "We are all terribly distressed to hear of the trouble you had been in—sick and alone, and fearful as you are of the consequences of those heart attacks. Mr. Cleary will be more impatient than ever now to get back home with you again, and stay with you. . . . You seem a good deal run down—you would never have the dysentery otherwise."

But Michael remained in Chicago. Also in July, Vera, seventeen months, became ill, too, and Peattie wrote on 17 July: "Indeed I felt most deeply grieved when I heard that she was ill. I do hope it has been one of those transitory ills of childhood which are frequent." In September, Vera was diagnosed as having typhoid fever. This time, Michael hurried home after an absence of six months, arriving on 6 September. The couple had already lost one child to the dreaded disease, and one can assume that Kate must have been nearly frantic, prompting Michael's immediate return to Hubbell. A week after his arrival, the local newspaper reported: "Baby Vera Cleary has been seriously sick with typhoid fever for the past two weeks but is considerable [*sic*] better at present." At the end of September, Vera apparently out of danger, Michael left again for Chicago. Although the newspaper reported that he would be gone for only a few weeks, he did not return to Hubbell until December, making an absence from home in 1895 of nine months.

Cleary poured out her feelings to Peattie that November, prompting this response on 3 December: "You seem to have got lost in the Valley of the Shadow, and to be wandering there, unable to escape. It is a bitter place, and the winds that blow there chill the soul. I wish I could lead you out of it, away from the fearful and eternal mysteries. The New Year is here, as you say, and must certainly mean growth or retrogression. We must each make our choice, I take it." Peattie understood Cleary's depression and empathized, "Of course I do not blame you for weeping. Why were tears given us if they were not to fall? I do not see any retrogression in the fact that you grieve. It is your right. But do not forget the blessings you have—do not overlook the joy that is yours still."

Knowing the need for personal confidences, Peattie urged, "Can you not come out here and can we not talk together? I hate letters—words seem even more futile when they are written than when they are spoken—and that is unnecessary, heaven knows. . . . We are all well and poorer than ever—in debt too. But what of it? The world is still ours. It's yours too, Kate. Let your tears flow. But remember: 'joy cometh with the morrow.'"

Michael returned in December, shortly after Kate's severe depression, and apparently remained in Nebraska throughout 1896. The Peatties were moving back to Chicago, and both Elia and Kate busied themselves with their families, the social life of their communities, and their writing. Her husband home and the children healthy, Kate's emotional load lightened.

Although the rural community of Hubbell was small and isolated from the larger cultural centers of Nebraska, the town buzzed with activity. In January, the social news for Hubbell in the *Hebron Journal* reported an ice skating party at Spring Branch, six miles north of town, a taffy pull, a G.A.R. Leap Year Ball, and several private parties where couples danced, played High-Five, and enjoyed large midnight suppers. Visiting and visitors also filled the days. Cleary traveled to Omaha the last part of February to visit Peattie, her son Jim stayed with the Peatties in April during a school break, and her brother Edward spent several weeks in Hubbell. When Edward fell ill in June, Cleary and the children accompanied him back to Chicago, nursing him for two months and visiting friends and family.

Michael occupied himself with his business, neglected during his absence. He traveled to the district court in Hebron, where he won two foreclosure cases against delinquent customers. The Hubbell Driving Park Association also claimed Michael's time, for he had served as secretary since its organization. Southwest of Hubbell, along the western bluffs of the valley on land owned by Hubbell Johnson, the association members had built an oval racetrack. They constructed an amphitheater on the west side of the course and a judge's stand across from it on the east side. The horse barns stood on the southwest corner, and the center served as a ballpark and fairgrounds. Celebrated for its good horses and enthusiastic betting, the racetrack drew flocks of people from neighboring towns in Kansas and Nebraska to share in the summer fun. Johnson, who prided himself on his own fine stable of horses, served as president of the association. For other summer amusement, the Clearys played tennis on clay courts with their friends and relatives or held shooting contests with their neighbors. Michael documented it all with photographs, and some of the rivalries even made the local newspaper's gossip column.

Cleary joined in the national craze of bicycling, a sport she had begun when she first moved to Nebraska. In a 12 June 1885 letter, her husband joked with her, "I think riding the bicycle would do you a world of good and in more ways than sleeking." Many families in Hubbell owned bicycles; more than twenty-two "wheels" were reported by townspeople in 1897. The Clearys numbered themselves among that group, with Jim taking special pleasure in his bicycle. The women of Hubbell even featured bicycles in their local celebrations. The newspaper reported that to celebrate Memorial Day, the women decorated their bicycles with flags and formed a procession to the cemetery and then to Johnson's grove, the community picnic area where citizens regularly presented speeches and listened to band concerts. Cleary and the children often took long rides down the hard-packed clay roads, exploring the countryside and enjoying the natural beauty of the plains. She even wrote a bicycle poem titled "A Bicycle Conundrum" that was accepted by *Puck* for its 28 August 1895 issue.

The biggest excitement of 1896, however, was the heated debate over the gold or silver standard and the presidential campaign between Republican William McKinley and Nebraska Democrat William Jennings Bryan. Nebraska townspeople formed political clubs for both sides, and torchlit rallies and parades with hundreds of participants stirred up the dusty streets of the tiny communities. In October, thirty-six women of Hubbell and the surrounding area formed a McKinley and Hobart club and elected officers, including six vice presidents. The next week, the membership swelled to fifty women, who paraded in gold capes and carried torches down the main street of Hubbell. According to the *Hebron Journal*, the Hubbell Bryan Club gave them enthusiastic opposition, sponsoring free-silver rallies that boasted of more than eight hundred participants.

Cleary, who was seven months pregnant in October, contented herself with politicking on the sidelines and by proxy. She wrote political speeches and poems upholding the Republican nominees, and her son Jim, age nine, recited them before enthusiastic crowds. Jim became a state and national celebrity because of his unusual abilities in the political arena, and he was called "The Boy Orator of Hubbell," a takeoff on Bryan's nickname "The Boy Orator of the Platte." Posters publicizing the rallies often featured Jim's name in print as large as that of the visiting politician's.

In its 16 October 1896 issue, the *Hebron Journal* covered a 10 October rally at which Jim had spoken and printed the entire text of his speech. The newspaper noted that the Republican committee had solicited Jim to give the address that was "written by Mrs. M. T. Cleary, who is a woman of literary ability and experience, being a contributor to many of the leading magazines and periodicals. . . . Master James is only nine years old and is gifted with a fine mind and memory. He is already a student and observer of political events, and his delivery of the address elicited hearty applause." The speech contained a thorough and hearty denunciation of Bryan's beliefs, with humor sprinkled throughout. Cleary added a local political appeal for a Dr. Wilcox of Hubbell: "In the blackest night he has come to our call. Through bleak storms he has hastened to our aid. He has congratulated parents when children came. He has mourned with them when some of us went away. He is young, brainy, capable. He has the courage of his convictions. He has the energy to enforce them. He is not to be bought. He has been nominated Representative from this district. He does better than ask your votes. He merits them."

Even the *Chicago Tribune*, undoubtedly upon information supplied by Cleary's brother Edward, featured Jim's portrait and a whole column report in its 29 October 1896 issue, with extracts of his speech from the Hebron rally. The *Tribune* reported, "In the matter of the 'Boy Orator' the political campaign has ceased to present a one-sided appearance. With strict impartiality, Nebraska, after sending out William J. Bryan with an opponent to his name expressive of juvenile declamatory ability, has put on the stump James Mansfield Cleary, 'The Boy Orator of Hubbell—not of the Platte,' on the other side of the question."

Jim, accompanied by his mother, also headed parades, proudly carrying Old Glory and leading marchers in "Shouting for McKinley," a seven-stanza song with a repeated chorus written by Cleary that was sung to the tune of "Marching through Georgia." The final verse proclaims:

> *We've put him in the White House and Protection on her seat,*
> *So we'll rest our weary voices and we'll rest our weary feet,*
> *And we'll eat and eat and eat and eat, and eat and eat and eat—*
>   *After shouting for McKinley.*

"Shouting for McKinley" premiered at the 21 November ratification meeting of the McKinley and Hobart Club held at the G.A.R. Hall in Hubbell. The meeting opened with "America," "The Star-Spangled Banner," and a speech, followed by Cleary's song and more speeches. A hearty meal of roast beef, bread, butter, pickles, and coffee capped the event. After the song was published in local newspapers, it gained an even wider public usage and acclaim.

Although Dr. Wilcox was not elected, McKinley did win the presidency, and Cleary turned her attention to her sixth pregnancy. Evidently her doctor expressed apprehension about the upcoming birth, and this worried Cleary. She wrote to her cousin Lizzie Dunne on 30 December 1896: "I am in daily dread and expectation, of course, now that the time is so near. I am anxious for the worst to come and get it over." She must have also written a letter to Peattie about her fear of dying, a well-founded concern especially for Cleary in her remote area of Nebraska, where capable doctors were rare, medical supplies rudimentary, and hospitals nonexistent. Her earlier childbirth complications surely deepened that anxiety.

Peattie wrote consolingly to Cleary in an undated letter: "Kiss all the children for me, and keep a good heart about the trial at New Years. It is a peculiar fact that things of that sort never turn out as physicians think they will. I just paused to think of seven or eight prophesies made by doctors to the effect that the women could never endure another child, and in each case they not only endured the ordeal but thrived on it." Peattie was right, for on 11 January 1897, Cleary gave birth to Edward Sheridan, nicknamed Teddie after his uncle. Both mother and son thrived.

Her restricted activities that winter during the latter part of her pregnancy and the days of confinement after Teddie's birth afforded Cleary the opportunity to finish another novel, this time a mystery set in Nebraska. *Like a Gallant Lady* is noteworthy for its vivid descriptions of the plains and pioneer life, its memorable minor characters, and its strong, intelligent woman as the central character.[15] On the title page, Cleary quoted Elizabeth Barrett Browning:

> *The World's male chivalry has perished out,*
> *But Women are Knights Errant to the last.*
> *And if Cervantes had been Shakespeare too,*
> *He'd made his Don, a Donna.*

Cleary used an appropriate quotation from Shakespeare to introduce each chapter, and she borrowed heavily from her favorite dramas: from *The Merchant of Venice,* the intelligent and strong woman protagonist; from *Hamlet,* the bloody apparition and mysterious death; from *Othello,* the unfaithful lover; from *The Taming of the Shrew,* the arduous suitors vying for a beautiful woman; and from *Romeo and Juliet,* the two lovers and the potion that causes a death-appearance that ultimately separates them.[16] Like Shakespeare, Cleary knew the importance of comic relief, so she added Peter Jennings, the foolishly pompous Englishman, and Mrs. McLelland, the good-hearted but unsophisticated undertaker's wife, to the novel's cast of characters.

The primary plot of *Like a Gallant Lady* revolves around an insurance scam.[17] Cleary's "Knight Errant," Ivera Lyle, a beautiful and wealthy young lady from Chicago, arrives in Bubble, Nebraska, after learning of the death of her fiancé, Mark Dudley, from her brother, one of his partners in a grain and real estate business. Her journey to the plains results from a mysterious dream she has that Dudley is calling out for her help. Ivera moves in with her brother, Rob, who has taken to excessive drinking since he arrived in the West, helps him straighten out his life, and proceeds to solve the mystery of her fiancé's death. Gallantly following all leads, she discovers that Dudley has not died but has instead been part of a scheme to defraud his and his partners' insurance company. With the unknowing aid of the morphine-addicted local physician, Dr. Eldridge, one of the partners, Prior, has concocted a serum that will simulate death and then formulated its antidote. Dudley was to take the potion, be declared dead, and be presumed buried. Then he was to be revived with the antidote, and the partners were to split the insurance claim. The antidote has failed, and Dudley remains in a vegetative state.

Ivera also discovers that her fiancé has not only been an excessive drinker like her brother but has also proved unfaithful and fathered an illegitimate child. To add the required romance to the tale, Jack Jardine, a young, handsome Englishman who has come to make his fortune in the West, becomes entangled in the mystery. After several misunderstandings and plot twists, Ivera begins to fall in love with Jardine. They meet later in Chicago, but Cleary did not supply the customary arbitrary marriage at the end; instead, she left the couple with "eyes only for each other" as Ivera tears an old letter into pieces and lets "the wind from the west waft them away" (292). Deftly weaving plots and subplots, Cleary employed classic literary traditions as well as popular sentimental conventions to guarantee the novel's success.

Cleary's use of local color and a western setting ensured added sales, and she featured the East-meets-West clash in the first few pages of the novel: "Suddenly a whistle sounded. The men in the saloon bolted for the door and tore wildly down the street. Jardine finished his whiskey, and, in leisurely fashion, followed them. The abrupt exodus signified the approach of the train from the East, which came in every second day. The population of Bubble invariably assembled in force on these occasions." As Ivera steps down from the freight car, "Her gown, the poise of her head, the way she walked, distinguished her as city-bred. Her glance swept her surroundings. She saw the dull, red depot and section-house, the staring crowd of flannel-shirted, top-booted men, of clumsy women, of gaping children; the brand new buildings, many in process of erection, straggling across riven corn-fields; the bluffs, some steep, some sloping, which encircled the bowl-shaped hollow of the embryo town" (2–3).

Cleary expressed the feelings of her love/hate relationship with the plains in "To Nebraska," the poem that she wrote to preface the novel, and this ambivalence surfaces throughout the work. In some instances, the beauty of Nebraska filled her with awe, and Cleary recorded, through her heroine, what may have been her own impressions of the West. Ivera comments to her brother, " 'It is different from what I imagined. I've always thought of Nebraska as level. I find its prairies are like the waves of a subsiding sea.' She was looking out across the billowy undulations all plaided with the dull amber of cornstalks, the vivid green of winter wheat, the delicate daffodil of withered grass. 'It is level, in spots,' he returned, laughing. 'This doesn't happen to be one of the spots' " (34).

Ivera's first impression of the plains is positive: "It was an idyllic morning, the sky blue and luminous, the earth wearing a fresh-washed face, the air crisp and caressing. There were shifting, silvery hazes on the distant bluffs, and to one city-bred the absolute absence of sound was by contrast strangely restful" (35). Later in the novel, after Ivera has spent the winter with her brother in a little shack on the prairie, she finds that same silence overwhelming: "The plains stretched away, boundless and mysterious. The sky, frigated with whitish clouds, loomed low and light. Between these crept the silence, the awful, op-pressive, overwhelming silence of the prairies. It seemed to close around the girl standing there in gigantic coils that crushed out indi-viduality—almost extinguished identity. An impulse to scream as if in a nightmare frenzy—anything to break the spell, came to her" (266). Although Cleary did appreciate the natural beauty of Nebraska, she did not romanticize pioneer life in her novel. As Ivera points out, "The only people who associate solitude, romance and all that sort of thing with the plains are those who write about them without having had any personal experience" (267).

Cleary's heart went out especially to the farm women, and in an attitude reminiscent of the characters of Hamlin Garland, her narrator, Ivera, outlines their plight: "I've been in the farmhouses and talked with the women. Such isolation! Such monotony! Such drudgery! And the hopelessness of ever escaping from these conditions accentuates the horror of them. One exceptionally intelligent woman I met asked me if I had read Kipling's story of the ride of Morrowbie Jukes, and the experience of those endeavoring to escape from the plague pit. 'We are like that here,' she said. 'When those accursed creatures tried to scale the walls that bounded their living grave, the sand sifted down on them, destroying their foothold. We try to escape, and there is the drouth one year out of three, sometimes oftener. In the odd years of prosperity the price of grain goes down, until the most a man makes after all goes but a short way toward paying the indebtedness incurred during the years his land yielded him nothing' " (63–64).

Cleary respected the courage and fortitude of these hardy pioneer women, and, interestingly, it was through Jack Jardine, the man whom Ivera came to love, that she voiced this admiration: " 'I have known instances where women have come out here who were no more fitted to endure the isolation, the intellectual poverty, the grinding routine of ignoble tasks, than a blooded racer is fitted for the plowshare. And yet, in a way, such a woman as one of these makes the most magnificent success of her life. Hardy says in one of his earlier novels that when a strong woman deliberately throws away her strength she is weaker than a woman who has never had any strength to throw away. I don't know if I make myself understood when I speak of such a woman as being lofty enough to submit, strong enough to surrender, passionate enough to be silent' " (277–78).

Comedy balances this bleak view of the frontier experience in *Like a Gallant Lady,* and Cleary's ever-present sense of humor and her Irish sensibilities surface in two minor characters. In one of them, Peter Jennings, a stereotypical Englishman who has come to the West to make a fortune, Cleary mocked the foolish foreigners who infested the West: "He wore a showy plaid suit, abbreviated as to coat and voluminous as to trousers. The helmet of the British tourist adorned his head. A massive gold chain, from which a bunch of seals depended, dangled across his vest. His satin tie was pink as the skin of a Bougereau nymph. In one yellow-gloved hand he carried two satchels. The other gripped a bundle of canes and umbrellas, and held a long, steel chain to which was attached a diminutive dog" (5–6).

Jennings serves as a foil to Jardine—another Englishman, but an intelligent, educated, and attractive one. Jardine has blended into the environment, appearing a part of the western culture, "blue-shirted and corduroy-clad, wearing battered top boots and an ancient hat" (6). Jennings, a western Cyrano de Bergerac, helps forward the love interest in the narrative when he convinces Jardine to write love letters to Ivera for him.

Most memorable, however, is Maria McLelland, a character who also appears in Cleary's stories and sketches. Even Mrs. McLelland's entrance into the narrative is momentous: "Suddenly the sunshine was shut out. A huge shadow wavered across the floor. A mighty tread set the dishes dancing. A gigantic form, gowned in clean and crackling calico, loomed up before them. A square, clean-cut, alert, shrewd old face beamed down upon them" (39). Collapsing upon a chair, Mrs. McLelland laments the problems she has with her legs: "I soak 'em in coal oil, an' I rub 'em with turpentine. Pa kin tell you I used up seven bottles of Shinsquinicook Indian Infallible Remedy on 'em, an' they're that stiff and hurtful yet I say to Pa sometimes I wish I was like that cobbler down to Bubble that supports a fambly on one leg—he ain't got two to bother with ef they git feelin' mean like mine does" (40).

By the end of the narrative, Cleary has rounded out Mrs. Mc-Lelland's character by revealing a more vulnerable side to this strong woman. At one point she confides her feelings to Ivera: "His first wife she was only a bit of a girl—friv'lous, I jedge, as they make 'em. She allus had pretty clothes, an' they say she could sing sweeter'n any bird. But she couldn't cook none to speak on, an' she never saved a carpet rag, or pieced a quilt. She was jest fearful friv'lous—Annie was" (276). Mrs. McLelland confesses, "Pa sets a heap by me. But somehow, when he talks nights—some folks does you know—I ain't ever heerd him propitiate my name. . . . It's allus her'n. Seems like he keeps a-dreamin' of that little thing that was berrid with her baby when she wasn't but nineteen come her next birthday. 'Tain't reel satisfactory after you've been layin' down by the side of a man fur mor'n thirty year to have him stir an' call you Annie when your given name's Maria" (276–77). Mrs. McLelland serves many purposes in the novel: as comic relief, as local color, and as a woman confidant. Perhaps a composite of several women Cleary knew in Hubbell, she represents the strengths and the shortcomings of the pioneer women Cleary encountered on the plains and her conflicting feelings toward them.

Besides describing life in a small frontier town at the turn of the century in rich detail and revealing the attitudes of a woman who had lived in the West for fourteen years, *Like a Gallant Lady* also contains much autobiographical information. Like Ivera (named after her daughter, Vera), Cleary was an intelligent and strong woman from the cultured East who was more sophisticated and intelligent than many of the women in her community. From the window of her two-story home, with its bulging bookshelves and well-stocked pantry, Cleary could view the crude log cabins, sod houses, and dugouts of her less fortunate neighbors. Although Cleary was well liked by the community and blended into the crowd as did her character Jack Jardine, a secret part of her remained intellectually above them—as did a part of him— as if always viewing them from her second-floor window.

With encouragement from her brother Edward, Cleary published *Like a Gallant Lady* with Way and Williams of Chicago in November of 1897. Perhaps Peattie, whose own collection of short stories about the West, *A Mountain Woman,* had been published by them the preceding year, put in a good word for her, too. Way and Williams, who would be Kate Chopin's publisher for *The Awakening* the next year, priced the clothbound book, with its gilt top, bold black lettering, and Will Bradley's ornate cover design of conventionalized corn on a light blue ground, at $1.25.

Although the book sold well and went into a second printing in 1900, the reviews of it were mixed. Eastern critics lauded the novel. The literary critic for the *Post Express* of Rochester, New York, wrote for the 15 January 1898 issue: "This book is a photographic reproduction of the living death of a woman's life on the prairies of the West, a tale of drudgery from dawn to dark, a study of life that is intellectual starvation. It is the biography of the life of a refined Eastern woman in a dreary Nebraska town. The pessimistic tone is in accord with the life portrayed, though there is no lack of grim humor. . . . 'Like a Gallant Lady' is destined to take its place with the best work of Hamlin Garland and Mrs. Peattie."

On 10 December 1897 a short critique in the *Baltimore Sun* noted, "The author understands Nebraska and its people, and has therefore made of 'A Gallant Lady' a novel that has reality in it," but the writer added that the book's action was "slow and full of trivialities, which have no bearing on the plot." The *Chicago Tribune*, on 11 November 1897, lauded the creation of Mrs. McLelland and compared her to Mrs. Malaprop in Sheridan's play *The Rivals*. Although the *Tribune* faulted Cleary for her tendency "to have things happen too suddenly— without sufficient raison d'etre," it classed *Like a Gallant Lady* as "a strong work by a novelist of high promise." The reviewer concluded, "It is a strong, realistic novel, embodying the hardy spirit and the cruel environment of Nebraska life."

The Nebraska reviewers also tempered their praise. The *Omaha Bee*, on 8 December 1897, praised the book's realism but squirmed at the negative image given to its state. After quoting the stanza of "To Nebraska" that describes the harsh aspects of the land, the critic begrudgingly wrote: "But dispiriting and untruthful as this introduction is, the story is full of a kind of life that appeals strongly to western readers." The newspaper admitted that "the village may not be unlike some that have existed in Nebraska in pioneer days, and, for that matter, in all states when far out on the borders of civilization. There is the rough border element in the town and the whole-souled hospitality prevalent, the freedom in social intercourse and the crude methods of amusement common to such places, while the characters are exaggerated and the situations overdrawn. The story is fairly well told, even if it does give some impressions of the west wholly unwarranted."

The *Nebraska State Journal* also qualified its generally positive 22 November 1897 review. Its writer praised Cleary's characters and local-color description: "The author is a Nebraska woman and her first venture of a serious nature in the literary arena is an undoubted success.

The scene of her story is laid somewhere in the Republican valley, in a new mushroom town she calls 'Bubble,' which is painted in very somber colors, and contains rather more than the average number of villains and ne'er-do-wells, but her characters are very strongly drawn and are all unmistakably alive. . . . Some of the eccentric characters are overdrawn, but they are all interesting." However, the reviewer regretted her tone: "Hamlin Garland's pessimism has to a considerable extent over-shadowed the spirit of the story and the indications are that the book has been written about two years, dating back to the drouth period which was so disastrous to western Nebraska." The writer justified this opinion by assuming that the introductory poem was written at a later date and forgave Cleary's negativism because she redeemed Nebraska as "a land that yet shall be / Fair and fertile, proud and free."

Entrenched attitudes about the frontier played a large role in the reviews of *Like a Gallant Lady*, with many in the East accepting the idea that the West was the Great American Desert and those in the West holding out in their belief that the land was a Garden of Eden. Despite their mythic preconceptions, however, all conceded that the novel realistically portrayed an important time and place in American history, and most reviewers favorably compared Cleary's writing to Hamlin Garland's.

Although Edward McPhelim shared in his sister's excitement about the publication of *Like a Gallant Lady*, he did not live to see the book come out in print. He died of tuberculosis on 11 June 1897 at age thirty-four. Again, Cleary's successes were tempered by sorrow. The day after his death, the *Chicago Tribune* ran a brief notice on the front page. On 13 June, the paper printed a longer article extolling his personal qualities and his writing abilities: "The death of Edward J. McPhelim at Elgin will touch the heart of every person who was privileged to know the man. . . . His tastes ran chiefly to literature, and for many years he devoted all his efforts to book work and dramatic criticism, and in both of these allied spheres he made an enviable reputation. He possessed the poetic instinct to a high degree, and it found constant expression in his prose writings." He was further eulogized, and one of his poems was reprinted on the literary pages he had helped to pen.

The only hint in the newspaper of the cause of Edward's death was a brief notation in the funeral listings that he died "after a lingering illness." About a month before Edward died, Michael went to Chicago and visited him in the Elgin hospital. On 7 May 1897, Michael wrote to Kate that he had spoken with Edward's doctors, who had told him that tuberculosis was causing Edward to hemorrhage. The *Chicago Tribune* reported at length on the funeral, held on 14 June, commenting on the many leading members of the worlds of drama, journalism, and literature as well as the various public officials who attended the rites. It is not known whether Kate was able to return for the funeral and to follow the cortege to the burial at Calvary Cemetery, where her mother, younger brother, and one daughter were already interred, but his passing left her with no members of her immediate family surviving.

Sickness again plagued the Clearys in the fall of 1897. Jim was seriously ill with typhoid fever through August and September, and then Michael was attacked with hemorrhaging of the lungs in October and November. With his lumber company failing because of the depressed economic conditions in Hubbell as well as his own poor health, Michael decided to sell the business and find a location more favorable for his condition. He announced his plans at a meeting of the Hubbell Driving Park Association, and on 21 January 1898, the *Hubbell Times* made the decision public: "Mr. Cleary, who has been secretary since the organization of the association, was compelled on account of poor health and his probable removal from Hubbell, to decline re-election. In Mr. Cleary's retirement from the duties of this arduous position the association loses one of its most active workers and one to whom is mainly due the splendid success which has attended all race meetings held under its auspices."

That winter, Michael made several trips to Lincoln on business and on 11 February 1898, the front page of the *Hubbell Times* announced the sale of Cleary Lumber and Coal, one of Hubbell's original businesses, to A. J. Bayse of Kansas. In another article in the same issue, Michael officially declared: "I hereby announce to my old friends and customers that I have sold my lumber yard to Mr. A. J. Bayse, and I also wish to thank those with whom I had dealings for so many years for their friendship and patronage. As I must leave very soon on account of my health I request all persons knowing themselves indebted to me to call and settle accounts." By March the business had been transferred to Bayse for $1,500, and by April Michael was on a train headed for the Pacific Coast in search of a better climate. Four weeks later, he returned to Nebraska after stops in Tacoma, Portland, and Seattle, cities he was considering as a new home for the family; instead of going west, however, the family decided to move back to Chicago. Michael remained in Hubbell for only one week before departing once more, this time for Chicago for another month's stay. It is odd that Michael chose to return to a climate that he had once left for health reasons, but economics may have played a major role in the decision.

Meanwhile, Cleary remained at home with the children, organizing lavish birthday parties for each of them, visiting friends and relatives in Hebron and Superior, making arrangements for the reburial of Rosemarie at Calvary Cemetery in Chicago, and taking care of last-minute business. She sold an empty lot in the Coon Addition to the Bayses for seventy-five dollars, donated to the town another lot upon which the town hall had been erected, presented the Methodist Episcopal church (whose services the family attended when the traveling Catholic priest was not in town) with a lamp to be placed in front of the building, and, as always, wrote and wrote, publishing mainly patriotic articles about the Spanish-American War for the *Chicago Tribune,* the *Nebraska State Journal,* and the *Havelock (Nebr.) Times.*

Cleary's husband returned to Hubbell in the middle of June to help with the final preparations for moving. He was just in time to attend, with three other Hubbell men, the extravagant Trans-Mississippi Exposition that had recently opened in Omaha. His descriptions of the fabulous buildings and exotic grounds inspired Cleary to pen probably the last story she wrote in Nebraska, "At the Omaha Fair," a tale about a poor farmer's daughter who attends the extravaganza and daydreams that she is a princess. Cleary transcribed the scenes her husband related to her and let her own memories of the Chicago World's Fair, newspaper photographs, and her imagination fill in the details as she fictionally transplanted a sheltered country girl to the fantasy world of the 1898 exposition: "Once she stood to watch a procession pass. There were Egyptians—supple, handsome, bronze-skinned creatures, flinging their shining swords in swift, sweeping circles from hand to hand. Chinese women, their black hair braided down their dough-white faces, weighted down with the golden embroidery on their silken gowns, tottered along on their poor cramped feet. . . . A sumptuous creature in crimson tights smiled from her pinnacle on a chariot. Indians, feathers in their hair, their naked bodies striped with paint, their grim visages emotionless as masks of bronze, rode slowly by."

The "princess" has to return from Omaha to her homestead and become once more merely a "thin, brown girl in a patched and faded cotton gown" who "stood at the door of a little shack, and looked out across the vast stretches of Nebraska prairie. Overhead was a burning sky. The sun blistered down. The crackling of the corn in the dusty wind was like the rattle of musketry." The girl's father has no use for "such notions" as those the girl dreams of, but Cleary knew that only beauty and imagination could keep a soul alive amidst such physical and emotional deprivation. The *Chicago Tribune* published the story on 4 September.[18]

Soon Cleary was saying farewell to the endless sweep of Nebraska prairie and the legions of emerald corn. She and Michael sold their home to L. P. Luce, packed their belongings, and on Sunday, 3 July 1898, departed on the train for Chicago. She must have had mixed emotions about leaving the house they had built, furnished, and loved, the home where she had begun to raise her children and had lost two of them. Perhaps, as the train pulled away from Hubbell's dull red depot and she looked down the dusty main street, Cleary felt again the ambivalent emotions she had expressed so well in the final stanza of her poem "To Nebraska." She was leaving forever the state that had "harbored bride, and slave and guest," a state that had "given worst— and best!"[19]

3

Back to Chicago:
1898–1903

In the summer of 1898, the Clearys moved to Austin, Illinois, then a western suburb of Chicago and a strongly Irish community of bungalows and "two-flats"—two-story apartment buildings. Jim had advanced enough in his education, presumably through the literary influence and tutoring of his mother, to enter Austin High School at age eleven. Little is known about the family's life during the next four years, except that Cleary belonged to the Austin Women's Club, that financial problems continued to harass the family, that neither Cleary's nor her husband's health improved, and that Cleary wrote and published persistently to "keep the wolf from the door." City directories for those years indicate that the family, listed under M. T. Cleary, lived an unsettled life.

In 1899, Michael Cleary worked as the secretary and treasurer for Dumont and Cleary, an advertising agency at 315 Dearborn.[1] W. D. Dumont was the president. The next year, the family moved to 109 South Central Avenue, and Michael worked at Weadley and Cleary at 59 Lake Street; he and Alfred J. Weadley specialized in bicycles. The family moved again in 1901 to 5002 Washington Boulevard, and Michael was now employed as a bookkeeper at 43 South Green Street. The next relocation, in 1902, was only to 5500 Washington Boulevard; Michael had opened Cleary and Company, a fruit store at 96½ Madison. By 1903, he had assumed a job as secretary for Templeton Lumber at 440 South Canal Street, working for Arthur B. Templeton. It was Arthur's brother John from Superior, Nebraska, who had married Michael's sister Josie and had helped Michael establish the Hubbell lumber business. Again, the family moved, this time to 2183 Monroe.

Until the job with Templeton Lumber in 1903, it appears that each of Michael's employment opportunities necessitated buying into or establishing a business. Although the sale of the Cleary home and business in Hubbell must have afforded the family a small relocation fund, since Michael's enterprises never lasted more than a year, these investments may have drained the family resources.

Cleary's publishing activity provides an additional source for biographical speculation. During her first year back in Chicago, Cleary published her best short stories, most of which were local-color stories about the West, many of them humorous. Distanced from the prairie town, settled back into her beloved Chicago, and with money in the bank, temporarily at least, she had the luxury to write and revise. The *Chicago Tribune* published an average of three of her stories a month in its Sunday Arts section, often featuring her work as the leading story as well as works by Bret Harte, Rudyard Kipling, Hamlin Garland, Edith Wharton, and Sarah Orne Jewett.

Upon her return to Chicago, Cleary found herself in the midst of a great literary explosion in the Midwest. Beginning around 1885, Chicago had risen in importance as a literary and art center. In *Crumbling Idols* (1894), Hamlin Garland asserted that "the rise of Chicago as a literary and art center is a question only of time, and of a very short time; for the Columbian Exposition has taught her her own capabilities in something higher than business." He believed that "the founding of vast libraries and art museums is the first formal step, the preparation stage; expression will follow swiftly, magazines and publishing houses are to come" (152). Garland's prophecy came true, for by 1905 Chicago was ranked second behind New York in book and job printing, and the "Chicago school" of writers, such as Garland, Theodore Dreiser, Frank Norris, and Henry Blake Fuller, were publishing widely. During the first two decades of the twentieth century, Chicago became recognized as the literary and cultural capital of America.[2]

Cleary outlined her philosophy of writing in "Apropos of Story-Writing," published in the *Writer* at about this time. She believed that, ideally, one should "write fully the red-hot idea when it is sizzling in your brain—when your pencil will not, for all your endeavor, run as fast as your burning thoughts. Verse, story, or essay is the better for being transferred to paper with all rapidity—and the manuscript then locked up." She also explained her process of revision: "When one has partially forgotten its existence, and can read it over with the dispassionate and coolly critical judgment one would give to the work of a stranger, the time for revision has come. For the writer there is only one good and sane rule, and that's a paraphrase: 'Write in haste and revise at leisure!' "

Aware of William Dean Howells's dictum to faithfully record the realities of the American scene, especially its "smiling aspects," Cleary kept an eye open for significant local detail and representative individuals. Many of her best stories revolved around her experiences in Nebraska, and she found humor and courage in the lives of the people she had observed there. Of course, she went beyond the "smiling aspects" in her more naturalistic stories, also recording the gritty aspects of life on the frontier, and for this she was denounced by some Nebraska critics.

Cleary's humorous western stories written during this period are among her most significant contributions—stories such as "An Ornament to Society," "Jim Peterson's Pension," "Sent to Syringa," "A Western Wooing," and "The Rebellion of Mrs. McLelland." In these stories Cleary employed the popular literary devices of the time: vernacular or dialect humor, malapropisms, caricature, exaggeration, and verbal witticisms. However, because of her strong education in and love of the classics, especially Shakespeare, the traditional comic personae of the *eiron* (the witty, self-deflating fool who pretends to be less than he or she is) and the *alazon* (the boastful impostor who appears to be more than he or she is) also appear in her texts.

Cleary usually narrated her stories from a third-person omniscient viewpoint or through the eyes of a minor character who serves as a sort of "straight man" to forward the plot. Whichever point of view she assumed, she maintained a sophisticated, almost superior detachment from her comic characters, viewing them with realistic objectivity. In this way, her comic types serve a broader purpose than simple entertainment; quite often they function satirically, to expose cultural flaws. This "literary habit of satire" had its roots in eighteenth-century Ireland, Charles Fanning believes, and was a typical response for Irish immigrants, whose tradition recognized words as a powerful offensive weapon.[3]

Cleary's western stories, especially "An Ornament to Society" and "Jim Peterson's Pension," not only realistically document life in the small towns of the American West but also point out the incongruities and absurdities of the idealized cultural images that had been imported, along with bustles and brocade, to a frontier in the process of formation. For Cleary, the idealized Angel of the House seemed even more out of place in the big outdoors of the West than in the parlor societies of the East. In her fiction she attacked the superficial education of the typical Victorian woman, criticizing the artificial ideals that were taught as well as the men and women who perpetuated them.

In several of her stories, Cleary constructed a New Woman, a New *Western* Woman, dedicated to the concept of individual freedom and personal growth. Her New Western Woman was strong enough to confront the Victorian Cult of True Womanhood and enjoy life to its fullest. Like Cleo Harrowsby in "An Ornament to Society," who chooses *not* to submit to traditional roles, not to be simply an "ornament," many of Cleary's female protagonists elect to take responsibility for themselves, to choose or to defy their husbands, to map their own destinies. A young woman, prescribed Cleary in her fiction, should have the freedom to roam where she pleases; she should be self-taught from nature; she should be physically active, even in those pursuits that are typically male dominated; and her activities should be eclectic, ranging from candy pulls to "literaries." As Cleary wrote of Cleo Harrowsby, "In those crisp, yellow autumnal days, whether walking miles and miles or skimming over the good, hard Nebraska roads on the bicycle her father had bought her, or shooting quail and prairie chicken along the short cuts and seldom used prairie ways, or racing the black horse to a distant candy pull or 'literary,' [Cleo] came nearer the full experience of content than she had ever known."

Cleary's western satires provide firsthand interpretations of life in the New West. Even though she exposed her neighbors' and friends' social facades—which were like the typical western building's impressive false front, designed to make it appear more imposing on the vast stretches of Nebraska plains—she also captured the diverse contents within. Never cutting or cruel, her humor mocked the pretenses of society, not the women and men striving to bring a reassuring civility to an isolated frontier.

In an article titled "Women Who Have Humor," published on 21 July 1898, the *Chicago Chronicle* paid tribute to three leading women humorists in that city, reporting that in one of them, Kate McPhelim Cleary, "with the laughter-loving temperament of the Irish race," readers discover "real pleasure and delight, to say nothing of success. She is a regular contributor to *Puck* and various other humorous periodicals, and talks as brightly and as vividly as she writes." The article described her as "a genuine bohemian, loving freedom and unconventionality as more ordinary women love matters of dress and household adornment. Her day, had she free and unhampered choice in this direction, would begin near midnight and end only with dawn." The critic called her a "natural humorist" and said she was respected by the people "whose cares she has lightened and whose sorrows she has rendered endurable by her kindly and sympathetic gayety." The article declared that "there was never yet the trouble which she couldn't make one smile over."

Cleary's humor may have lightened the burdens of others, but for her, the ability to be "cheerful and gay" throughout "adverse and trying experiences" was hard earned. In 1900, she abruptly began to write only formula fiction for the "Story of the Day" in the *Chicago Tribune*. This transition may have had several causes. First, the newspaper discontinued publishing the more creative fiction by established writers in its Sunday edition; instead, it began the daily story, featuring short, sentimental, popular fiction appealing to a female audience. Second, since it does not appear that she even tried to publish anywhere else, financial problems may have been a motivating factor in her churning out stories quickly for an accessible market.

A larger problem may also have confronted Cleary as a writer. In the period from 1885 to 1920, Chicago writers grouped themselves into the three well-defined writing worlds of the university, the studio, and the newspaper. The academics of the Chicago universities occupied themselves with literary criticism, not creative writing. The "Harvard gang," as they were called, were intrigued by the image of the New Woman. Although they allowed women equal status within the teaching community, the male intellectuals nevertheless dominated the writing group. Studio life, on the other hand, was controlled by elite society, mainly women; this "artistic gang" drank tea and socialized with the "right people" in groups such as the Little Room, the Cliff Dwellers, the Chicago Club, and the Fortnightly. Art was judged by how well it pleased these wives of the Chicago business leaders. Finally, the "journalistic gang," whose function was not to please the exclusive few but to entertain the larger public, formed the Press Club and the White Chapel Club, which were restricted to newspapermen, businessmen, and male politicians. They believed that "good writing" should be contemporary in subject and realistic in local-color depiction and should contain human interest. They did not abide by the "social intolerance of the 'silk-stocking' puritans" who were "openly anti-semitic, anti-immigrant, and anti-Catholic."[4]

Although Cleary's writing fit in all three worlds, the critical, the literary, and the popular, she could stand only on the borderline of each. With higher education a closed avenue for her because of her domestic and financial situation, not her intelligence, she could never be a part of the university scene; the newspapers were the only outlets where she could earn a living as a writer, yet the studio pets considered any newspaper writing to be sub-literature; and she was denied entrance into the "old boys' " journalistic order because of her gender—she could publish in newspapers, but she could never "belong." Since Cleary needed to write to provide for her family, she did what she had to do to survive and remained isolated from any supportive community of writers.

Cleary soon discovered that the most lucrative publishing opportunities came from syndicates such as the Daily Story Publishing Company, the McClure Syndicate, Associated Magazines, and the Authors' Syndicate. As a result, her formula stories began appearing regularly in the *Chicago Tribune,* the *Chicago Daily News,* the *Chicago Record Herald,* and the *Chicago American,* as well as in newspapers across the United States that subscribed to the syndicates. She also entered national story competitions like those sponsored by the *Detroit Herald* and *Collier's,* hoping to win but also knowing that runners-up often had their works published, too, if only at the "per-word" rate.[5]

A typical "Story of the Day" written by Cleary centered on romance, featuring either a wealthy and beautiful young girl, usually between seventeen and twenty, whose major dilemma in life was choosing the proper gown and the right mate, or a wealthy and handsome bachelor, usually in his mid- to late twenties, whose elegant but lonely apartment and meaningless life needed a woman's warmth. Cleary knew what would sell, so she wrote for an audience that still believed in the same fantasies that she had capitalized on in her first short story published twenty years earlier. Most of her stories are set in Chicago or at the resorts of the idle rich, but several of them have western settings or a western protagonist confronting the big city.

Even Cleary's potboilers have a graceful style and creative or satiric edge that make them captivating. Often their plots have unusual or ironic twists, and many strong and memorable women protagonists add depth to the narratives. Cleary took pride in the descriptive details and psychological realism she used in these works, terming them her "good bad stuff."[6] In a humorous poem published in *Puck* on 13 December 1893 entitled "A Warning to Novelists," she tells writers that "the novel of the future" may be "didactic," "humorous or wise," or "of themes transcendent treat," but warned

> *Oh! soon and swift the wrath will fall,*
> *And swift will be the slaughter*
> *Of those whose heroines shall trail*
> *Their fingers in the water!*

One popular Cleary story, "A Lenten Costume," published in the *Chicago Tribune* on 31 March 1900, employs the traditional mistaken-identity plot. Nannie, a Cinderella-like young lady, surreptitiously wears her wealthy sister-in-law's new Lenten dress to church when the lady is too ill to attend. Nannie is mistakenly introduced as her widowed sister-in-law to the wealthy Major Ardene. He promptly falls in love with her and marries her, even after the accidental ruse and her poverty are discovered. In this piece, Cleary adroitly and humorously satirized the superficial Christianity of women who attend church to show off their elaborate Parisian costumes rather than to worship God. Several of Cleary's popular stories contain autobiographical elements, reflecting her life in small-town Nebraska and in big-city Chicago. In "The Price Paulina Paid," published sometime in 1900, a "well-known novelist from the east" visits the "dull little town of Braxville," and Paulina, a local celebrity because of her published volume of sentimental poetry, eagerly anticipates the event. Mrs. C. Browning Delamere appears before the Braxville ladies' group, looking "monumental and out of her element in the unpretentious best room of the largest private house of the village." The novelist's speech is "liberally decorated with quotations, and punctuated with platitudes. But none of those who listened lost sight of the fact that she was a successful city author and club woman—least of all Paulina Wright." When the famous writer snobbishly proclaims that she has never heard of Paulina's poems and snidely asks if there are any other "celebrities" in Braxville, Paulina replies, "We have gentlewomen in Braxville, Mrs. Delamere! Occasionally we bring celebrities here—and pay them for amusing us!"

Cleary had to end the story happily to satisfy the public, so she concluded it with Paulina running out into the rain, humiliated and humbled, and being rescued by her Prince Charming. Paulina learns that "her life's best happiness must come to her in John Litner's love, and in 'The sweet, safe shelter of the household fire.' " Despite the syrupy, disappointing ending, Cleary's satire of the pomposity of so-called celebrated eastern writers gives the text a subtle edge. Nor could she suppress self-mockery of her own "felicity in writing melodious verse" that was "so simple and—and—and sweet" that the townspeople made themselves "sick crying over" her poems about dead children.

"The Romance of a Ring," published on 27 June 1900 in the *Chicago Tribune,* is a simple tale of a man who finds a diamond ring in a washroom of the Chicago Public Library and returns it to its owner, a young woman who is wealthy enough to have her own library to share with him. The plot is predictable, but delightful autobiographical paragraphs weave in and out of Cleary's narrative: "John Burroughs got into the habit of taking a dose of literary browsing every afternoon. Indeed, he went as regularly up to the aloof and delightful rooms of the Crerar or Public Library as other men dropped into their favorite haunts for a glass of Madeira, or a Frenchman stops to sip his 5 o'clock absinthe. To be sure, the reading of good literature was his only intemperance. And love of the arts can never be an objectionable mania, although occasionally it proves an unprofitable one." Cleary represented her own love for literature in this piece, as well as her admiration for the splendor of the new Chicago Public Library erected in 1897, specifically its public rest rooms, with their rows of marble basins: "He wheeled around, gave his hat to the attendant, removed his cuffs, and turned the hot water faucet. A sense of gratitude to the founder of this particular library, and to the individual who suggested a public lavatory, came over him. One of these days, when he had made his pile, he would see that his money reverted to those who should be benefited in a manner at once as worthy and artistic as the former, as utilitarian as the latter." Although Cleary could now experience such classic elegance only in public places, she dreamed of the time when she, too, would make her "pile" and could afford to share beauty with those less fortunate.

In her formula fiction, Cleary's depiction of the competition of the courtship ritual and the struggle for social position, money, and prestige as well as against parental domination epitomizes the values of turn-of-the-century Chicago society. "The end of love in Chicago must be marriage," asserts Hugh Dalziel Duncan in *The Rise of Chicago as a Literary Center.* "It is a Darwinian world in which the battle is to the swift and to the strong. It is only characters who will play the game according to the rules stated in these terms who are depicted at all" (89). Although all the conflicts in Cleary's stories, as in most popular fiction of the time, are quickly resolved through marriage, tension often exists within the heroines themselves, who fluctuate between dependence and self-reliance.

Finally, in late 1901, the prestigious *McClure's* accepted two of Cleary's stories, and in 1903 *Cosmopolitan* published another. As her payments increased, so did her fame. When *McClure's* chose Cleary's story "The Stepmother" to open its September 1901 issue, a flurry of reviews followed. In an undated clipping from the *Chicago Tribune*, one reviewer wrote with approval, "One of the most powerful stories in the September magazines is 'The Stepmother,' by Kate M. Cleary, published in *McClure's*. It is a story of Nebraska—and after that statement is made it goes without saying that the story is a tragedy." After describing the plot, the reviewer continued, "Dan Carr loved his stepmother, had some appreciation of her courage, her patience, her longing for beauty, her desire to live a dignified life, worthy of the admiration of those around her. He gave her the admiration which her husband withheld, and mingled with it a tenderness which a boy feels for his mother. . . . Mrs. Cleary is to be congratulated upon the somber strength of this tale."

The *Omaha World-Herald*, however, took offense personally to "The Stepmother" and entitled its 28 August 1901 review "A Libel on Nebraska." The reviewer proclaimed, "To those who live in Nebraska—eye-witnesses to the prosperity of the farmers, the splendor of its big cities, and the thrift of its smaller cities and towns, will naturally be surprised if not indignant at the publisher of *McClure's* magazine for permitting such a libel on a great and powerful commonwealth to appear on its pages. The statements of the story are absurd; but unfortunately while this is known here, it is unknown to the people of the east where the magazine largely circulates." After listing the gross errors of the narrative, the *World-Herald* reviewer argued that "there is not a 'rocky farm' in Nebraska," that "Nebraska farmers are not dyspeptic. They are not maudlin drunkards," and that "the Nebraska farm woman does not distinguish her speech with a 'lingual slovenliness,'" and concluded that "the author's unfortunate 'Stepmother' is not indigenous to Nebraska soil."

Two days later, another local review added to the moral outrage in Nebraska, pointing out more inaccuracies in Cleary's text. This reviewer agreed with the *Omaha World-Herald* that there were no rocky farms, bad farmers, or dust storms in May in Nebraska, and added that Nebraska women are "direct descendants of women of the East and in the main they are educated, cultured women to whom the vice of slovenliness is a stranger." Moreover, the reviewer wrote, " 'oceans of oats' are not raised in Nebraska," and "the wind does not 'bellow up from Kansas' in Nebraska. The only winds that bellow out there are the winds from the northwest and east." This critic concluded, "We do not agree with the World Herald in attributing to the author of the story or to the publisher of the magazine any unworthy motive. Ignorance of the West—the real West—is probably responsible for this remarkable picture of life in one of the most prosperous, enlightened, and progressive states of the Union."[7] Cleary, who had endured the Nebraska droughts of the nineties, observed the depressed farmers in the notorious state-line Hubbell taverns, spoken to uneducated farmers' wives and immigrant women wrestling with the English language on their rare trips into town, and struggled against the typical south winds, probably laughed out loud at the ignorance of editors whose western experience did not extend outside Omaha's city limits.

Articles about homemaking also proved lucrative for Cleary after her return to Chicago. Ten years earlier, she had profited from her culinary skills and published a series of articles in *Good Housekeeping* and the *Housewife,* giving recipe variations and cooking tips. Remembering these successes, she added some research to her homemaking background and wrote a series of articles for the *Home World,* a new women's magazine edited by Miles Benjamin Hilly that was to begin publication in 1902.[8] Undoubtedly impressed by her skill, sophistication, and straightforward approach, the editors asked Cleary to write the introductory article for the first issue, coming out in February 1902, and she complied: "By way of making one's bow to the readers of the *Home World,* it may be well to state explicitly the purpose and scope of this little magazine. The need has been observed and recognized of giving people of refined tastes the opportunity to keep in touch with modern furnishings and the current fancies in house decoration, which go so far to making one's abode a place of esthetic charm as well as of rest and comfort."

Cleary's articles for the *Home World* were eclectic, ranging from "The Uses of Denim," "The Children's Hour," and "Notes about House Decoration" to "Cooking Over," "The New Furniture," and "The Literary Mother." All reflected her love of culture, her individuality, and her belief that making a home for one's family could be an intellectual endeavor. In "Culture and Cooking," published posthumously in *Ex-*

tension in February 1910, she expounded on this philosophy, "Cooking is an accomplishment of value and distinction. More—it presupposes intelligence. A stupid man or woman is never a first-class cook." She agreed with a French poet who said, "An ideal cook must have a great deal of the poet's nature, combining something of the voluptuary with the man of science." The *Home World* evidently did not last long, perhaps for only a few issues, for it is not even recorded in the Library of Congress.

Although Cleary's prodigious writing alleviated her family's financial straits, it placed a heavy burden on her. Not only did her husband's health remain unstable, preventing him from holding a steady job, but Cleary was suffering, too, for she had never completely recovered from the childbed fever she had nearly died from in 1894 after the delivery of her fifth child, Vera. Taking care of the house, the four children, and a sick husband while sandwiching in time to write exacted a high physical and emotional toll. Before her oldest son, Jim, received his diploma from Austin High School in 1902 at age fifteen, the youngest pupil ever graduated from a Chicago high school, Kate admitted herself into a private sanitarium—for morphine addiction.[9]

Women's sanitariums proliferated in Chicago at the turn of the century, filling the classified ads of the newspapers with promises of "nervous debility successfully cured" and "skillful and scientific treatment of all diseases peculiar to women."[10] With privacy assured and hope kindled, Cleary finally admitted she needed help. According to family history, Cleary's addiction had begun eight years earlier with the childbed fever, when her doctor had given her morphine for the pain. Cleary's recovery process had been a slow one, and this allowed the morphine to take control of her body. She must have attempted to stop using the drug later that year and throughout 1895, for in her letters to her friend Elia Peattie she complained of "heart attacks," "dysentery," "depression," and "weeping"—all symptoms of morphine withdrawal.[11]

However, the timing of her attempts to quit taking morphine could not have been worse. It was only nine months after Vera's birth that Marguerite fell ill. Cleary, still weak from her own illness, nursed her daughter during her typhoid fever, only to lose her in December 1894, a little over a year after her own mother had died of pneumonia. Then Michael's health worsened, and he departed for Chicago in February of 1895, leaving behind a sick and grieving wife to manage the family by herself. That April, the frail Rosemarie, too, became sick and died. Kate had to care for her daughter, plan the funeral arrangements, and grieve alone. Hardly had she adjusted to the death of Rosemarie when Vera came down with typhoid fever. Although Michael came home in September and stayed until Vera was out of danger, he again left for Chicago. It is understandable that Kate's attempts to stop taking morphine met with little success. She must have felt she needed all the strength she could muster, in whatever form.

Quinine, morphine, and alcohol were all therapeutic mainstays for many doctors in the late nineteenth century, and most had little fear of their effects.[12] They found morphine to be a powerful painkiller and calming agent. Its use, after the invention of the hypodermic syringe in 1853, had become widespread during and after the Civil War. In the later part of the nineteenth century, the opium derivative was readily available without a prescription and had a standard strength. Many doctors considered morphine the ideal analgesic, for it was inexpensive, was not toxic even after extended use, had few side effects, and was easily administered. The one drawback, of course, was that, once addicted, the user had to have his or her daily dose of morphine to feel "normal." It was this need to function as usual, rather than a desire for euphoria, that caused the dependence.[13]

Morphine, as well as cocaine, laudanum, heroin, and alcohol, were also used in countless multi-drug patent medicines advertised to cure every conceivable ill. According to Glenda Riley in *The Female Frontier*, "Prairie women also turned to patent medicines for relief both from their maladies and from frequent pregnancies. Based on morphine, quinine, or alcohol, these remedies were supposed to relieve menstrual pain, female diseases of all sorts, and problems associated with childbearing and birth" (50). For women living in isolated frontier communities, these patent medicines could easily be purchased through the mail or at any general store.

In some cases, unregulated medicine manufacturers consciously sought to addict their customers to assure a steady business, and even so-called cures for drug dependence contained opiates. It was not until 1906, after the Bayer Company in Germany had developed heroin in 1898 and used it as the main ingredient in their cough medicine, that the United States government passed the Pure Food and Drug Act.[14] This act, however, merely forced patent drug manufacturers to state the alcohol and narcotic contents on the label; it did not eliminate the drugs from the medicine or limit their availability to patients with doctors' prescriptions.

It is not known whether during her severe illness Cleary became addicted to morphine through patent medicines, whether she took morphine capsules, or whether she injected herself hypodermically, but clues in her writings reveal some interesting insights. One is that she was aware of morphine addiction and its links with doctors' "cures." Hubbell historians relate, moreover, that it was general knowledge not only that the local physician was a morphine addict but that he had addicted other residents as well.

While writing *Like a Gallant Lady* in 1896, probably two years into her own addiction, Cleary took literary revenge for her doctor's addicting her to morphine by inventing the fictional Bubble physician, Dr. Eldridge, for her scapegoat. She described the country doctor "driving over the prairies in his ramshackle buggy, glancing from parched sod to pitiless sky . . . being fortified by frequent administrations of morphine," and believing "that there was no God in heaven, no compassion nor supreme intelligence anywhere" (249–50). Throughout the text she criticized the doctor as "a drugged fool" (251) and berated him, saying, "You stick to your hypodermic syringe, will you, and leave other people's affairs alone" (254).

Cleary was also aware of patent medicine claims. In *Like a Gallant Lady,* when Ivera helps an immigrant girl with her sick child, she discovers that the family has been giving the baby patent medicines that would even "cure chickens." Ivera retorts, "But that isn't the right kind of medicine. That will not help him any" (121). Even when the stalwart Mrs. McLelland becomes depressed, she takes down her black vial of "Composition Tea," which is "warmin' and soothin' " (216).

Later, Cleary's negative attitude toward herself and her six-year morphine habit surfaced in a short story with the sadly ironic title "The

Boy's Mother," published on 8 February 1900 in the *Chicago Tribune*. In this narrative, the son of a brilliant statesman has just died, and people sympathize with the family, especially with the boy's mother, who is supposed to be an invalid. However, unknown to anyone but the family, the boy's mother is really a morphine addict, and it was "knowing her case was hopeless" that took from the son his "wish to recover." Cleary showed no compassion when describing the mother's need for the drug: "We don't know how she got it, sir. She must have bribed one of the nurses—she's that cunning. I'd suspected something for the last week—she was that quiet. But we caught her with a syringe and an ounce of the drug last night—just as she was going to use it. She's wild for it now. The doctor has just been here. He says when a case goes on as long as this—five full years—there's only an institution left." The story continues to describe the completeness of the woman's degradation as she begs, "Give it to me—give it to me! My God, I'll go crazy if you don't. The point of the needle is broken off? What do I care? You can tear my arm in pieces—only give it to me! Just a little bit of morphine—you can take my rings for it, Jane! Here—here! Only a few grains! Then I'll be still—so still."

At the same time, Cleary's literary career was not proceeding as she had hoped. A parallel to her own trials might be seen in "The Destiny of Delores," a popular story Cleary published sometime in 1901 shortly after the *Chicago Tribune* reported on the front page the suicides of three women who drank carbolic acid.[15] In the story Delores, a small-town girl, leaves home naively believing she can be a writer: "I have been scribbling all my life. I want to be a writer. I shall not be content with a little success. I must become famous. And I shall. I've been reading a great deal about women who have succeeded. They almost all went to cities. Many worked hard for a time on newspapers. I can do it—I know I can. It's my destiny." Delores finally realizes that "she had exaggerated ideas of the facility with which one, imaginative, although untrained, might earn a living by literary work. And she did not dream that in such work experienced mediocrity counts for more than crude, unpolished talent." Just as Delores reaches her lowest point, the voice of an old admirer startles her, and the bottle of carbolic acid she is in the act of drinking from to kill herself falls and splinters on the sidewalk. Delores may not achieve her destiny as a writer, but she is rescued by love.

"The Boy's Mother" and "The Destiny of Delores" were not bylined, so the author of these tales remained anonymous to the public. Cleary must have realized the depths to which her addiction was pulling her as well as the negative effect it was having upon her family, especially her beloved son Jim, and she must have feared that the popular fiction she had to pen for survival was jeopardizing her literary career.

Drugs were considered a major problem in Chicago at the time, and Cleary's stories about their abuse would have interested a wide audience. The *Chicago Tribune* proclaimed in "Cocaine in Chicago" that "victims of the deadly drug are numerous and its use is increasing." The article blamed doctors for abusing all drugs and accused them of prescribing opiates "rashly, foolishly, almost criminally."[16] Cleary's sanitarium cure was unsuccessful, and by May of 1902, she had relapsed into her morphine habit.

In the fall of 1903, Cleary arranged for the children's schooling. The younger ones left for boarding schools in Bourbonnais, Illinois, south of Chicago: Vera, nine, had transferred to Notre Dame Academy from St. Catherine's in Austin, and Gerald, twelve, and Teddie, six, attended St. Viator's Academy. As the family was moving to yet another address, this time 415 Jackson Boulevard, Cleary collapsed. On 13 October 1903, she was admitted to the Illinois Northern Hospital for the Insane at Elgin. The case book listed her occupation as "Housewife," the duration of her addiction as four years, the form of her disease as "Mania (morphine)," and the assigned cause as "Alcohol and Morphine."[17] What Cleary endured at the hospital can only be surmised. Contemporary medical books and articles, Cleary's weekly letters to her son Jim, and a book entitled *A Year at the Elgin Insane Asylum*, published in 1902 and written under the pseudonym Kate Lee by a woman who was a patient there from 1899 to 1900, all help to reconstruct the seven months Cleary spent at the hospital.

During the sixty days between her admittance on 13 October and her transferral to the "well" ward in the second week of December, Cleary underwent treatment in the infirmary. According to medical articles and texts of the time, opinion varied on the best methods for the treatment of morphine addiction; however, by today's standards, all are appalling.[18] Most doctors considered a fifty- to sixty-day treatment period to be the minimum necessary and believed in a preliminary period of "purging" to eliminate all bodily fluids capable of storing the "poison." To achieve this end, doctors employed strychnine and calomel (chloride of mercury), powerful cathartics to empty the intestinal tract; Seidlitz water, a laxative consisting of sodium bicarbonate, tartaric acid, and Rochelle salt, which is a crystalline compound used in making mirrors; and pilocarpine, a poisonous compound used to induce sweating.

Unfortunately, as Sarah Stage explains in *Female Complaints,* calomel was not only "therapeutically useless" but also dangerous, for it "broke down in the intestines into a virulent mercurial poison" (49). Moreover, Stage laments, "doctors quick to see the evils of patent medicines showed a remarkable blind spot when it came to the misuse of calomel, quinine, alcohol, morphine, and other dangerous drugs they used with abandon. In retrospect, it seems likely that medical doctors in the nineteenth century were responsible for at least as much promiscuous poisoning as the patent medicine vendors they attacked" (63).

When the patient was completely dehydrated, the withdrawal of the morphine began. Most doctors believed in the complete and abrupt cessation of morphine administration, for although the struggle was severe, the patient suffered for a much shorter time. Typically, doctors administered hydrobromate of hyoscine (scopolamine, used as a sedative and as a truth serum) or chloralamide (a hypnotic to promote sleep) until the patient reached a state of intoxication characterized by restlessness, dilated pupils, dry throat, and hallucinations. Doctors maintained this state for twenty-four to forty-eight hours, with the assistance of a strong and competent nurse to protect the patient from self-injury. Often doctors found it necessary to give the patient strychnine (to stimulate the central nervous system), nitroglycerin (to dilate the blood vessels), or digitalis (to stimulate the heart) for cardiovascular complications due to the stress of the treatment. A few doctors even endorsed heroin or cocaine for the treatment of morphine addiction.

Once the crisis period was over, withdrawal symptoms lasting eight to ten days set in: delirium tremens, acute manias, insomnia, severe diarrhea, intestinal colic, nausea, vomiting, and labored and deficient heart action. The cliché that doctors would either "kill or cure" a patient seemed to be especially true in the treatment of drug addiction. At the end of thirty days, on 14 November 1903, Cleary was able to write her first letter to her son Jim from the infirmary. Patients at Elgin were allowed to write only two letters per week, and these were often screened. According to Kate Lee in *A Year at the Elgin Insane Asylum*, "The letters are placed, open, in some place from which the ward physician can conveniently take them up as he goes through. They are then read by one or more doctors, and if approved are stamped and forwarded. Not all the letters that are written are passed and some are returned to be altered before sending" (39). Thus, Cleary's letters to Jim had several audiences. First they may have had to pass hospital inspection, and then they needed to live up to her own personal standards—to comfort rather than burden her son. In addition, Jim shared the news in her letters with his brothers and sisters, and occasionally read parts to his father. For the most part, however, Cleary wrote specifically to Jim.

In that first letter, Cleary apologized for not writing sooner, alluding to the hospital rules and admitting her weak condition. She also gave some insight into the events precipitating her collapse: "As you probably know the loneliness, the brooding over the absences of you children, and the arduous work of arranging with teamsters, warehouses etc—and getting things packed and moved, resulted in complete collapse—mental and physical. I lost 24 lbs in the three weeks after you left, but now, by persistently eating, and drinking a great deal of milk, I am creeping back and have got up to 96 lbs."

A typical day's menu at Elgin, Lee reported, consisted of coffee, oatmeal, sugar, white bread, butter, stew of potato, and a little beef for breakfast; tea, white bread, brown bread, butter, gravy, cauliflower, corn starch pudding, and a very little milk for dinner; and tea, sugar, white bread, brown bread, butter, and molasses cake for supper. Occasionally, boiled beef or pork and dried fruit sauces would supplement the fare (71).

Hoping to be allowed to spend Thanksgiving with her cousins Ed and Lizzie Dunne—Cleary's first cousin, Elizabeth Kelly, was married to Judge Edward F. Dunne—Cleary also looked forward to seeing her son soon. She seemed optimistic about her future, telling Jim, "Of course I will come back here until I am stronger physically, but I hope and think I will be able to leave for good, and buckle down to work not later than Christmas. You know how necessary it will be in the future to keep my typewriter busy. If I had done more writing and less housework I would be better off in every way today." Her first letter closes with concern for her children: "Answer this, like a dear boy, and tell me all you know about the others. I am aching to see you all and counting the days—almost the hours. Those here are kind, but the enforced idleness, the dragging monotony of the days, and the melancohly [*sic*] misery of those surrounding me have a depressing effect which it takes every effort of my will to combat."

By 27 November, Cleary's spirits were high even though she remained in the infirmary. She wrote to Jim: "Dear boy, the recovery is absolute. I never said that before. Indeed, I wrote the reverse to the *other* sanitarium the day after you graduated. And I have been told that I am not being detained for any reason concerning my physical or mental conditions, but merely to 'make sure.' The Judge [Edward Dunne] told me this morning that as there was no case on record here of a patient making a complete cure in the time I have, they were unwilling to have me leave. But he also says that he can imagine nothing more torturing than absolute idleness and now, with a sound mind in a sound body, I am chafing against inaction. I shall not soon take up housekeeping in any case—chiefly for the reason that it will pay me better to write."

An encouraging personal letter from S. S. McClure provided Cleary with even more incentive to recover. She reported to Jim what the famous publisher had written to her: "You have a power that is all your own, and when health is restored you ought to use it, and I know you will use it for the benefit of a wider circle of readers than you have hitherto known, and I will help you to do this, as far as a publisher can help an author." Cleary added modestly, "Wasn't that nice?"

The letter also voiced concern about her husband's health: "And do send me any news you hear of your Papa and his latest letter to you, as I hear he still is ill, and I am worrying a great deal over the fact." Michael was ill, as she had feared, but he was staying at the home of his sister, Bessie Cleary Keefe, and her husband, Jim, a doctor; Kate felt somewhat relieved to hear this. Her own health, however, had improved markedly, enough for her to be transferred to the "well" ward the second week of December.

On 12 December, Cleary shared her good news with her son: "I was transferred to the 'well' ward last Tuesday. It is much more pleasant than being in the infirmary. You would fancy coming in that you had entered a clean and comfortable hotel. There is a piano, a library, and we have the current magazines. It is not exactly pleasant having to go down two flights and then traverse a long corridor open to the elements in order to reach the dining room—but I'm glad to have an appetite that makes me willing to go. I find climbing the stairs hard on my heart—or perhaps it is dispensing with the medicine I took three times a day in the infirmary. But as this does not last and I am absolutely well otherwise, I cannot complain." She spoke of plans to visit the Dunnes for the Christmas holiday, in hopes of seeing her children.

Cleary also revealed in the 12 December letter that she would not be released from Elgin soon, so she was settling in and making plans to begin writing again. She continued reassuringly: "It is likely I shall return here later—*only* for the sake of the quiet while I am finishing that Nebraska novel which has hung for so long. I've had another letter from McClure's urging me to finish the story and let them see it. First, I must get the MS out of the warehouse—and secure the typewriter too." Meanwhile, Elia Peattie wrote Cleary regularly and visited her in the hospital often, providing moral support and literary encouragement: "Mrs. Peattie spent a couple of hours with me last week, and said she had not known me to be and look so well since we came back to Chicago."

Cleary's relationship with the Dunnes proved politically important for her, for Edward Dunne was serving as judge of the circuit court at this time and would later be elected mayor of Chicago and then governor of Illinois. His power and prestige presumably provided Cleary with special privileges at Elgin. According to Kate Lee's account, only those patients who were soon to be dismissed were assigned to Ward A2, "the best, or 'going home' ward," or as Cleary referred to it, the "well" ward. Lee's description concurred with Cleary's, and she described it as well furnished and, most importantly, "comparatively secure" from the more disturbed patients. Those in A2 enjoyed a carpeted room with lace curtains and, "beside the bed, a good dresser, a table with two shelves, an iron contrivance which serves as a washstand without taking up space, a comfortable low rocker, and another chair" (56). Although Cleary appears to have moved directly from the infirmary to the "best" ward, most patients had to work their way up to A2 after serving time in other wards. Cleary may even have had a room of her own.

At first, Cleary did not want the children to visit her at the hospital. On 20 December she wrote Jim, "By the way, Doctor Whitman told me that Judge Dunne told him, that Kittie Kelly [Cleary's aunt] had told him, that Papa had told her—he was going to send 'some of the children' down to see me during the holidays. I do not understand how this can be, as Papa promised me after the trial that only you alone should ever know that I had come here. Dearly as I would love to see them, I cannot bear the thought of their later associating me with this place,—and for their own sake. For there are some very charming men and women recuperating here, I can assure you. But Gerald and Valentine might have morbid imaginings when they were older." She selflessly added, "I shall not go up [to Chicago] this week however, because I do not wish to interfere with the beautiful time the trio will be sure to have at the homes of their father's relatives. I could not be in the same city with them without wanting to see them—and if my doing so would detract ever so slightly from their enjoyment of the festival— well, I hope I am unselfish enough to endure this bleak exile a little longer." In a letter to Jim two days later, her resolve had weakened, although she remained fearful of the consequences to the younger children: "Kittie K. [Kelly] has written me you are to bring the children here on Thursday. I shall expect you. If Valentine does not know the character of this Institution, don't tell her. It might only worry her years from now. And I would not for worlds have anything detract from the pleasure of your Christmas. I hope you all will enjoy every hour out of school, and will take back only joy and pleasant memories when you return."

Cleary's health continued to improve, and in her 12 January 1904 letter to Jim she noted that she had gained forty-one pounds since her arrival at Elgin, adding, "What do you think of that for a well Mamma? And a Mamma who is going to keep well too!" In addition, she informed her son that she had begun to write again, but not at her typical pace. She complained, "Mrs. Peattie seems to think I ought to get a great deal of writing done here, but between going up and down those stairs you traversed three times a day to meals, and twice every day to walk, the time is so cut up it is hard to get good connected work accomplished. I'm doing my best however—and trusting in God."

Cleary had somehow acquired a typewriter during the middle of December, and by the middle of January, she began receiving checks. On 18 January 1904, the day before Jim's seventeenth birthday, she wrote to her son: "Well, I did get fifteen dollars from the Daily News on Saturday, and meant to go downtown today if I was allowed, and get you something, or at least send you part of the money, but find I cannot legally sign the check until I am released from here. So you see if I cannot do that, it is no wonder I could not sign the other paper you wished me to! But the check will keep, and so will the promise."

Then, in a rare moment of emotional candor, Cleary confided to her son, "My own dear boy, it is mighty hard for me to say what I would like to you tonight. I will say that I do hope no other sorrow will ever come into your young life. If it does it will not be your mother's fault. And perhaps, when you are older and have a wife of your own, and know more of women and their needs, you will admit I was not altogether to blame. But dearest, it must be a happiness to you to know how good and gentle, and forbearing you have always been. I am rich in having a son like you—if in nothing else. And the thought of how dearly your father and I love you—how proud we are of you—how we depend on you, ought to give you a glad consciousness through your hardest hours of study and most tiresome ones of work."

Throughout her life, the devotion and pride Cleary felt for her children was all encompassing. Jim, since he was the oldest, served as his mother's emotional support. This bond developed during the long years in Nebraska when Michael's health necessitated his frequent absences. Cleary had good reason to be especially proud of her eldest son during these difficult years. Intelligent and a hard worker, Jim graduated from high school at age fifteen in 1902 and began working as an order clerk for Sears, Roebuck, and Company. Then he was hired by the Corn Products Company and worked in the chemical research department, saving his twenty-five-dollar-a-month salary to pay his tuition so that he could attend classes at the Central YMCA night school. He entered the University of Illinois in 1903, paying his university expenses by "tending furnaces, washing dishes, and managing a boarding house." These were hard years for them both, with Kate fighting her drug dependency and Jim supporting himself and attending the university at such a young age.[19]

Since she rarely unburdened herself on her friends or family, Cleary, in her letter to her son a week later, 26 January, apologized, "I have your lovely letter, and it does cheer me up so much! I've been ashamed ever since I wrote to you as I did, for I feel it was a cowardly thing to do. You have had too many of our troubles to bear all your life, and I should not have written a word to give you an unhappy moment. But it seemed that night, being so worried about Teddie and other things, that I had to blurt out a bit of my heartache to someone. So—I talked out to you. And as I say your reply has helped me wonderfully, and makes me patient—which does not at all excuse my having written so to you."

In an attempt to persuade her son that everything was fine, Cleary continued, "I wrote six short stories last week, and have sent them. I am not trying to do magazine work, as it is rather a strain here, where there are such peculiar and not always pleasant interruptions. But I'll get enough syndicate and News stories done to be a bit ahead one of these days." She even added a little humor for the first time since her admission to Elgin: "Dear, it is time to join the motley throng, travel downstairs and out to dinner. But nothing matters much when you are all well, and—there's a star in the sky!"

In a postscript, Cleary mentioned the big news item of the day, the tragedy at the Iroquois theater on New Year's Eve, when fire caused by sparks from a spotlight ignited the frayed edge of a nearby curtain, killing 572 people because the fire exits were locked. The *Chicago Tribune* published lists daily, often with photographs, of those consumed by the fire.[20] All of Chicago mourned, including Cleary: "I knew eight who were fatally burned in that fire, but missed poor Mrs. Kennedy's. That makes nine—and Ryan, dying by fire the same week makes ten in Chicago whom I knew personally. Poor Mrs. Fitzgibbon's money will not go far to console her now! I am glad I never set my heart on wealth—only on people. But it is pretty hard when those you love fail you."

By February Cleary was keeping the typewriter busy, and on the fourth she wrote to Jim that she had finished ten short stories the week before, had started on a special article for some Chicago doctors who promised her twenty dollars for the piece, and had just received fifteen dollars from the *News*. The amount of writing that Cleary accomplished while at Elgin is also evidence of her special status at the asylum. According to Lee's account, the state required inmates to do a half-day's work every day "to pay for board." This usually involved cleaning as well as work in the kitchen, dining room, or laundry. Lee complained that "to write at Elgin Asylum would be next to impossible. A few little notes might be made, and carefully looked after, but it is difficult to see how even the doctors could help one to write, without allowing her a room in the Center, which would be a very unusual favor. . . . And not only can no *work* be done, but everything else must be abandoned. No business can be carried on, no trips taken, no visits made" (103). Cleary undoubtedly received preferential treatment. Besides being the judge's relative, her admittance record states that she was being supported by a bond and lists M. T. Cleary, husband, and Edward B. Healy as bondsmen. This indicates that Cleary was not a ward of the state, not an "object of charity," but one of the "bond patients," someone whose relatives guaranteed that her hospital costs would be paid. However, once released, she would be responsible for repaying those bonds, and this was a great burden for her as she struggled to support herself after leaving Elgin.

In that same letter to Jim, Cleary burst forth with good news: "I had a telegram from Robert Peattie yesterday, saying Elia would be out tomorrow, Friday, to make arrangements to have me leave here.

Dear Lord, but I'll rejoice!" Inmates of Elgin were not formally discharged until after they had completed a three-month parole, and, as
Lee explained, "any one who remains out for more than three months
is considered to be 'cured,' and is restored to her full rights" (130).
Cleary had good reason to rejoice, for it seems that Dr. Whitman believed her to be cured and ready to leave Elgin. Unfortunately, Michael
refused to sign for her parole. Such incidents of cured patients' not
being released were not unusual. According to Lee, "It sometimes
happens that . . . when the doctors are willing to let one go, they cannot
get any one to come for her" (113). Lee wrote of the case of a woman
who had been at Elgin for four years, "not insane for the latter part of
the time, at least; but she was unable to get any one to take her out.
At last some friend, apparently not a relative, came for her" (78). She
noted, "With few exceptions the inmates of the Asylum were like birds
vainly beating their wings against a cage in the effort to get out" (91).

According to Elia Peattie's memoirs, the doctor appealed to her "as
Kate's nearest friend," saying that "he had done all he could for her,
that he regarded her as sane but that she certainly would not remain
so if she had to stay in the asylum."[21] Evidently not wanting to go
against Michael's wishes, Elia hesitated to intervene until she felt a
spiritual presence in her garden, "the sweet and beseeching face of
Kate's mother, long since in her grave." That evening, working late in
her library, she again felt someone standing beside her, and she looked
up: "There again stood Margaret McPhelim, her dark hair parted and
rippling away from her low brow, her face maternal, sweet and as
before, imploring." Elia promised, "I'll take her out, dear."[22]

4
The Lonely Road:
1904–1905

From the time of her release from the Elgin hospital in February through May 1904, Cleary resided with the Peatties in their home at 7660 Bond Avenue in Chicago, where, Elia Peattie reported, she was "faithful to her parole."[1] Once again, Cleary devoted her time to writing. On a Saturday morning, one week after gaining her freedom, she wrote to Jim that she had been very busy. She said she had been writing, working on a project for a doctor that would pay her twenty-five dollars, but lamented, "If I did not have to buy everything new for myself, I'd be some ahead. . . . I write every day when I need not go down town, and sew every evening." She also completed a seven-thousand-word story for a competition for the *Metropolitan*, which offered prizes ranging from six hundred to eight hundred dollars. Proud of the psychological strength of the characters in her entry story, she believed that if she didn't win the contest, she would have no trouble selling it. Although frightened by the sum she would have to pay the warehouse to retrieve her belongings, she found some extra money for material to sew some clothing and a lounging robe for daughter Vera and to buy some mittens for Teddie and some reading materials for Gerald. She added optimistically, "I've not failed in anything I've attempted since I got physical health and mental clarity back, and I don't feel that I will fail now."

This same letter to Jim may also give some clue as to why Michael might not have wanted to sign for custody of his wife during her parole.

Kate stated in the letter, "Papa tells me that he has a very comfortable room at Annie's and every care. Of course he ought to have good accommodation for the sum he pays. I am not at all worried about him now, for I know he is where he would most prefer to be, and with those for whom he cares most—apart from you children." We learn from this not only that Michael was living with his sister, who had returned to Chicago from Nebraska, and was paying rent, with no home of his own, but that unhealed wounds seemed to exist between Kate and her in-laws. In an undated letter to her husband written at 11 P.M. at about this same time, Kate wrote, "I know it is almost impossible for you to think well of me but—there are those who do. In hearing your family chorus of 'Poor Sonnie' which was for more than a year dinned into my ears, you may fail to realize how many say, 'Poor Kate.' "

Public attitudes toward morphine had changed by the turn of the century. Fueled by the growing uproar against alcohol created by Frances Willard and the Woman's Christian Temperance Union and continued by the Anti-Saloon League, as well as changes in the medical practices of doctors, society considered morphine no longer a miracle drug but rather a demonic threat to family and society. By 1900, Cleary would have been firmly entrenched in her morphine addiction. Just as a diabetic needs insulin to remain functional, Cleary had become dependent upon morphine and its ability to make her pain from neuralgia, angina, and headaches tolerable and to help her complete her routine daily tasks. Morphine relieved her physical and emotional pain and anxiety, enabling her to take care of her family and home, deal with the family's financial stresses, and continue writing. As the years progressed, Cleary would have required larger doses to achieve the same effect. To counteract this growing tolerance, she evidently turned to alcohol, as did many addicts, to heighten the morphine's effects or, perhaps, as a substitute.[2]

Apparently, pressure from his family overwhelmed Michael. Caught in the middle of shifting societal attitudes, his family's anxiety, and his own poverty, Michael did not have the strength to act in support of his wife. Kate, entangled physically, emotionally, and socially in the conflict, had only Elia Peattie and her cousins to turn to for support. In a poem she titled "A Knowledge," Kate mourned,

> *I used to think, in days gone by,*
> *No fate more sad could ever be*
> *Than that you whom I loved should die,*
> *And go afar away from me.*
> *But older now and wiser grown,*
> *This fate more bitter there could be,*
> *Is to my trembling heart made known —*
> *That you could lose your faith in me!*

Despite her disappointment in her husband, before February was over, Cleary agreed to meet him downtown. She described their visit, the first since she had left for Elgin, in a letter to Jim dated 22 February 1904: "I was shocked to find him looking weak and aged, but after we had talked things over—sensibly and amiably on both sides, with a judicious evasion of references that might hurt the other, he seemed to brace up wonderfully. We had supper together, and stayed downtown watching the Chinese celebration on Clark Street for some time. He was much relieved to hear I hoped to have a place out here where I could take care of the children next summer, and that I was in the health to do so. . . . Indeed, he seemed so much encouraged and more content after the several hours we spent together, that I am hopeful his physical health will be likewise improved. He kissed me goodbye, and I came home feeling that I had done right to meet him, and was not influenced by all the advice that has been given me to the contrary."

Displaying her concern for her husband as well as allusions to their marital problems, Cleary continued: "I think for a while—as he *then* did not wish me to know his address, that he possibly feared I would resent his living with Annie and Kattie [his sisters]. Indeed, I was more than glad to be assured of that fact, and it lifted a big load from my mind. I was dreadfully worried at the thought of him alone in a rented room. Where he now is he has the comfort and care he needs—also the pleasant companionship, and I would be not only selfish but malignant, to try to alter conditions at present even if I wished to do so."

Cleary closed her letter with assurances to her son: "Dont [*sic*] send him any of my letters to you, for I could not write freely to you if I thought you were doing so. And I am sure that you will be glad to know that after all our dark days, there remains no unfriendly feeling between us. To no one else would I write or speak as fully as I have to you, because it was you who suffered most in a way from your sense of 'divided duty.' Dear boy, we love you—and bless you. And let me know if your pocket-book gets too attenuated for comfort."

A few days later, the relationship between Cleary and her husband had warmed even more; on their twentieth wedding anniversary, 26 February, they had supper together at the Cafe Brauer and went, afterwards, to wander around at the public library, Cleary's favorite haunt. She wrote Jim, "We had a happy evening. He was in much better health and excellent spirits."

The months of Cleary's parole passed swiftly and successfully. She wrote tirelessly, living precariously from story payment to story payment, spending what little extra she had on train fare to visit her children at their schools and on little gifts to take them. Her social life also improved, and she boasted to Jim in an undated letter written Friday at 10:30: "I have only 4 social engagements for tomorrow. I'm going to a lecture on Tolstoi in the morning, then to a luncheon with Mrs. Gillis, a new friend of mine, then to meet two Elgin girls for an hour, and then out to dinner at Miss Morgan's. I'll stay there overnight. Mrs. Peattie makes me go out. She insists that I shall not work all the time." She also had met with Michael again: "Papa looks first rate and says he feels very well."

Retrieving her belongings from the warehouse where they had been temporarily stored became Cleary's chief concern. During the months she spent at Elgin, the bill had mounted rapidly. The warehouse held all of her books and several unfinished manuscripts, and until she could make payments, they remained out of her reach. On 21 March, she wrote Jim, "About the books you mention—they are in warehouse, and not at Kellys' as I thought. . . . You shall have them as soon as I get things out, but first I must have a place to put them. I've paid five dollars storage, and will pay five more this week, but that will still leave forty to be paid the first of May."

Cleary also began room-hunting, for she did not want to impose on the Peatties any longer than necessary. She began searching the Windsor Park, Hyde Park, West Side, and Wabash Avenue area lodging houses, but without success. Finally, Robert Peattie suggested the Palace Hotel, an apartment run on the European plan by a friend and former newspaperman, H. B. Humphrey. It stood on the corner of North Clark and Indiana Streets, and upon investigating it, Cleary found a room, number 305, that she could afford. In an undated Sunday night letter, she described it to Jim: "It is a respectable place, comfortable but not luxurious, steam heat (I've had no heat in my room the last two months [at the Peatties'], and have felt the cold a good deal), gas, bath, elevator, etc.—It is seven minutes walk from the court house—so I'll have no carfare. I've been paying 30 cents every day I came in town. I got a small room on the 3rd floor for 3.50 a week. I'll take my meals out."

Reconciled to the location and pleased that the children would be able to spend some time with her, Cleary affirmed in an undated Monday morning letter to Jim: "I don't pretend that this is precisely the place I would choose to live, but it is convenient and satisfactory for the present. It is chiefly a theatrical house—whole companies stopping here, but it is respectable, and strictly conducted—in this respect differing from others in the neighborhood. . . . In any case, I only want a warm spot in which to work, and room for my typewriter. Then the deal of time I used to spend on the cars I can put to remunerative use. By night I'll be tired enough to read for a while and go to bed. I am trying to take care of my health. I think you'd hardly know me, for I've grown—heaven only knows how! to look so much younger. I know it isn't flattery when every one tells me so. Regular work, regular hours, and the determination not to worry over the tragedies of my past— these, and faith in God, keep me comparatively contented—persistently hopeful."

With the addition of rent payments to her budget, monetary concerns harassed Cleary even more. In her next letter, written on a Monday, she noted that although the *Red Book* magazine bought a story, she had been down to her last nickel and needed the money to buy Vera her First Communion clothes. Evidently her old health problems began troubling her again, too, and in an undated Saturday 8 A.M.

letter, she again confided her troubles to her son. His letter of reply, brought to her room by a little neighbor boy, eased her depression: "He . . . brought me up your dear, good, inspiriting letter. And—I needed it. Not that my mental need is as great as it has been. Now that I've got—through suffering, and your prayers perhaps—so close to God, I dont [*sic*] feel the necessity for human companionship as I once did. But I've been battling with physical pain for the past week, and it has rather worn on my courage. Neuralgia. Papa wanted to get me quinine the other evening, but I've such a dread of all drugs now, I would not take even that—so I'm fighting it out. But three nights of insomnia from pain—well, never mind! I'm free from it now. It seems to be only bad at night. And I'll be better tomorrow. It is absurd to growl about bodily aches anyhow. Every time I pass that dreadful Iroquois Theatre, and I do frequently for I always walk into town, I remember what I said to God on the 31st of December. 'If my children were not in that hell, I will never again complain, no matter what further unhappiness you may call upon me to bear!' "

Cleary's faith, always an anchor in her life, grew even stronger after her struggles with her addiction. In the same letter to Jim, she discussed a book, *Honor toward God,* that Peattie had been having problems reviewing. The author had lofty ideas but wrote badly. Cleary said that she told Peattie, "Give him full credit for that which he tries to say. Never mind the failure—so many of ours in life are passed over by the Great Critic!" Philosophically, Cleary continued to Jim, "Anyhow, all this ramble gets me back to the idea with which I started—life really resolves itself into a compact—into honor toward God. It seems to me if we keep that inviolate according to our inner conviction, which is not always associated with creeds, that nothing else matters much. Or rather, that all other things that do matter,—such as love, confidence, peace, respect,—will 'be added unto us.' "

Embarrassed by her sermonizing, she apologized, "Heavens! What a dreary monologue I've been betrayed into! But its [*sic*] the dark, the rainy morning, the weariness from lack of sleep, and the satisfaction from your friendly letter which are responsible, I think. Dear, I get so desperately hard up sometimes for a single soul to talk to who will understand. Elia Peattie would—but I wont [*sic*] talk with her. Our friendship is a good deal I fancy like that of two men, who detest effusion and display, and know that to preserve silence on certain subjects is more honorable than could be any speech. And dearly as I love her, of my actual heartaches I have said to her never a word. I think she divined one of them though. For—good friend that she is—she says to me occasionally: 'Jim is such a comfort—such a son to be proud of! And—I'm sure he loves you!' That helps every time."

Cleary's loneliness is evident in this letter, one of the longest that she wrote to Jim. Even Michael was trying to be supportive: "[Papa] asked me to stay and have supper, but I was too tired after my rambles [to the Lincoln Park Zoo] with Vevie [Vera] and told him I'd rather come back here, and that he'd better go out home to his regular supper. But later, as I was sitting reading in the twilight, he walked in with a very dainty luncheon—broiled spring chicken, bread, potatoes, etc.— also a plate, knife, and fork—rather indispensable adjuncts. Wednesday he telephoned that he would come over and go around town with me any evening I felt lonely. But I answered that I'm tired enough to go to bed by the time night comes."

Michael continued in his concern, despite Kate's sometimes stubborn pride. She wrote: "Thursday evening he came over however, and brought me some nice fruit. He told me to call on him if I ever got out of money! I wonder I survived the shock! I only said, 'I shall never do that—never in all the world!' And—I never will. I had less than a dollar in the world at the time—but I did not tell him so."

Determined to be self-supporting and indebted to no one, Cleary described her financial concerns and outlined her literary plans: "Yesterday I got fifteen dollars from the Daily News. I'll have to pay ten of this though, at the warehouse, as I must get out my papers if I want to compete for the Collier competition. Without the faintest hope of winning a prize, I still might get the five cents a word they offer for all other accepted stories. . . . The reason I especially wish to get out my papers, is that I want to send in a Nebraska story, and I've the material among my other MSS. William Allen White is to be one of the judges. He ought to recognize a faithful story of the plains."

Fortunately, after a prolonged search, Cleary found her unfinished manuscript, "A Woman of Nebraska," and began revising it. Then, in an undated Friday morning letter, she reported to Jim that in the midst of her creative fervor her typewriter had broken down: "On Tuesday I wrote eight hours steadily, and on Wednesday seven, only pausing for Lunch." She complained, though, "Part of this time I was over-hauling this old machine, which was daily out of order." Nonetheless, she completed the eight-thousand-word manuscript, and after she had mailed it off to *Collier's*, she took her typewriter to the Hammond office for repair. Relieved when she discovered that the machine sim-ply needed a new shuttle arm, which only cost her fifty cents, she lamented, "I wished I had taken it earlier, and not have wasted my time and patience, trying to do it myself."

Collier's offered prizes of $5,000, $2,000, and $1,000 for its story competition. Twelve thousand stories were typically submitted, and "trained magazine readers" narrowed the field to nine entries. These top stories then went to the judges, Henry Cabot Lodge, Walter H. Page, and William Allen White.[3] White probably never even read Clea-ry's story. She did not place, nor did *Collier's* publish her story; even worse, the manuscript is missing, so it was probably never returned.

Meanwhile, with the help of Robert Peattie, Cleary tried unsuc-cessfully to find "steady work of a congenial kind." She explained to Jim in a Monday noon letter: "You know I dont [sic] want to do ordinary reporting. But I must get something that will pay me a certain salary, so that I wont [sic] have to worry continually about my room rent, etc. The time I spend thinking of that I ought to put in thinking stories and so on. Well, the Journal has changed hands, and been bought by men of great wealth who are bombing it." Peattie suggested that Cleary could become their literary editor, and he volunteered to recommend her to the new publisher. Unfortunately, this opportunity dead-ended, too.

Including a letter from Elia Peattie in one of hers to Jim, Cleary explained, "The enclosed letter will interest you. The part I tore off had an uncomplimentary reference to your father. [Elia] thinks he ought to appreciate more the plucky fight I am making for a living, and for rehabilitation. Well—I believe he does, in his heart. The ref-erence at the end, means that I said, if I let myself be depressed every time he was blue over his business troubles etc, that I'd never get any work done. Of course I let him talk if it does him any good, and I sympathize with him too, but you know he always did look on the darkest side, and that I'd be foolish to sit down and fret, when I can go ahead and work. I have sold four stories to the McClure syndicate, which means forty dollars, but I've not yet got the check, but will shortly. Well, now I'll get at those editorials. I do hope they'll go."

With her resources so low, Cleary could not afford to buy clothing for herself. Too ashamed to visit her children in her shabby condition, she apologized in a Friday morning letter, "Dear, I see no hope of going down before your vacation begins. I always said I would not go down unless I had good clothes. I haven't anything except the suit I bought last February, and that is pretty well played out. Just to keep going and my current expenses paid, is all I have been able to do so far. You know my rent alone comes to 15 dollars a month. I'd love to see you but can only keep working—hoping—praying. These three generally work together to good effect in time." To pay her bills, Cleary frequently pawned personal items, such as a favorite bracelet, her grandmother's earrings given to her by her mother on her thirteenth birthday, or even her mother's engagement ring, a present to her on her fourteenth birthday. She then wrote frantically to earn enough money to redeem them.

Meanwhile, Michael continued to telephone and visit Kate in her apartment. Their relationship was curious. The couple dined regularly at a nearby hotel and then spent the afternoons or evenings taking pleasure in the inexpensive entertainment that the transit system offered. In addition, Michael read the drafts of her stories, occasionally bought her meals, and brought her medicine, as she related in an undated Friday morning letter: "I had some serious suffering with indigestion, but now that I take three—instead of two meals a day as I had been doing, and supplement this with the excellent medicine that Papa brought me, I am feeling well again."

As much as she seemed to enjoy his company, Kate refused to live with Michael, and we can only guess at her reasons. As she commented in her first letters to Jim from Elgin, "I shall not soon take up house-keeping in any case" and "If I had done more writing and less house-work I would be better off in every way today." Perhaps Kate's desire and need to make a living by writing, coupled with her husband's ill health, sporadic employment, and downhearted approach toward life's problems, made her wish to live independently. In an undated Wednesday letter to Jim, she mentioned that Michael was "rather blue and complaining of a headache," and in an undated late evening letter to Michael, she chided him, "Put all of your problems and troubles and perplexities aside," and urged him not to "whine" and be "just a good fellow."

Michael, typical of most husbands at the turn of the century, would have expected Kate, as his wife, to care for the house, the children, and him—cooking, cleaning, and washing, as well as mending his clothes and his ego, and that would have taken precious time away from her job of writing. Living alone, she could come and go as her own flexible schedule allowed, and her writing would not have to be interrupted to fix a meal, do the family's laundry, or turn out the lights and come to bed. Moreover, she would no longer have to be responsible for her husband's financial support. Her comment in an earlier letter, "it is pretty hard when those you love fail you," adds an emotional angle to the mystery.

For Michael, living with Kate during her drug and alcohol dependency days certainly would have been trying, too, especially when heaped upon his own health problems and business failures. The emotional scars inflicted upon their relationship and doubts about her recovery would have been difficult for him to disregard.

As the summer of 1904 wore on, Cleary's health began troubling her again. She wrote to Jim in an undated 8:30 A.M. letter, "That horrid neuralgia seemed to go to my head—or the place where that romantic disorder is supposed to be located. I tossed around in wretchedness till dawn." On 21 July 1904 she wrote, "I'm ashamed to say I've been very idle this week on account of the intense heat and a nervous ailment not to be unexpected at my age—I took things quite easy."

Deciding that a rest in the country would do her good, as well as give her a chance to be with her children, Cleary arranged to rent a cottage in the country. In an undated Tuesday evening letter to Jim, she described it as being "two miles from a telephone—literally five miles from a lemon, for those had to be bought at Kankakee, seven from a railroad." The children, delighted in the vacation, played with the farm animals and explored the countryside. However, "four days in that solitude gave me all I could stand of it," and it became "too much for my nerves," she wrote Jim. "I got a dreadful nervous attack— the feeling that I used to have at Elgin, that for me there was no escape, unless I left while I still had strength to go." Worse, the trip cost her twenty-two dollars, and she defended her sudden decision to leave by saying, "That was the wisest thing I could have done. If I'd stayed any longer they'd have held me up for my shoes. I never met such rapacious people in my life."

By the end of the summer, both Cleary's spirits and her health had declined further. She revealed to Jim in a letter written on Labor Day that she felt "weak physically" and that her imagination seemed "at low ebb." She complained, "Where I used to do several stories a day, I find I can write only one now. . . . But just now I'm behindhand— not having a single story on—or under—consideration at the NEWS. You know the ten I wrote in one week for the McClure Syndicate they took at seventy-five dollars. But so far I've found it impossible to get ahead. The good restaurants are so expensive—and the other kind make me sick. Interest also, eats up a lot. But—never mind. I'm holding my own, and paying my way."

Cleary boasted in a 22 August 1904 letter of selling a tale that involved only two hours' work to *Ainslee's* for forty dollars. The money trickled regularly in, and her letters documented her publishing successes. In an undated Sunday night letter she told Jim, "Dear, I sold last week 2 stories to the News, 2 to the Associated Magazines and one poem."

In the fall of 1904, Cleary's health and spirits renewed. Upon Jim's suggestion, she began attending Mass at the Holy Name Cathedral on North State Street, a parish that encompassed the wealthiest as well as the poorest neighborhood in Chicago, rather than the Italian church she had been attending, probably the Assumption Church on West Illinois, with its exquisite stained glass.[4] She and Michael resumed their long transit rides. In an undated Sunday letter, she exclaimed, "Papa was saying how fine I am looking. I feel first-rate again and am gaining flesh. While I don't weigh as much as I did when I came back last spring, I still weigh thirty-seven pounds more than I did this time last year. And I feel—oh, so differently mentally—so hopeful, capable, and intelligently content." She had paid the last of her doctor's bill and the six dollars' rental on her typewriter and was completing her eleventh story that month. Worried, though, about Jim's financial straits, she added, "Papa tells me your expenses will be heavy this year. I do hope I'll be able to help you after awhile, but I haven't got all my debts paid up yet—not got my bracelet back. But I will, please God! I get a little blue and lonely sometimes—especially when it gets too dark to write, but I never despair. There is always the thought of you children to cheer me, and books to read, and sometimes in the evening I run over to the Cathedral for a little while."

Michael's name reappeared several times in this letter, demonstrating their warming relationship: "And of course having Papa so much of a lover again is pleasant, although I continue to think that my suggestion we live as we are doing, is for the best." He even seemed to be on warm enough terms to give her business advice: "Papa thinks I ought to pay five dollars a month on a new typewriter, instead of three dollars rental. Five, would go on the payment of the machine, and they'd take my old one at fifty dollars. I suppose he is right—but I'm so afraid to incur an obligation of fifty dollars just now."

So the rented typewriter continued to churn out story after story until finally Cleary decided to buy a new typewriter. She announced to Jim on 12 November: "Please be duly conscious of the honor I am doing you! The first work attempted on my OWN BRAN-NEW [*sic*] typewriter is—a letter to you! The men have just brought it over, and taken away my old rattle-trap and their rented one. This is a beauty, and runs like velvet. Of course the price is steep—a hundred dollars. But they allowed fifty for the old one, and I've paid Twelve dollars on this. I signed notes for the remaining thirty-eight dollars due."

Optimistic as Cleary was, her financial situation was still tentative. In the same November letter she wrote, "Papa was down Wednesday evening, and when he left he sent up half a hot roast chicken from the restaurant. He tipped the bell-boy ten cents to bring it up to me. He did not know, and I did not tell him, that I had that day spent my last cent for lunch, and not even one penny—let alone a whole nickel in the world. But I knew I had stories out, so I prayed good and hard, went to bed and slept soundly and was wakened by the bell-boy knocking at my door. He handed me a check for $25 from the News. Out of this I've paid six to my doctor, six on this machine, and two to get my white dress from the cleaner's. I'll pay five on my rent today, so you see, taking out current expenses since Thursday, I'll not be able to take the children very much if I go down tomorrow—as I hope too."

Cleary moved to a better room that fall at the Monarch Hotel across the street, also at the corner of Indiana and Clark. Not only was it twice the size of her old abode, she wrote Jim on 29 November, but it was "cozy, warm, and quiet," and every article in it was new and "artistic." Although the movers charged her one dollar and she had to make an advance rent payment of eleven dollars, she was "dee-lighted," especially since she would now have room for her books.

Cleary's letters to Jim, most of them undated except for the day of the week and the hour, taper off toward the end of 1904. No letter with a 1905 date exists. Cleary was beginning to rely more upon the telephone, and with Jim especially hard-pressed for time, working and attending the university, this may have been a viable solution. In an undated Monday letter, she asked her son: "Dear, if your telephone is not one that eats up a nickel every time, I wish you'd telephone me occasionally that I may keep track of you. My number is 2016 North. Your father generally calls me from 5 to 5.15. I do not wish to be so selfish as to take any part of your badly-needed vacation from you, but I do want to hear your voice once in awhile, and know that you are having a good time."

Whatever the case, the close relationship continued. This long letter, possibly one of the last she wrote to Jim, affirmed her love: "This is only to say that while we did not talk much to each other yesterday, I was happy to be near you. You are so very very like that dear lost brother of mine, I experience a certain embarrassment when with you. I dont [sic] know if I can make myself clear, but I think I'm trying to say that while I can talk with facility and a fair vocabulary to people for whom I care nothing—I rather choke a bit with emotion when it comes to—you! Quite probably your own intuition explains this semi-apology."

Explaining her special relationship with her brother Edward, Cleary continued, "Dearly as we loved each other, Ned and I, and congenial as were our tastes, we would be together hours without speaking. Some clever person has said that silence—where neither is bored, is the true test of congeniality. We both detested an effusive display of affection in public. We considered it bad form. But when we did kiss each other—we meant it. And once in awhile he wrote that he loved me, just as Teddie pats my cheeks with 'I do too-see!'—and we understood." She continued resolutely, "I have long meant to write something of this sort to you—especially since the time you last were here, and I want you not to toss this aside until you fully—understand—and then we shall not refer to the subject again." That emotional topic concluded to her satisfaction, the letter turned to an update on her work: "I had a note of acceptance from Mr. Taylor of a tiny poem today. He must be very kind—or have—as he wrote me—loved Ned very dearly. He has taken every last line I've sent him—and seems to be looking around for something else to pay for! The News takes everything I send—and I've nothing at all out now, except five stories that the McClure Syndicate have accepted, but—they pay on publication. So—I must get busy! I suppose you remember that play of 'Busy Izzy' we saw two years ago—on your birthday! I do wish one might buy a little vial containing 'Essence of Energy,' and get our work done speedily."

Nothing is known about Cleary's life during the winter and spring of 1905. Her popular stories continued to appear in the daily newspapers, and *Youth's Companion* published one of her poems, "The Day Between." Cleary also continued her voracious reading, for in February, after the publication of Willa Cather's short story "The Sculptor's Funeral" in the January *McClure's* magazine, she wrote the now famous Nebraska author a letter. On 13 February 1905, Cather responded, pleased with Cleary's encouragement. Cather noted that many critics had claimed that she exaggerated life west of the Missouri River, and she said she appreciated Cleary's acknowledgment of the lack of culture and the discouraging lives of many western people. Cather remarked that they both understood life in small western towns.

Cleary truly did understand Cather's pioneer stories and settings, for Hubbell and Red Cloud, Nebraska, not only shared similar historical backgrounds but also were both border towns in south central Nebraska, and they were only fifty-two miles apart. In addition, the two women moved to Nebraska within a year of each other. Cather, at age nine, arrived in Red Cloud in 1883, and Cleary, at twenty, came to Hubbell in 1884. Cleary began publishing her works about the West, many of which are similar to Cather's earlier works in theme and tone, in about 1895, the year Cather graduated from the University of Nebraska.

Inspired by "The Sculptor's Funeral," Cleary dashed off an unpublished response to it that she entitled "About Being Super-Sensitive": "The genius who allowed his cows to become 'foddered' while he watched the sunset over the marshes—is worth while. His friend who had the decency to go and get drunk at the proper time is very well worth while also. But the direct and definite lesson taught is this: one may not judge that one among us upon whom has descended the pain—the poignance—the passionate pleasure of Pentacostal [*sic*] fire!"

In her letter, Cather also thanked Cleary for her interest in her upcoming collection of short stories about art and artists, *The Troll Garden,* to be published by McClure, Phillips, and Company.[5] In a postscript to the letter, Cather asked whether Cleary knew Elia Peattie. Cather's query solicited an immediate reply from Cleary, to which the young author responded on 25 February. Cather wrote admiringly and at length of Peattie, closing with the hopes of visiting both of the women on her next trip to Chicago. Cleary must have mentioned her interest in Cather's upcoming collection again, for Cather thanked her for her encouragement and hoped that she would not be disappointed in it.[6]

Cleary's popular stories continued to appear regularly in the *Chicago Daily News,* and she also wrote a series of feature articles on Judge Dunne and his family to help campaign for his election as mayor of Chicago. However, the stories stopped after 29 April, when "On the Highway" was published. Suddenly, on 6 July 1905, Michael entered a petition in the County Court of Cook County to have Kate committed again to an insane asylum.[7]

The petition alleged that "Kate M. Cleary a resident of Cook County, is insane, or suffering under mental derangement, and unsafe to be at large, and that the welfare of herself or others requires her restraint and commitment to some Hospital or Asylum for the Insane." The sheriff of Cook County was "commanded to arrest said Kate M. Cleary forthwith, and convey and deliver her to the Keeper of the Department for the Insane in Chicago, Cook County, Illinois; and said Keeper is hereby commanded to receive and keep said Kate M. Cleary in safe custody until the 6th July A.D. 1905, at 9 A.M., at which time said Keeper is commanded to have her before our County Court, and then and there to await and abide the result of the trial."

Terror and anger must have consumed Kate when she arrived at the County Court building. That morning, Dr. Charles J. Whalen examined her and testified in writing: "This is to certify that I have examined Kate M. Cleary and that I have found her to be insane." The testimony of one man, her husband, and a cursory examination by a doctor summarized in nineteen words was enough to force her to stand trial for insanity.

A jury of seven men, one of them another doctor, O. R. Bluthardt, M.D., heard the evidence and declared that "the said Kate M. Cleary is not insane, and is not a fit person to be sent to a State Hospital for the insane." A ten-dollar fee was assessed, and Cleary was free to leave. The sudden emotional shock seems to have upset Cleary's delicate health, and she returned to her room and stayed in her bed.

Ten days after Michael petitioned for Kate's arrest, he brought two of the children to visit her. He sent Teddie, age eight, to Kate's room to see her while he and Vera, age eleven, waited below in Stoltz and Grady's Drug Store. Kate went downstairs with Teddie, and she and Michael greeted each other and then stepped outside of the store to talk privately. Moments later, the 17 July *Chicago Tribune* reported, "angry words were heard passing between husband and wife and it was seen that Mrs. Cleary was becoming pale. She left her husband abruptly and went into the drug store, where she was given restoratives. After a short rest Mrs. Cleary got up and started upstairs to her room, followed by the little boy. Just as she reached the door of her room, on the third floor, she fell dead at her son's feet. Frightened and unable to realize that it was his mother's death that he had witnessed, the little fellow ran downstairs to his father and told him that 'Mamma fell on her face.' "

Besides detailing Cleary's tragic death, the *Chicago Tribune*, typical of the times, sensationally exposed the personal details of her life. The article described Cleary as "well known in Chicago as a newspaper and magazine writer" and Michael as "M. T. Cleary, 340 Ashland boulevard, a lumber salesman." The reporter added that "although never legally separated, the couple agreed at the time they parted that the father should care for the children, while the mother, at her request, was permitted to contribute to their support, with the understanding that her husband would bring the children occasionally to see their mother."

The article concluded with the information that "only ten days ago her husband brought her into court in an attempt to prove her insane, but failed. Several years ago Mrs. Cleary was confined for a short period in the Elgin Asylum for the Insane. She was the sister of the late E. J. McPhelim, for many years a dramatic critic on the *Chicago Tribune*, and was a cousin of the wife of Mayor Dunne."[8]

On 18 July, the *Chicago Record Herald* added more sensational details to the incident. The paper reported, " 'Heart disease' was the verdict of the coroner's jury which yesterday held an examination into the sudden death Sunday afternoon at 102 North Clark Street of Mrs. Kate M. Cleary, the writer." Then the news story began to read like one of Cleary's own tales: "Mrs. Cleary was 42 years old. For years she had been a victim of the drug habit and had been detained in the Elgin Asylum for the insane but had been released. She had been separated from her husband, M. T. Cleary, and her four children for a considerable time. Pathetic above all was the intense love of the woman for her children. On the table in the little room in the lodging-house where she died was found a poem, penned a short time before her death, and entitled 'Teddie.' 'Teddie' is the name of her youngest son." The *Chicago Record Herald* printed six stanzas of the eleven-stanza poem that documented Cleary's passionate love of life and love for her children as well as her disappointment in the "love of man" that "did betray."[9]

Repeating the incidents leading up to Cleary's collapse and death, the *Chicago Record Herald* added a tribute to her writing and a cause for her addiction: "For many years and up to quite recently Mrs. Cleary was one of the best-known woman magazine writers in the country. Her pen products were frequently seen in the leading periodicals and her name was well established before the public. Sickness led to the use of drugs and the breaking down of her health."

Again mystery surrounds Cleary's life. Had she returned to using drugs? Her letters to Jim document the pain that she had been experiencing after her release from Elgin, pain that could have prompted her to find relief again in patent medicines, morphine, or alcohol. She complained of "neuralgia," "congestion of the womb" [menstrual irregularity], "insomnia," "headaches," "indigestion," "nervous ailment due to my age," and occasions of near blindness that her physician decreed was "induced by chronic heart trouble." Even Michael, his relationship with Kate seemingly renewed and protective, had been bringing her medicine, perhaps unknowingly resurrecting her addiction. Elia Peattie in her memoirs commented, "For the three months she lived with me she did not once touch the drug that was her ruin; but the day after the expiration of her parole she returned to it. She died miserably."[10]

Cleary's death certificate lists the cause as "fatty degeneration of the heart accompanied by fatty degeneration of the liver." Although disproved today, this was the typical cause of death then assigned to morphine addicts; rarely was an autopsy performed since most believed that a fatty degeneration of the heart was caused by drugs.[11] The heart attack Cleary suffered may have been caused by a terrified attempt at withdrawal on her own, for the newspaper reported that she "had been ill and confined to her room for ten days." The withdrawal process usually lasted five to ten days and often caused notable loss of weight and body fluids and, most significantly, elevations in blood pressure. Modern experts agree that withdrawal can be life threatening; this would be especially true with someone who has a history of heart problems. However, Cleary's letters also documented her dread of all drugs and her desire to remain free of them, as well as the nature of her relationship with Elia Peattie, who had earlier called her "my best friend and my worst enemy."[12] Peattie had stayed with her invalid husband while writing to support her family; she may not have approved of Cleary's separation.

Cleary's death may also have been caused simply by a heart attack, for she had suffered from heart problems most of her adult life. In a 7 May 1897 letter to Kate, Michael had urged, "I hope you take those cactina pellets. *You should never be without them.* Please take care of yourself for your boy." Her use of cactina, a substitute for digitalis, points to a primary heart disease. Even in his letters before their marriage, Michael had urged Kate not to stress or overwork herself, and her doctor's concern and her own fear before her last pregnancy may have been fear of heart failure.

In addition, Chicago was suffering record-high temperatures the month Cleary died. The *Chicago Daily News* reported on 19 July 1905, "Not since July 21, 1901, when a temperature of 103 was recorded, has such heat been experienced in Chicago. Even nightfall failed to bring relief in the congested districts where the fiery temperature seemed to be absorbed and retained by walls and pavements." The newspaper, publishing lists of heat-related deaths, twenty-one as of that date, declared, "A trail of deaths and prostrations told the story in the blistering streets, where banks of heat had rolled untempered by wind or precipitation. Many of the dead were felled by the sun's rays yesterday and Monday." The heat in Cleary's third-floor apartment in the middle of downtown Chicago must have been unbearable.

Whatever the reason, Cleary's weak heart, undoubtedly stressed by the traumatic treatment while at Elgin, the emotional events of the insanity trial, and the record temperatures that week in Chicago, could not endure. Her funeral was held on 19 July 1905 at St. Jarlath's Church, and she was buried in a private ceremony in Calvary Cemetery beside her beloved mother, brothers, and two daughters.[13]

Shortly before Cleary's death, Houghton Mifflin had been negotiating with her on the publication of a collection of her short stories. One editor wrote that they "showed many aspects of western life better than any stories I have seen, and . . . had more atmosphere of the

Nebraska summer in it than I have found in all of the books of the West I have read."[14] Unfortunately, the book was not published, nor does any record remain of which works were to be included. As with many authors before her, Kate McPhelim Cleary's death abruptly halted her writing career before it could reach its full potential.

Cleary entitled one of her more poignant stories "The Road That Didn't Lead Anywhere." Alone in her Chicago apartment, unable to fully participate in the literary circles of the Midwest, Cleary must have, as did the mother in this tale, seen the lonely and dusty road she had traveled through life as a dead end. Her life metaphorically paralleled her young protagonist's: "Staggering a little under the weight of her burden, she stepped carefully down the slope to the road, picked her way across the strip of sandy loam, and, climbing the hill beyond, set the child down in the shade of the sod wall. She leaned back, panting a little, and looked away down the road that went writhing and twisting out of sight among the innumerable draws and bluffs of southern Nebraska."[15] Cleary, too, staggering under the heavy burdens of family responsibilities, poverty, ill health, and the societal constraints placed upon nineteenth-century women, saw the road she wished to travel twisting out of sight.

Although the specific circumstances of many overlooked writers' lives vary, quite often the causes for their obscurity are strikingly parallel. Tillie Olsen dedicated *Silences* to women like Kate Cleary, the "silenced people, century after century their beings consumed in the hard, everyday essential work of maintaining human life. Their art, which still they made—as their other contributions—anonymous; refused respect, recognition; lost."

Exemplifying the struggles of the nineteenth-century woman to stand strong against all personal, physical, and social odds, Cleary personifies the difficulties America's literary foremothers faced in their attempts to unfetter their creative talents and to break into the closed circles of the literary community. Not only did they need to find the time and energy to write while raising children, but they often had to shoulder their families' financial responsibilities through their publishing efforts. Because of Cleary's persistent will and her unremitting desire to write, to record her life and times both realistically and creatively, she has increased our knowledge of our pioneer and Victorian past and added significant writings to our literary heritage. Charles Fanning agrees: "She deserves to be remembered as a good writer and a courageous woman."[16]

Cleary typifies America's neglected women regionalists, whose work, although deeply rooted in place, represents universal human emotions and conditions. Emily Toth, in her introduction to *Regionalism and the Female Imagination,* argues in favor of "finding the women buried under the label 'regionalist,' bringing their work to light, and giving the careful analysis it so richly deserves," adding that works by such women let us "feel and taste the texture of real lives" (9, 10). Toth suggests a redefinition—"not only of regionalism but of what constitutes significant literature and useful literary criticism" (11). A few women regionalists at the turn of the century, such as Edith Wharton, Sarah Orne Jewett, and Willa Cather, did succeed and lead full literary lives, becoming internationally acclaimed authors. Others, however, such as Kate Chopin, Rebecca Harding Davis, and Charlotte Perkins Gilman, have only recently been "discovered" and allowed to assume their rightful places in America's literary heritage.

Cleary, too, deserves recognition for her contributions to American literature. In her poetry, Cleary's romantic sensibility and pastoral subjects reflect society's continuing intrigue with the natural world, especially the new American Garden of Eden of the frontier. Although much of her verse is sentimental and stylized, many of the lyrics contain vivid images and deep emotional insights. Others, especially her humorous poems, are realistic with a keen sense of wit or a critical satiric edge.

As a popular writer, Cleary created conventional characters and plots that appealed to Americans who wished to escape to a fantasy world where problems could be solved by the love of a good man or woman. Acknowledging that women must function within the context of society and family, her romantic and sentimental writings fulfilled the myth of female domesticity as well as meeting the emotional needs of a culture reeling in the aftershocks of the Industrial Revolution, the economic depression of the nineties, and the Spanish-American War. Her stories presented models for success in the competitive social world of the turn of the century and serve as cultural documents for readers today.

Cleary's more realistic and naturalistic works set in the Nebraska prairies, on the other hand, provided an opposing view to the idealized agrarian myths. Her powerful depiction of the hardships of the pioneer West, viewed firsthand by a woman who endured the droughts and blizzards of Nebraska and who knew its inhabitants on a first-name basis, is a truthful record of the difficulties of settlement times.

Perhaps Cleary's strongest contribution to American literature lies in her humorous stories, sketches, and poems about the West that realistically depict the lives and customs of its inhabitants. Her soft-hearted satire reflects the personal and social concerns of the time. She gently mocked the absurdity of the idealized Cult of True Womanhood, the foolishness of social pretension, and the perennial battle between the sexes while she upheld the values of simplicity, sincerity, and self-reliance.

When Elia Peattie penned her 1893 tribute to Cleary in "A Bohemian in Nebraska," she could not foresee the difficulties Cleary had yet to confront. She wrote with ironic prophecy: "I think that anyone who has broken down the obstacles, who has proved that the art of living is not a thing controlled by circumstances, is a fine example to us all." However bleak her prospects, Cleary always saw the beauty in life and rose to its challenges. A line among her last written words, "I love the world with all its brave endeavor," reveals her courage to rise above adversity and persevere. Cleary truly traveled her precipitous road like a gallant lady.

Kate and Michael pose proudly on the porch of their new home in Hubbell, Nebraska, on 11 September 1884. Michael Cleary (standing), Kate Cleary (sitting on railing), Billy Templeton (standing on railing), Josie Templeton, John Templeton (standing), James Mansfield Cleary (in top hat), and Jack Cleary. All photographs are from the Cleary family scrapbooks.

In a very candid photograph for Victorian times, Michael photographed Kate with her hair down in July 1890, two months before Gerald was born. Daughter Marguerite is in the foreground. The background shows the sparse population of the town. Photo by Michael Timothy Cleary.

Kate kept her typewriter busy as she wrote stories, sketches, poems, and novels from her Hubbell home. When this photograph was taken on 1 February 1891, she had already published a novel and numerous short stories, sketches, and poems about the West. Photo by Michael Timothy Cleary.

Kate and her mother, Margaret Kelly McPhelim, promenade on the wood sidewalks on the main street of Hubbell with Gerald on 13 February 1891. Photo by Michael Timothy Cleary.

Guests were heartily welcomed by the Clearys and often boasted of the elegant meals and warm companionship found in the Hubbell home. E. A. Downey visits Michael and Kate on 24 March 1891.

Elia Peattie, Kate's closest friend, and her daughter, Barbara, visit the Clearys in Hubbell in 1891. Photo by Michael Timothy Cleary.

Michael Cleary was one of the first businessmen in Hubbell.
This is his office at M. T. Cleary Lumber and Coal.

Kate sat for this formal photograph in October 1897, the month of the publication of Like a Gallant Lady.

*Kate vacations with her children, Jim, Gerald, Valen-
tine, and Edward (Teddy), at South Haven, Michigan,
in July 1901.*

Kate Cleary: Time Line

1819   Kate Cleary's father, James McPhelim, is born in Ireland.

1834   Kate Cleary's mother, Margaret Kelly, is born in Ivy Lodge, Borrisoleigh, County Tipperary, Ireland.

1855   Michael Timothy Cleary is born in Clonmel, County Tipperary, Ireland, on 26 April.

1856   Margaret Kelly marries James McPhelim in New Brunswick, Canada.

1863   Kate McPhelim is born in Richibucto, New Brunswick, on 22 August.

       James Mansfield Cleary and son Michael, age eight, emigrate to St. Louis; they move to Chicago, where James Cleary joins a wholesale liquor firm.

1865   Kate Cleary's father dies at age forty-six.

1877   Kate, fourteen, publishes her first poem.

1878   Kate, fifteen, publishes her first story, "Only Jerry," in *Saturday Night*.

1880   Hubbell, Nebraska, is established.

       Kate's mother moves with her three children to Chicago.

1881   Burlington Railroad completes its track through Hubbell and runs four trains through daily; the first school is established and the Presbyterian Church built.

1883   Michael Cleary travels to Hubbell with plans of resettling in the West. He decides to begin a lumber business with the help of his brother-in-law John Templeton of Superior, Nebraska.

1884   Kate McPhelim marries Michael Cleary on 26 February in Chicago and moves to Hubbell, Nebraska.

       Kate Cleary publishes novel *The Lady of Lynhurst.*

1887   Son James Mansfield is born on 19 January.

       Cleary publishes novel *Vella Vernel, or An Amazing Marriage.*

1888   Elia and Robert Peattie move to Omaha to work for the *Omaha World-Herald.*

1889   Daughter Marguerite M. is born on 18 January.
Brother Francis Albert McPhelim dies of pneumonia on
14 April at age twenty-four.

1890   Son Gerald Vernon is born on 8 September.

1892   Daughter Rosemarie Catherine is born on 19 May.

1893   Cleary's mother dies of pneumonia on 4 August at age fifty-
nine.
Cleary's poems are read at the Chicago World's Fair in
June.

1894   Daughter Vera Valentine is born on Valentine's Day. Cleary
falls dangerously ill from childbed fever.
On 2 December, daughter Marguerite, nearly six, dies of
typhoid fever.

1895   Michael Cleary leaves for Chicago in February; his lumber
business and health are failing.
Daughter Rosemarie dies in March at age three.
Kate Cleary has a series of "heart attacks" and dysentery.
Baby Vera Valentine becomes seriously sick with typhoid
fever; Michael Cleary returns home briefly.

1896   Kate Cleary, with son Jim, is very active in the McKinley
presidential campaign.
The Peatties return to Chicago to work for the *Chicago
Tribune*.

1897   Son Edward Sheridan ("Teddie") is born on 11 January.
Brother Edward Joseph "Teddie" McPhelim dies of tuber-
culosis on 11 June at age thirty-four.
Cleary publishes *Like a Gallant Lady*.

1898   Michael Cleary sells the lumberyard in February.
Rosemarie is reinterred in Chicago's Calvary Cemetery.
In April, Michael leaves for the Pacific Coast; Kate and
children remain in Hubbell.
In May, Michael returns home for one week before de-
parting for Chicago.
In July, the family moves to Chicago.

1902   At age fifteen, James becomes the youngest high school
graduate in Chicago.
Cleary commits herself to a private sanitarium for treatment of morphine addiction, but without success.

1903   Cleary collapses, and on 13 October, she enters the Illinois Northern Hospital for the Insane at Elgin for treatment of morphine addiction.

1904   Cleary is released from Elgin on 5 February. She lives with the Peatties for three months on probation and is released sane on 5 May.

Cleary and her husband, although separated, celebrate their twentieth wedding anniversary at the Cafe Brauer.

Cleary rents a room at the Palace Hotel; in the fall, she moves across the street to the Monarch Hotel.

1905   Her husband obtains a court order on 6 July to commit Cleary to an insane asylum; a jury finds her sane, and she is released.

Cleary dies on 16 July at age forty-one; she is buried in Calvary Cemetery.

1911   Edward Sheridan Cleary dies of rheumatic heart disease on 7 June at age fourteen and is buried in Calvary Cemetery.

1917   Michael Cleary dies in South Haven, Michigan, on 7 September at age sixty-two.

1922   Cleary's children publish a book of poetry by Cleary, Edward McPhelim, and Margaret McPhelim entitled *Poems*.

1958   James Mansfield Cleary edits a collection of Cleary's stories, *The Nebraska of Kate McPhelim Cleary*.

1971   Gerald Vernon Cleary dies on 19 May at age eighty.

1972   James Mansfield Cleary dies on 4 March at age eighty-five.

1980   Vera Valentine Cleary Bullard dies on 26 January at age eighty-six.

Notes

1. FROM NEW BRUNSWICK TO NEBRASKA: 1863–1891

1. For sources consulted on the Cleary family and on Hubbell, refer to the works cited section. Much information throughout this biography, unless otherwise noted, was supplied by Cleary's grandchildren Marguerite Cleary Remien, Aileen Bullard Droege, Joel Bullard, Mary Evelyn Cleary Sundlof, and Jeanne Cleary Goessling through personal interviews, personal letters, scrapbook clippings and memorabilia, and telephone conversations from 1993 to 1996. My research in Hubbell, Hebron, Omaha, Lincoln, and Chicago newspapers and historical archives supplied other historical and biographical details.

2. "Midnight Mass under Three Flags," 13–14.

3. "To My Darling Katie on Her 14th Birthday," *Poems*, 5. Unlike this poem, many of the poems, articles, and short stories quoted in this work are from the scrapbook, clipping, and original manuscript collections of the Cleary family and are, for the most part, undated and with few references to the publishers. Where a date and publisher are known, they are noted in the bibliography.

4. *Hubbell Heritage*, 4.

5. Neither the Library of Congress nor the National Union Catalog lists *The Lady of Lynhurst*. The only reference to it is in an 18 November 1884 letter to Cleary from Street & Smith, New York, informing her that her novel would be number eight in their "Leading Novel" series.

6. When they published *Vella Vernel, or An Amazing Marriage*, the editors at Street & Smith announced that it was by the author of *Little Goldie: A Story of a Woman's Love*, published in 1868 and reprinted in 1879 by George Munro's Sons; however, since Cleary was born in 1863, it is clear that she did not actually write *Little Goldie*. The pen name Mrs. Sumner Hayden may have been a series name used by authors for George Munro's Sons and affiliates, for another of their books carries the same pseudonym: *The Midnight Mar-*

riage, or Whose Wife Was She?, a sentimental novel first published in 1879 and later reprinted in Munro's Library of Popular Novels in 1894. Curiously, *Family Romance, or A Friendly Chat between Two Old Cronies upon a Matter of Life-Time Interest*, a narrative advertising the Eclectic Life Insurance Company published in 1870 in Boston, also claims Mrs. Sumner Hayden as its author. None of these works resemble writings by Cleary in style, tone, or technique. The only other connection might be that Cleary's mother, Margaret McPhelim, wrote these three works and Cleary borrowed her mother's pen name. That, too, seems unlikely, as Mrs. McPhelim wrote mainly poetry.

7. I obtained information on Elia and Robert Peattie from the following autobiographical works: "The Star Wagon," Elia Peattie's unpublished memoirs; *The Story of Robert Burns Peattie*, by Robert Burns Peattie; *The Road of a Naturalist*, by son Donald Culross Peattie; and *The Incurable Romantic*, by son Roderick Peattie. Additional information came from critical sources including Sidney H. Bremer's introduction to *The Precipice*, Peattie's 1914 novel about a Chicago woman social worker, and Joan Falcone's *Bonds of Sisterhood in Chicago Women Writers: The Voice of Elia Wilkerson Peattie*. I wish to thank Noel, Mark, and Alice Peattie for their permission to quote from the Peattie letters and from Elia Peattie's memoirs.

8. Leavitt, *Brought to Bed*, 154–55; Wertz and Wertz, *Lying-In*, 121.

9. *Poems*, 87; also in *Nebraska of* KMC, 235.

10. *Belford's Monthly*, April 1893; also in the selected works section of this book, and in *Nebraska of* KMC, 59–68.

11. Wertz and Wertz, *Lying-In*, 127.

12. *Chicago Tribune*, 14 May 1899, 42; also in *Nebraska of* KMC, 135–49.

13. Hoffert, "Childbearing," 279.

14. *Chicago Tribune*, 27 December 1887, 6; also in *Nebraska of* KMC, 27–36.

15. Bessie Calhoun, a Hubbell historian, described the Clearys' house in a taped interview by Lois Mannschreck in February 1988.

16. Peattie, "A Bohemian in Nebraska," 7; also in *Nebraska of KMC*, 5–13.
17. *Good Housekeeping,* November 1891, 223–25; also in *Nebraska of KMC*, 195–202.

2. THE DIFFICULT YEARS: 1892–1897

1. *Puck,* 28 May 1896.
2. "Building for Nebraska Exhibits," *Chicago Tribune,* 18 June 1892, 13.
3. *Nebraska of KMC,* 10.
4. Undated, unidentified newspaper clipping in the Cleary scrapbooks.
5. Undated, unidentified newspaper clipping in the Cleary scrapbooks.
6. If that failed, according to the 1882 *Encyclopedia of Health and Home,* ed. I. N. Reed, "the tincture of the muriate of iron, in doses of ten or twenty drops in a wine glassful of water, repeated every hour, will generally be found superior to every other remedy" (633–35).
7. The exact nature of Rosemarie's illness and the cause of her death are unknown. She may have died from complications surrounding her partial paralysis.
8. *Nebraska of KMC,* 44.
9. Originally published as "On the Hubbell Hill," *Chicago Tribune,* 4 August 1895, 34; also in *Nebraska of KMC,* 45–48.
10. *Chicago Tribune,* ca. 1895; also in *Nebraska of KMC,* 49.
11. *Poems,* 46.
12. *Nebraska of KMC,* 231.
13. *Poems,* 122; also published in a slightly different version in *Extension* magazine, ca. 1910.
14. Peattie, "Star Wagon," 10.
15. Cleary, *Like a Gallant Lady* (Chicago: Way & Williams, 1897). Subsequent references are from this edition and are given parenthetically in the text.
16. Introductory chapter quotations are taken from *All's Well That Ends Well, King Lear, Julius Caesar, The Winter's Tale, King Richard II, As You Like It, Antony and Cleopatra, Hamlet* (2), *Othello* (2), *Romeo and Juliet* (2), *The Merchant of Venice* (2),

Much Ado about Nothing (2), *Henry VI* (2), and *Two Gentle-men of Verona* (3).

17. On 14 October 1900, the *Chicago Tribune* published a history of insurance scams in "Incidents in Famous Attempted Insurance Swindles" (45), attesting to contemporary popular interest in such subjects.

18. *Chicago Tribune*, 4 September 1898, 42; also in *Nebraska of KMC*, 41–43.

19. *Gallant Lady*, front pages. The complete poem is included in the selected works section of this book.

3. BACK TO CHICAGO: 1898–1903

1. The numbering system of Chicago streets was revised in 1909, so the numbers given here do not correspond to present-day street addresses.

2. Duncan, *The Rise of Chicago*, xvii, 69.

3. Nancy Walker's article "Alegaste or Eiron: American Women Writers and the Sense of Humor" also notes that "by pretending to be innocent" the protagonist can point out "society's faults through his own naive questioning of the world around him" (105). Fanning, *The Irish Voice in America*, 37.

4. Duncan, *The Rise of Chicago*, 114. Duncan's book provided the background for this analysis. Information on the Chicago literary groups is in his chap. 8, 104–22.

5. Letter from Kate to "Sonnie" (Michael), Saturday 8 A.M., no date.

6. In her "Literary Reviews" column titled " 'The Spring Song' and Other Fiction," Elia Peattie made reference to Cleary: "The book comes under the head of what my friend, Kate McPhelim Cleary, used to call 'good bad stuff.' " Peattie herself called this type of writing "whoopla" fiction: "It follows the old theme of mistaken identity, and the usual strain is put upon credulity. But devoted readers of fiction are accustomed to that strain and are willing to bear whatever burden it imposes, if only the story be absorbing enough" (undated clipping in Cleary scrapbooks).

7. Undated, unidentified newspaper clipping in the Cleary scrapbooks.

8. These articles are collected in their entirety in the Cleary scrapbooks, but I have been unable to find any record of this periodical. From 1908 to 1941, E. C. Baldwin published *Home World* in New Haven CT, but it does not appear to have any connection to the one for which Cleary wrote. Miles Benjamin Hilly published a book called *Rugs from the Orient* in 1896, but he is unlisted in nineteenth-century biographies.

9. Letter from Kate Cleary to Jim Cleary, 27 November 1903.

10. Advertisements from the *Chicago Tribune*, 27 January 1904, 13.

11. Terry and Pellens, *Opium Problem*, 442, 545, 549, 605.

12. Stage, *Female Complaints*, 62.

13. Musto, *American Disease*, 2–3; Rublowsky, *Stoned Age*, 127–28.

14. Musto, *American Disease*, 3; Stage, *Female Complaints*, 166; Rublowsky, *Stoned Age*, 130. Another factor in the legislation of the Pure Food and Drug Act, according to Austin, *Perspectives*, was the need to stop the widespread use of cocaine in patent medicines and popular beverages. In Europe, Austin explains, Angelo Mariani introduced Vin Mariani, an extremely popular preparation of coca and wine, and he was awarded a gold medal and cited as "a benefactor of humanity by Pope Leo XIII, a frequent user." At this time, Sigmund Freud also praised cocaine as "a magical drug" and suggested its use for treatment of morphine addiction. Patent medicine manufacturers began to exploit it, too. It seemed "the perfect drug for the 'industrious' Americans," according to Austin, and the "Great Cocaine Explosion" lasted from 1885 to 1905. To compete with Mariani, John Styth Pemberton of Georgia in 1886 invented Coca-Cola, "a soft drink made from a syrup based on coca and caffeine" (*Perspectives*, 228, 229). To appreciate how extensive opiate abuse at the turn of the century was, Charles F. Levinthal points out in *Drugs, Behavior, and Modern Society*, one must compare the very conservative estimate of 250,000 opiate-dependent people in the United States one hundred years ago with the estimated 300,000 opiate (chiefly heroin) addicts today in a population four times larger (156).

15. *Chicago Tribune*, 8 November 1900, 1.

16. *Chicago Tribune*, 2 February 1896, 38.
17. Kate M. Cleary: Case #8228, Case Book, Illinois Northern Hospital for the Insane, Elgin IL. Records are available only to family members through court order.
18. *The Opium Problem*, by Terry and Pellens, published in 1928, is still considered the most authoritative source on the history of drug abuse and treatment. I have used the information from turn-of-the-century sources in this text, pages 442–551, to arrive at what I consider to be the methods of treatment Cleary probably received while at Elgin in 1903–4.
19. Jim Cleary received his B.A. in 1906 and entered Northwestern Law School, working as a reporter for the *Chicago Tribune* to pay his tuition and support there. He was admitted to the bar in 1909. By 1912, he was serving as an executive for the *Chicago Tribune* in sales and advertising. In 1913 he took a leave of absence to help the *Los Angeles Times* establish its promotion department. Upon his return, he organized the *Tribune*'s copy and art bureau and its business research department, and established the promotion department there. He left the *Tribune* in 1925 to join Studebaker as advertising director, followed by positions as vice president of Studebaker–Pierce Arrow–Rockne Sales Corporation and president of the White Company, Cleveland. After 1932 he was a partner in the Roche, Williams, and Cleary, Inc., advertising agency in Chicago. From 1937 to 1943 he served on the board of trustees of the University of Illinois, including a term as president. In 1943 he worked with the War Department, Washington DC, settling and terminating contracts. He supported several civic and charitable commissions and associations, and he was named Press Veteran of the Year in 1967 by the Chicago Press Veterans Association. He died in 1972.
20. *Chicago Tribune*, 1–17 January 1904.
21. Quoted in Falcone, *Bonds of Sisterhood*, 42.
22. Peattie, "Star Wagon," 301–2.

4. THE LONELY ROAD: 1904–1905

1. Peattie, "Star Wagon," 250.
2. Liska, *Drugs and the Human Body*, 154–59.

3. Information about the writing contest can be found in *Collier's*, 27 February 1904, 5; and 11 February 1905, 13. Unfortunately, Cleary's manuscript and any evidence of its possible publication in any other magazine have been lost.

4. Lane, *Chicago Churches and Synagogues*, 37, 49.

5. Willa Cather to Kate Cleary, 13 February 1905; in the personal collection of Connie Koepke.

6. Willa Cather to Kate Cleary, 25 February 1905; in the personal collection of Joel Bullard, Cleary's grandson.

7. County Court of Cook County IL, Case 27837 on the "Lunatic Docket," 6 July 1905. Apparently Michael's petition was entered on 6 July and Kate stood trial the same day.

8. The *Hubbell Standard* published this obituary on 21 July 1905, p. 5: "Mrs. Kate M. Cleary died very suddenly of heart disease, Sunday, at Chicago. Mrs. Cleary is remembered by our people as the brilliant and talented wife of M. T. Cleary, a former popular and highly respected citizen of this place. The family moved to Chicago in 1897."

9. This version is different from the one published in *Poems*. The newspaper did not print several stanzas detailing the beauties and joys of life. The poem published in *The Nebraska of Kate McPhelim Cleary*, edited by her son Jim, on the other hand, omits the stanza that begins "And love of man—the love that's worth the winning," which the newspaper included.

10. Peattie, "Star Wagon," 250.

11. Cook County Coroner, Certificate of Death #15069; Terry and Pellens, *Opium Problem*, 186.

12. From the Peattie article "Of Extravagant Economy," clipping in Cleary scrapbook.

13. At Cleary's death, all of her possessions still in storage were lost. Michael Timothy Cleary, who wanted his children and grandchildren to be taught "to love Ireland," died in 1917 at age sixty-two in South Haven MI. He was associated for a time with his son Gerald in a real estate business, taking it over when Gerald served in World War I. Up to his retirement, he was connected with Jones, Coates, and Bailey of Chicago. He was buried beside Kate in Calvary Cemetery.

   Gerald Vernon Cleary attended Northwestern University. In 1917, he interrupted his career in Chicago real estate to enlist in the army; he trained at Fort Sheridan. He served as a lieutenant at Camp Joseph, Jacksonville FL, and in Givres, France. After the war, he sold life insurance for Reliance Life and Lincoln Life and was a member of the Two Million Dollar Roundtable. He married Emily Goodwillie in 1922, and they had two children, Gerald Vernon Jr. and Emily (Scanlon). He died in 1971.

Vera Valentine Cleary graduated in 1911 from Notre Dame Academy in Bourbonnais IL at the age of seventeen and attended Loyola University, studying social work and assisting at the early settlement houses of Chicago. After her father died in 1917, "Val" lived with her brother Jim and his wife, helping care for their children. Around 1923 she opened the first of a series of bookstores in the heart of the Chicago Loop. The store was a welcoming place for writers to frequent, with comfortable wicker chairs and plants; its walls were covered with autographed pictures of authors and poets. Charles Bullard, an attorney and an aviator, stopped in one day, and he and Val were married in 1927. Charles was working for Chicago Trust, which moved him to South Bend IN. There the couple made a home, raised two children, Joel and Marna Aileen, and enjoyed their twelve grandchildren. Val died in 1980. Teddie (Edward Sheridan) died in 1911 at age fourteen of rheumatic heart disease and was buried beside his mother in Calvary Cemetery. For biographical information on Jim Cleary, see chap. 3, n. 19.

14. *Nebraska of KMC*, 3.
15. *Chicago Tribune*, 14 May 1899, 42; also in *Nebraska of KMC*, 135.
16. Fanning, *The Irish Voice in America*, 180.

Works Cited

Austin, Gregory A. *Perspectives on the History of Psychoactive Substance Use.* Rockville MD: National Institute of Drug Abuse, 1978.

Bremer, Sidney H. Introduction to *The Precipice.* 1889. Urbana: Univ. of Illinois Press, 1989.

Calhoun, Bessie. Taped interview, by Lois Mannschreck. February 1988. Thayer County NE Historical Society.

Cleary, James Mansfield. *The Fogartys of Tipperary — 1600–1832.* Chicago: n.p., n.d.

———. *On My Father's Side.* Chicago: n.p., 1956.

———. *On My Mother's Side.* Chicago: n.p., 1952.

Cleary, Kate McPhelim. *Like a Gallant Lady.* Chicago: Way & Williams, 1897.

———. *The Nebraska of Kate McPhelim Cleary.* Ed. James M. Cleary. Lake Bluff IL: United Educators, 1958.

———. Unpublished letters. In the private collections of Marguerite Cleary Remien, Aileen Bullard Droege, and Joel Bullard.

———. Unpublished stories, articles, poems, memorabilia. In the private collections of Marguerite Cleary Remien, Aileen Bullard Droege, and Joel Bullard.

——— [Mrs. Sumner Hayden, pseud.]. *Vella Vernel, or An Amazing Marriage.* Street & Smith's Select Series, no. 3. Chicago: Street & Smith, 1887.

Cleary, Kate McPhelim, Margaret Kelly McPhelim, and Edward Joseph McPhelim. *Poems.* N.p.: Published by Vera Valentine Cleary, Gerald Vernon Cleary, and James Mansfield Cleary, May 1922.

"Dies at Her Son's Feet." *Chicago Tribune,* 17 July 1905, 3.

Duncan, Hugh Dalziel. *The Rise of Chicago as a Literary Center from 1885 to 1920.* 1948. Totowa NJ: Bedminster, 1964.

Falcone, Joan. "The Bonds of Sisterhood in Chicago Women Writers: The Voice of Elia Wilkinson Peattie." Ph.D. diss., Illinois State University, 1992.

Fanning, Charles. *The Irish Voice in America: Irish-American Fic-*

tion from the 1760s to the 1980s. Lexington: Univ. Press of Kentucky, 1990.

Garland, Hamlin. *Crumbling Idols.* Chicago: Stone & Kimball, 1894.

Hoffert, Sylvia D. "Childbearing on the Trans-Mississippi Frontier, 1830–1900." *Western Historical Quarterly* 22, no. 3 (August 1991): 273–88.

———. *Private Matters: American Attitudes toward Childbearing and Infant Nurture in the Urban North, 1800–1860.* Urbana: Univ. of Illinois Press, 1989.

"Hot Wave Is Broken." *Chicago Daily News,* 19 July 1905, 2.

Hubbell Heritage. Collected by Hubbell Public School Eighth Grade. Hubbell NE: n.p., 1963.

Keezer-Clayton, Jean. "The Poetic Metaphors of Kate McPhelim Cleary: Bride, Slave, Guest." Paper presented at the Western Literature Association, Vancouver, Canada, October 1995.

Lane, George A. *Chicago Churches and Synagogues: An Architectural Pilgrimage.* Chicago: Loyola Univ. Press, 1988.

Leavitt, Judith Walzer. *Brought to Bed: Childbearing in America, 1750 to 1950.* New York: Oxford Univ. Press, 1986.

Lee, Kate. *A Year at the Elgin Insane Asylum.* New York: Irving, 1902.

Levinthal, Charles F. *Drugs, Behavior, and Modern Society.* Boston: Allyn & Bacon, 1996.

Liska, Ken. *Drugs and the Human Body: With Implications for Society.* 4th ed. New York: Macmillan, 1994.

Makowsky, Veronica. *Susan Glaspell's Century of American Women: A Critical Interpretation of Her Work.* New York: Oxford Univ. Press, 1993.

Melendy, Mary R. *Perfect Womanhood for Maidens, Wives, Mothers: A Complete Medical Guide for Women.* Chicago: Hoey, 1903.

Musto, David F. *The American Disease: Origins of Narcotic Control.* New York: Oxford Univ. Press, 1987.

Olsen, Tillie. *Silences.* New York: Delacorte, 1965.

Peattie, Donald Culross. *The Road of a Naturalist.* Boston: Houghton Mifflin, 1941.

Peattie, Elia. "A Bohemian in Nebraska." *Omaha World-Herald,* 23 April 1893, 7.

————. "The Star Wagon." Ed. Joan Falcone, Mark R. Peattie, and Noel R. Peattie. Unpublished manuscript.

————. Unpublished letters. In the private collections of Aileen Bullard Droege and Joel Bullard.

Peattie, Robert Burns. *The Story of Robert Burns Peattie.* 2d ed. Ed. Mark Robert Peattie, Noel Roderick Peattie, and Alice Richmond Peattie. N.p.: Published by his children, 1992.

Peattie, Roderick. *The Incurable Romantic.* New York: MacMillan, 1941.

Reed, I. N., ed. *Encyclopedia of Health and Home: A Domestic Guide to Health, Wealth, and Happiness.* Vol. 1. Chicago: I. N. Reed, 1882.

Riley, Glenda. *The Female Frontier: A Comparative View of Women on the Prairie and the Plains.* Lawrence: Univ. Press of Kansas, 1988.

Rublowsky, John. *The Stoned Age: A History of Drugs in America.* New York: G. P. Putnam's Sons, 1974.

Saur, P. B. *Maternity: A Book for Every Wife and Mother.* Chicago: L. P. Miller, 1888.

Shannon, T. W. *Perfect Manhood: How Inherited, Attained, and Maintained; How Wrecked and Regained.* Louisville KY: T. W. Shannon, 1911.

Stage, Sarah. *Female Complaints: Lydia Pinkham and the Business of Women's Medicine.* New York: Norton, 1979.

Terry, Charles E., and Mildred Pellens. *The Opium Problem.* 1928. Montclair NJ: Patterson Smith, 1970.

Toth, Emily, ed. *Regionalism and the Female Imagination: A Collection of Essays.* New York: Human Sciences Press, 1985.

Walker, Nancy. "Alegaste or Eiron: American Women Writers and the Sense of Humor." *Studies in American Humor* 4, nos. 1 and 2 (spring/summer 1985): 105–25.

Wertz, Richard W., and Dorothy C. Wertz. *Lying-In: A History of Childbirth in America.* New York: Free Press, 1977.

Willard, Frances E., and Mary A. Livermore. *A Woman of the Century.* Buffalo NY: Charles Wells Moulton, 1893.

"Woman Writer's Death Due to Heart Disease." *Chicago Record Herald,* 18 July 1906, 5.

Selected Works

An Ornament to Society

Cleary often utilized local personalities as prototypes for her characters, and in this story, published in the Chicago Tribune *on 9 April 1899, she focused on the town's founding father. An article in the* Hubbell Times *on 15 April 1897 described him: "H. H. Johnson, Hubbell's jolly auctioneer, cried a sale for Mrs. Andy Mitchell . . . and it is conceded by almost everybody that he is the best auctioneer in this or adjoining counties." Johnson's daughter attended a convent school, according to the* Hebron Journal *of 24 December 1897: "H. H. Johnson went down to Concordia Saturday and brought Miss Jessie, who is attending the convent school there, home." However, the story's plot is pure fiction; the Hubbells were one of the wealthier families of the community, and Martha Hubbell died at age eighty-one in 1925. This humorous story satirizes the superficiality and absurdity of the Victorian Cult of True Womanhood, especially its inappropriateness on the frontier.*

JACK HARROWSBY WAS THE ONLY one of the men who had a chair. Some sympathizing woman had carried it out in the back yard and placed it for him. It did not seem proper that the lately bereaved husband and chief mourner should sit on the woodpile or the end of the horse trough as did the half dozen men who had dropped in to condole and smoke with him.

It was early—not yet half past 5—but the lifelong habits of the farm were continued in the town, and the process of "reddin' up" was well under way in the kitchen as one might judge by the clatter of dishes and the subdued but incessant chatter of women's voices that proceeded from the rear of the dwelling. The pungence of boiled coffee still lingered on the air, and the appetizing odor of fried bacon.

"There was jest three things she allus had her heart set on," remarked Jack, taking his pipe from his mouth, and looking with an air of mild reminiscence at the floating smoke. "One was to quit the farm and live in town. Any town would suit her. She'd never lived in a town—only on a farm. And the farms we rented when we came out here to Nebrasky thirty-five years ago was pretty lonely places. She wasn't but a young thing, an' she was skeered to death of redskins. She might well be—might well be!"

The hand that held the pipe shook. "There wasn't never a time when I had to be away but she kept her white pony saddled at the door, an' the rifle loaded. You know that stone shed half way inter the hill over onto Johnny MacGowthan's place—where he keeps his horses?"

His hearers nodded solemnly.

"That there was a fort when we come. Fifteen years later they made it a postoffice—the only one for the Lord only knows for how many miles. Mail come once every two weeks. You'd see 'em streakin' in all over the prairie fur long afore the messenger got there, an' squattin' around clean played out just waitin' fur a word from the folks back East. So it all was purty lonely fur a woman, you see. An' that's how Hat got to thinkin' that folks as lived in a town was most as blessed as them that ain't got a derned thing to do but keep their crowns on straight an' play on harps. Once she got reel het up. She said as how we'd stuck here long enough, an' weren't much better off than when we come. She took a notion she'd like to go farther West. So we hitched up an' drove to Colorady. She wasn't just herself that year—Hat wasn't. Seems like there come spells when if a woman could cuss good an' hard she'd feel better. But Hat was allus a church member—a full-blooded one. But when the children kep' a-comin' an' a-goin'—if 't wasn't a birth it was a death—if not a cradle that was bein' fixed it was a coffin, she got contrairy. She had cryin' spells. She didn't sleep none to talk on. But the work was there to be done. She done it. She couldn't stand Colorady though, so we come back."

He paused again. The men nodded once more, and one more

acutely sympathetic than the rest held out a bag of tobacco. Harrowsby mechanically accepted it—as mechanically shook out his pipe and re-filled it.

"Seems like what she couldn't stand out there was the want of greenness an' the mountains. 'Twasn't the dryness—there ain't nobody who can tell a Nebraska body a single thing about that. But there's greenness here—the timber, an' the criks, an' the rye, an' winter wheat. There it looked drab where it wasn't gray, an' brown where 'twasn't purple. She couldn't look up at the mountains. She 'lowed as how it made her dizzy—like lookin' down a deep well. She'd never had to look up—only level. She couldn't do it. So we give Nebrasky another show."

Higher rose the sun and all the east was one dazzling sheet of amber flame. The blue morning mists which filled the little low-lying town curled up, went floating away in shreds, in filaments, in dissolving, illusory mists. The distant Kansas bluffs elbowed their way forward until they stood, dusky and fir-clad, bold against the brilliance of the young day. People were stirring at cottage doors, in barnyards, and gardens. Already heavy wagons were rumbling into town. The freight train from the East came puffing leisurely along the track at the farther end of the village. A capricious breeze set the marigolds by the porch nodding, and fluttered the streamers of crape which hung from the knob of the side door.

"They'll be a heap of folks into the funeral," ventured the village carpenter. "Most everybody in the county knowed Mis' Harrowsby."

"She was a good woman," said Jack Harrowsby; "slews too good fur me."

"You was never mean to her, Jack. You let her feed the hull Salvation Army—all of them that come to town for revival. You let her go on the train to St. Joe when you was goin' in with cattle. You met her there, an' let her see the shops, an' buy what she wanted. You even left the farm to please her."

"That's so. But—great Scott! all the nights I've come home full. An' I never could keep from swearin'. Never meant nothin' by it—it just come nat'ral. Then, when I used to go to Chicago with hogs—but we won't talk about that. An' the way I laughed at her mission-meetin's, an' her prayer-meetin's, an' all! It wasn't the square thing—she bein' a Christian—a full-blooded one. I'm glad now I bought this house, though she ain't had but one month's wear out'n it. She's goin' to have the second thing she wanted, too. It's a little late, perhaps, but she's going to git it."

The agent tipped his hat back and shifted his quid of tobacco from one cheek to another.

"What was that, Jack?"

"A silk dress—a black silk dress. Hat often said the genteelest thing she knowed of was a black silk dress trimmed with beeds [sic]—the shiny kind."

"She could have had it most any time," put in Kipperton. He was a bald, gray-mustached little chap, who had got a bullet in his leg at Shiloh, and who gloried in the resultant limp. The limp had a way of being more or less noticeable, according to the occasion. It was barely obvious when he walked the streets in a campaign procession, but on Memorial Sunday and Decoration day the admiring small boys observed with awe how extremely difficult it was for Elijah Kipperton to keep up with his veteran comrades on their way to church or cemetery. The patriotic limb troubled him a good deal, too, on the day of the month when he drew his pension.

"Yes, she could. But she was savin'. Even after the railroad come through here, an' the site of this here town of Bubble was fixed right in the middle of my cornfield, she kep' on savin'. When corn went up, an' hogs went up, an' two good years come jest a-hoppin' after each other, I says to her: 'Hat, now's your time. Git the silk dress. You ain't never had one. I don't have to skimp. Things is comin' my way. I bet I got more money now than any man in Thayer County, except old Hiram Hicox, an' I'd hate to be the skinflint he is. Git the dress.' But she'd say: 'I've waited so long, I'll wait a bit longer. Cleo ain't growed up yet, an' girls need a lot of clothes now. I've been waitin' fur that dress sence I was 15. A few years more won't hurt.' She was 55 last week. She's got the silk dress today. There's Mrs. Magee comin' with it now."

A woman carrying a bulky bundle under her arm was turning at the side gate.

"I telegraphed to Omaha fur the goods night before last when Hat died. There wasn't any goods in town nice enough. That cost a hull dollar a yard. An' I told 'em to send the shiniest beads they had. The things come yesterday, an' Mrs. Magee's been sewin' sense. I told her not to spare any frills—to git any help she wanted, an' make it the latest style—I'd pay."

There was a murmur of approval from his listeners.

"What was the third thing, Jack?" asked the lumberman.

"The third gits me—it jest gits me. It's about Cleo. She's the only one that growed up you know. All the others died. Even Cleo's twin died."

"I didn't know as Cleopatra was a twin," put in the veteran.

"She was. The other was named Helen—Helen of Troy."

"Helenoftroy?" said the carpenter interrogatively. "I never heerd no such name as that."

"No more did any one else, hereabouts. That's why Hat was so taken with it. She got the names from a district school teacher who was boardin' to our house when the girls was born. He said they was beauties, an' how we ought to give them the names of two beautiful women. He told us them names. He was a nice fellow, but the board had to send him off. He didn't know about anything but books. That kind ain't never of much account. Well, Hat allus wanted as how Cleo should grow up to be a ornament to sassiety. Them's her own identical words. I've heerd her say hundreds of times as how she hoped her daughter would be a ornament to sassiety. I'd like awful well to please Hat about it, but—what fetches me is—what is a ornament to sassiety?"

There was no haze in the clear air now. A vast, golden effulgence brimmed the little bowl-shaped town up to its roof that was green-blue as a robin's egg. A buggy drew up before the palings of the house of mourning. Figures came trickling from different parts of the town, and passed in at the little swinging gates. Chickens flocked around the group in the back yard. Harrowsby looked inquiringly from one to the other of the half stolid, half sympathetic faces surrounding him.

"I'd say," declared the agent, "that a young lady who could take a hand at playing the organ in church, and sing some, and take an interest in reading polite literature," the phrase sounded so felicitous he repeated it, "reading we'll say polite literature was a ornament to society." But Kipperton shook his head.

"That ain't enough. She ought to be able to speak pieces about the war at the Memorial day services, an' other pieces at other occasions, like at the Baptist Church Christmas tree, an' the old settlers' reunion, an' the G.A.R. picnic, an' the Fourth of July popular demonstration. I should say a young lady who could do all that was a ornament to sassiety."

"She ought to dress stylish, an' always have her hair frizzed," decided the hardware man, who was young, and sustained the reputation of a gallant.

"Fancy work," put in the lumberman, "fancy work—that's the most refined thing I know. Drapes, tidies, doilies, centerpieces, headrests—to be a real ornament to society a young lady ought to know how to make those."

Now, whereas the lumberman had but lately espoused a certain Miss Stella Celeste Jones, whose proficiency in decorative needlework was well known, his enthusiasm on the subject and the glibness with which he repeated these mysterious words failed to impress his hearers as the utterances of one quite impartially interested. A chilling silence followed. Harrowsby sighed helplessly.

"I got to figure it out some way," he said. "If I can be sure just what's a ornament I'll see she's made one. Here she is, now. Hallo, Cleo!"

"Hello, pap!"

She crossed over from the back door to where the men sat—an angular, awkward young creature in her ill-fitting black gown. A sun bonnet shaded her face—a tanned, girlish countenance that at once attracted, repelled, provoked. There was evidence of her father's coarser nature in the heavy line of her chin, and the square fullness of her red lips. But this was contradicted and redeemed by the look in the gray eyes—a look of ignorant spirituality, of reserve, of loyalty.

"Is—is it time to git ready?" Harrowsby questioned.

Farm wagons were rolling up beside the fence, women were climbing down over the wheels from their board seats covered with home-made bed quilts. A block off the minister could be seen walking in the direction of the church.

"Most time," she answered. She did not lift her eyes. She was looking at the bow of black ribbon on the end of the yellow braid she had pulled over her shoulder. Harrowsby lumbered to his feet.

"I'll git on that coller now," he said.

They went into the house together. The funeral was an imposing one. The prayer and sermon of the minister were of unusual length. The church was packed. The line of teams outside the walk extended quite to the main street. Jack Harrowsby was known and liked throughout the county. His great voice had bellowed many an auction on many a farm. His bluff geniality, his hearty manner, even his amiable vices had tended to win him friends. As for his wife, she had been the model of all the hard-worked farmers' wives around. Her unceasing labor, her rigid religious views, her unrelenting resolution to never spend a penny for pleasure, her stern attitude toward sinners, especially those of her own sex, her liberality to heathen missions, her conservatism, her inflexibility, her passionate penuriousness, these had constituted her a social power to be admired and a leader to be reverenced.

When, in all the splendor of the new black silk, coveted for forty years, she was laid away in the little hillside cemetery, a different life began for Jack Harrowsby and his daughter. He brought a widowed niece to live with them, a flippant little woman, with round black eyes and a perpetual smile. She insisted on having a hired girl, and although Jack wondered if Hat would not turn in her grave could she hear the startling suggestion, he consented. So there were five around the dinner table now, for Frank Stanley was still with them. He had been chore boy for many years in the Harrowsby household, and under the stern regime of the mistress had developed into a worker after her own heart, bent on accomplishment and insensible to fatigue. After her death Harrowsby came to depend on him more, and to seek his advice in business matters. He was an erect, muscular, young fellow, bold as a lion when "rounding up" or stock lading, but of lamblike meekness of demeanor in the presence of femininity. With his niece Harrowsby discussed the best method in which to make Cleopatra an ornament to society. He discovered that her views on the subject were those of Kipperton and the lumberman combined, with the addition of one strictly original opinion of her own.

"Fancy work," she said, "and nice clothes, and never to do any kind of housework—not even dishwashing, so that her hands will be white. That ought to make her an ornament to society."

"I don't think," he said hurriedly, "that her mother quite meant the—last one." A hundred recollections of the heavy farm work which had so frequently been placed upon the girl recurred to him.

"An ornament to society is a lady," his niece returned promptly, "and a lady never does any work except play on the pianny—or the organ if she hasn't a pianny—and make fancy work."

So the delayed education of Cleopatra Harrowsby was duly begun. She took music lessons, and lessons in painting, and lessons in crewel work, and crochet, and ribbon embroidery. She did not take kindly to the unusual tasks. Her fingers were skillful enough in caring for turkey chicks, or feeding the young calves, or dosing a sick colt, or handling the reins from the seat of a harrow, or even when gripped confidently around plow handles. The black and white keys on the organ board bore too strong a family likeness to be promptly identified, and the needle became an instrument by which self-torture was involuntarily and frequently administered. Nevertheless, the result of her labors in the field of art became gradually apparent. Pictures were hung upon the walls—pictures in six-inch gold frames. Painted snow shovels also appeared, and trays, and rolling pins tied up by the handles with blue ribbons, and gilded piepans, and triangular satin banners, on which flaunted such flowers as never saw the sun of heaven shine. Mrs. Maltby—the name of Harrowsby's widowed niece was Mrs. Maltby—looked on with satisfaction as the collection increased, and Jack himself used to make an excuse to take his particular friends through the sacred room of state and seclusion.

"Cleo did them," he'd say airily, with a wave of his pipe. "She painted all of them—hand-painted them. Every blame one—they're all hand-painted."

"Drapes" multiplied also, strips of silk with lace sewn between, pincushions, sofa cushions, wool mats, and various other elaborately constructed articles. One evening when the latest artistic achievement had been duly exhibited by Mrs. Maltby, Frank Stanley ventured to congratulate the young person responsible.

"You're doing fine," he said. "Seems like you've learned an awful lot since she died."

"Fine!" She flared out on him, her face crimsoning. "It's rubbish—everything I try to do. I know it—you know it, too. The people who try to teach me know I'll never learn to do them things well—not if I live to be a hundred. But they get Pap's money. That's all they care about. Pap is the only one who really thinks it's fine. Do you suppose I'd keep on at it if it wasn't for him?"

A few days after that the girl saw Frank coming towards the house. A hot wind had raged that day—was still raging. Through the swirling clouds of brick colored dust she descried the colossal young figure, and the creature that only his powerful hand upon the bridle kept in check—a prancing, coal-black, beautiful creature that flung its delicate head high, and danced sideways with many curvettings. An instant later she had flung down her colored silks, was out of the room—out of the house.

"Where did you get it—the beauty?" she cried. Her hand was stroking the horse's satiny neck, her finger-tips tingling with the delight of feeling the quivering muscles grow calm beneath her touch.

"Your father's bought it. I'm going to take it out to the farm tomorrow to break it in. It's never had a saddle on."

"O!" said Cleo. Her gray eyes were shining, and she breathed more quickly. Then, "Did pap get off to that auction?" she asked.

"Yes. He won't be back till tomorrow night. He don't need to hold auctions. He is too well off. He's most too old for the work anyhow. But he hates to give up. Everybody expects him, and he likes meeting his old friends."

She started. "You were saying—yes," she murmured absently. Her hand fell from the horse's neck. She moved away towards the house.

The next day she was not at home for her music lesson, nor for her painting lesson, nor yet for her rick-rack lesson. The old mare, Molly, was gone from the barn, and so was the black horse. When Frank found her that noon she was riding the black horse homeward in leisurely fashion. It was dripping, trembling, and flecked with patches of foam. He noticed that she was white. Even her lips were white. But her eyes shone triumphantly.

"We had a grand time," she cried, "a lovely time! It took four hours' hard work, but I broke him. He's as mild as old Molly now. O, it was splendid, but—but—" she lurched a little in the saddle. Frank sprang down—put his arm around her. "I think he—he broke my arm about—an—an hour ago. He threw me, and fell against—"

"Cleo, my dear—my girl—"

Dr. Eldridge was cutting the sleeve from her arm when she regained consciousness.

"A dislocated shoulder," he declared. "Bad? Yes, it's bad, because it has been so long neglected."

When Harrowsby heard the story his heart gave a queer leap of exultation, but his expression was one of dismay. He could hardly reconcile with the opinions which had been forced upon him that breaking wild horses and having your arm jerked out in the accomplishment of this gentle pastime was quite the most approved manner of becoming an ornament to society. So, when Cleo was well enough to resume her interrupted career of culture, he betook himself one evening to the abode of Mrs. McLelland, and to that wise and outspoken matron gravely stated his doubts and the difficulty of his position.

"Do?" echoed Mrs. McLelland, "you'll send her to a convent—that's what you'll do. I sent my daughter to a convent—the only daughter I ever had—Eliza Louise. Do you know what they done with her? They transmogrified her. They made a lady of her—yes, sir, a real lady. I don't hold with the religion of convents—I'm a Baptis' myself—but when it comes to genteel manners, an' the kind of behavior Queens has when they switches their trains straight an' stands up to receive their courtiers an' penitentiaries—some of them havin' as many as ten given names to one hind name—then I say, 'Give me a convent.'"

So to a convent—a convent over in Kansas—Cleopatra Harrowsby was duly dispatched. Letters came from her at intervals. These letters Harrowsby showed to every one in town. The writing was laboriously symmetrical, and wherever a word had been misspelled it had been carefully scratched out and one in which no orthographical error could be detected duly substituted. They were the mildest kind of letters—

the most irreproachable and dutiful of letters. Harrowsby thought of
Mrs. McLelland with a glow of gratitude warming his breast. One
month passed—two. There was to be a cattle fair of importance in
Kansas. Harrowsby had injured his hand in the door of a stock car, so
sent Frank Stanley in his place. It was only the matter of a little horseback ride of twenty miles out of his way for Stanley to go to see Cleo.
He went. That young lady, rushing into the reception room, flung herself into his arms in a paroxysm of homesickness broken loose—gone
mad.

"O, Frank, I can't stand it. Take me away. The letters? You
thought—of course you did. That was all for pap. Unkind? Dear, no.
They are kind enough—but they don't understand. The barred doors,
and the time to walk out, and the time to stay in, and the time to say
your prayers—why, I get wild!—wild! I want the old farm—the good
times we had there before we came to live in town. And the dogs—
the dear dogs! And the riding—and the corn-shucking—and the creek!
O, I want the creek! The oak tree with the seat—you put the seat up
there for me, Frank! And the berrying—and the nutting—and the
wading when your feet were hot and the water was cool—O, I can't
stay here! Not if I was to be ever such an ornament to society—I
can't—I can't!"

Just then the Superior came in. Her gentle counsel, combined with
Frank's friendly advice, prevailed. At least it seemed to prevail, but
when, two days later, Frank got home from the cattle fair, he found
the daughter of his host cuddling a young litter of puppies in the barn.

"The darlings!" she cried. "No—pap doesn't mind now. He did at
first. He's bought a new farm at Guide Rock, and he's so much interested in it he doesn't mind much that I ran away."

Harrowsby was interested in his new farm—so much so, indeed,
that he went up there more frequently than one versed in farm lore
would consider necessary, considering that he looked upon his tenant
as competent and trustworthy. At home affairs went rather more happily than they had done since the morning of the funeral of the mistress
of the house a year and a half before. Mrs. Maltby had gone on a visit
to relatives in the East. Frank's time was taken up on the farm, and he
seldom came to town. Cleo made friends among the young people,

lived almost all her waking hours in the open air, and left the drudgery of the household to the maid who was paid to attend to it. In those crisp, yellow autumnal days, whether walking miles and miles or skimming over the good, hard Nebraska roads on the bicycle her father had bought her, or shooting quail and prairie chicken along the short cuts and seldom used prairie ways, or racing the black horse to a distant candy pull or "literary," she came nearer the full experience of content than she had ever known. Life was such a good thing—and health—and energy—and the vast sweep of the immeasurable world around and companionship with birds, and animals, and trees, and streams, and all nature's delicious, ever-varying, never satiating sweetness!

"How pretty Cleo Harrowsby is growing!" people in Bubble began to say. Remarks were current, too, as to how she would endure a stepmother. For it was hinted that Jack Harrowsby's frequent visits to Guide Rock were not wholly in the interest of his new farm. They said his tenant had an attractive sister. They said Cleo would do well to take the hardware man or the new doctor, both of whom were her ardent admirers. They said Cleo wouldn't stand out of the way for any woman, and they said—indeed, they said a great deal.

Harrowsby, coming in from the West on the train one evening, found quite a number of his old comrades at the depot. There was going to be a turkey raffle at the saloon. They wanted him to preside. They'd have a drink first—two or three drinks—and a bite of supper in the restaurant—some oysters, say, and then the fun would begin. But Harrowsby jostled his way through their ranks.

"Not tonight, boys. Important business on hand. Got to git home. One drink—haven't time. 'Pon my word, boys—got to!"

And he strode up the town to his home, and into the sitting-room where the table was set for supper and a wood fire burned in the cylinderical [*sic*] sheet-iron stove.

"Cleo!"

She came running to him, pushed him into a chair, tossed his valise in the corner and his hat after it.

"Cleo," he choked a little and then coughed. "I've got something to tell."

"So've I, pap."

"You first, then."

"No." She sat down on his knee. "You first. Go on."

"Cleo, you know my tenant up to Guide Rock? Yes; well, he's got the nicest sister you ever seen. She ain't overly young—not young enough to be silly. She's maybe 35. We'll say 35."

"Yes, pap. Go on."

"She ain't ever worked reel hard. She's had all the heavy work done fur her. So she's kept that cheerful an' rosy—it would beat you! She's easy on the hands, but they don't impose on her—they like her too well. She ain't reel strong on foreign missions, but the minister he told me she was the best home missionary he ever knowed. She sings, an' as fur playin'—well, I never heerd the like except when I was to a show once. An' the cookin'—my! You know your ma didn't go much on cookin'—jes plain fried pork, an' coffee, an' now an' then plum sass or crullers she 'lowed was good enough fur plain folks—with bread and potatoes throwed in, of course—of course! But the things Esther makes out'n just milk an' eggs an' sech common truck—'twould astonish you, Cleo!"

"Yes, pap."

"An' when it comes to dressin', she allus looks so trim. Don't seem to think any old thing is good enough to wear around to home like your—like some folks does. Bottom gownds that's right pretty, an' when she goes out the kind of style a man likes to see when he's goin' along, an' knows she'll be pinted out as his wife—got the feelin' besides that he kin afford it. She's kind, too—kind an' lovin'."

"Yes, pap."

There was silence in the dim room.

"That's—I reckon that's all, Cleo."

"All?" She leaned forward and swung open the door at the end of the wood stove. A flare of light fell full upon his face. "Is it all, pap?"

"Well, all except that I thought some—in fact, I was figurin'—to be square—we was allus square with each other, Cleo—I calculated—that I'd—you ain't got no objection, have you, Cleo?—that I'd—I'd marry her."

The logs crackled merrily by way of comment. Their sweet, summertime smell, silence, and firelight filled the room.

"Dear—dear me, no!" She took his handsome old head between her hands and kissed him. "And when will you be married?"

"I was thinkin' some of a month from now, Cleo."

"Dear—dear!" she said again. "And it's just three days since I was married."

"Cleo!" he sprang to his feet.

"Yes. Esther wrote me about her engagement to you. She thought she could break it better to me. I told Frank, and—well, we were waiting until you should be at home, but he said—I said—we thought—"

"By—thunder! Well, he's a good fellow—but they tell me you could have had the hardware man or the doctor, Cleo. But if you're happy—"

She kissed him again.

"I'll give Frank the farm, an' half the hogs—an' them hundred young steers. Are you sure you're willin' to go back on the farm, Cleo?"

"I'm glad! I've ached fur the farm, pap."

"But after all you've learned! An' now you won't ever be—"

She put her hand over his mouth and laughed.

"Never—never!" she said.

The New Man

*Published in Puck on 10 July 1895, this essay exemplifies
Cleary's strong personality and testifies to her position as one
of the progressive New Women of the turn of the century who
wished to be judged on her own merits, not on the way she
fulfilled prescribed female roles.*

*Two newspaper articles written about Cleary later, one
headlined "Woman and Her Ways" and another, "Women
Who Have Humor," were amazingly free of domestic references. Neither, however, could completely resist the temptation. One boasted, "She depicts graphically the terrors of frontier life, but with her keen Irish perception she also sees its
humor," but it added, "Mrs. Cleary's friends declare she was
born with a talent for cooking as well as for writing, and her
delicious dinners are the envy of all." The other described her
as a bohemian and "a natural humorist," but it carefully noted
that "despite these unconventional tendencies, she is a tender
and devoted wife and mother, holding her numerous little ones
in as warm and passionate regard."*

"HERE," SHE SAID, IMPRESSIVELY, "I have a book personally
descriptive of American female writers and their admirable contributions to literature."

"I shall take it—," he began.

She beamed, and opened her order-book.

"—if," he continued, suavely, "it does not say of a certain writer:
'She is prouder of her pork pies than of her poems.'"

"I—I believe in one biography there is mention of something of the sort."

"Is there an assertion than another author pays attention to every detail of her house-work, and takes particular pains that dust shall never be permitted to gather in her domain?"

"I—I think there is."

"Does one paragraph declare that a well-known novelist makes a boast of darning her table damask with number one hundred fifty thread?"

"I recall a reference to that effect."

"And is it averred of another celebrity that she fashions and re-models her gowns with such skill that her neighbors and associates believe them Parisian-made?"

"That is, indeed, said of a brilliant poetess."

"And is it also asserted in any part that a popular woman of the pen takes more pleasure, in the knowledge that the suppers prepared in the chafing-dish by her own hands are exceedingly successful, than in the popularity of her novels?"

"There"—(faintly)—"is something of the sort."

"So I supposed. When you bring me a book, dealing with what women have done in literature, without any apology for their having presumed to do it, I shall gladly buy the volume. I have not read that Ruskin put his ability for chopping kindling-wood above his brilliant criticism. I never heard that the chief argument in favor of Howells was his deftness in putting up stovepipes. It is yet to be announced that Riley takes less pride in his poems than in whitewashing a cellar. There may be people who think that a compensatory domestic sop should be offered to the Cerberus of mediocrity by every woman who ventures to send her soul beyond the four walls of the kitchen. But such people would not buy the book, anyway. They would borrow it. They shall not borrow it from me. Good morning!"

Disciples of the Little

In this editorial published in the Chicago Record Herald *on 21 August 1904, Cleary satirized women who waste their time with artificial art and ignore the true art of nature. In a news clipping in her scrapbooks about her poem being read at the Chicago World's Fair, the reporter called her a "poetess." Not wishing to be associated with those women aspiring to false "culture," she boldly crossed out "ess."*

A CYNICAL WRITER LATELY SAID that some men wished Adam had died with all of his ribs intact. He may have had scornful reference to the woman who apotheosizes the insignificant. And she is especially provoked if she possesses ability that if worthily exercised would give enjoyment to others, or add to the world's accumulation of beautiful objects.

For instance, one observed last week a woman who is an excellent artist, spending time, eyesight and concentration on the task of fashioning a collar out of a ten-cent handkerchief.

"How long have you been working on that?" she was asked.

"About three hours. I'm hemstitching it, you see."

"And how long did it take you to paint that lovely impressionistic aquarelle of the lagoon at Garfield Park?"

She sent the picture a cursory glance. "Oh, I dashed that off in a couple of hours."

Now, it's dollars to doughnuts that if that woman had not been trying to make a collar out of a handkerchief she would have been striving to make a handkerchief out of a collar. She had succeeded in spoiling a good handkerchief, in injuring her weak eyes, and in wasting time that might have been given to the production of a picture which, like the one mentioned, would be restful and refreshing to gaze upon—an inspiration and a joy forever.

Chicago's brilliant woman journalist who died a few months ago said in reviewing a certain book intended for women of the fussily domestic sort: "The ardent student of the volume may learn eventually by patience and application how to make a nightcap out of a sheet."

Some of these petty, poky, puttering women, everlastingly fidgeting over trifles, are so blind to beauty that nature receives no tribute from their veiled vision.

One such on a certain morning in the past winter was called to the window by an enthusiast. The spectacle revealed was superb, for snow and sleet had fallen and frozen in the night. The earth was one shining sweep of ermine, all jewel-sown. The trees were cased in white armor—gleaming, beautiful. And the silver birches had all their delicate, frondlike stems hung with gems, that glowed like rubies in the effulgence of a glorious red sunrise.

"Just look at those trees!" cried the enthusiast.

"That's only frost. I can make branches with twigs dipped in gum arabic that look just like those. You melt the gum arabic, and you take some diamond-dust, a teaspoonful, and—"

She turned from the window, all animation now.

But she who worshipped the work of the great Artist had fled.

Feet of Clay

A somber view of the pioneer experience, "Feet of Clay," pub-
lished in Belford's Monthly *in April 1893, is a tale much like*
those of Hamlin Garland's in Main-Travelled Roads, *for it em-*
phasizes the negative effects on women of the environment and
the isolation of frontier life. The title alludes to the biblical tale
of Nebuchadnezzar and his dream, which Daniel interprets —
a great image of gold, silver, and brass, but feet of iron and
clay that crumble and "do not cleave to one another, even as
iron is not mixed with clay" (Dan. 2:43). Likewise, Margaret
is "partly strong, and partly broken" (Dan. 2:42).

SOMETIMES IT SEEMED TO HER that she could endure everything
save the silence. That was terrible. Days when Barret was too far in
the corn for the rattle of the machine he drove to reach her, she could
feel the silence settling down upon her like a heavy cloud. Then, if she
were washing the dishes, she used to clatter them needlessly to make
some sound. But all that was before she began to hear the voices of
the corn. Perhaps she would not have dreaded the silence and isolation
so much if she were a happy woman. There is little woman cannot
bear if she has the kind of thoughts in her heart which make her smile
unconsciously. But one who has lost interest in the present, hope in
the future, and dares not look into the past lest the old delights mock
and sting, does not smile when alone.

The worst of it was that she had brought it on herself. Young, delicate, cultured, the only child of wealthy parents who adored her, was

Margaret Dare when she married Barret Landroth. She had been brought up in such a hot-house atmosphere of luxury, had been such a gay girl always, and so fond of balls and theaters and parties that her friends heard with incredulity the announcement that she was to marry a Western farmer, and live her life with him on a Kansas prairie. She had met him at the house of a mutual acquaintance. That he was impressed from the first was evident. He was thirty-five then, tall and largely built, with a heavy, regular-featured face, pale blue eyes, and reddish hair and mustache. He did not possess the manners of the men she was accustomed to meeting. He lacked their repose, their subtle deference, their habitual courtesy. Recognizing this, the infatuation which controlled her found in it cause for admiration. For the superficial defects she accredited him with unrevealed perfections. "Unpolished," she admitted, "but profoundly truthful; awkward, but honest to the heart's core!"

It was with a gentle contempt she listened to the protests of those privileged to advise her. How petty must be their ideals, how restricted and conventional the confines of their affections! The attractions of which they spoke, the material comforts, the social pleasures, even the intellectual and artistic stimulus which one finds only in cities, became minimfied [sic] when weighed in the balance with the devotion of a true heart. Hers was the sacrificial spirit of youth which is glad to make surrender of things dear. To the man she loved she gave the devotion of a perfect wife, which embodies triply the tenderness of a mother, the passion of a mistress, and the reverence of a child. It was a chill, gray November afternoon when the train which had borne her westward on her bridal journey slacked speed in the little Kansas town, south of which Landroth's farm was situated. It was a raw, new, straggling settlement, lacking all that was picturesque, even in suggestion. North of the trim, red-roofed station-house the brown prairies melted into a sullen sky. South of the track lay the town, about twenty houses huddled on the sunburned, withered grass. Some of the buildings had been moved from a decaying Bohemian village, others were in process of erection. There was a livery-barn, and a lumberyard also—at least lumber was piled on an unfenced bit of ground, and a rough box of a shed did duty for an office. "Better wait inside till I get a team, Margaret," Landroth advised, and strode away. But she did not go into the hot, stuffy waiting-room. She stood on the platform, where he had left her, and looked up the one deserted street, where the mud was axle-deep. Involuntarily she shuddered at the desolate stagnation of the place. Far in the west were bluffs, curving with refreshing boldness against the amethystine sky, but south—and there her home lay—were level plains, blank, boundless and unbroken. A skurrying [*sic*] wind, that peculiar wind with a wail in it, which springs up in the west at sundown, came rioting along, tore an auction poster from the boarded wall of the depot, and blew backward the skirt of her soft cloth gown. Two men, plodding by, looked at her with the stolid curiosity of cattle in their eyes—no more, no less. They were not impressed by her gentle beauty, by the elegance which was the appropriateness of her attire, nor by the distinction of her air; still they were duly conscious of her aloofness from the women they knew intimately.

"From Back East, I reckon," grunted one.

"Reckon so," indifferently assented the other.

Landroth drove up, and, getting down, assisted his wife into the buggy. When they were well out on the darkening road, with the wind that was like the wind of the sea, blowing from off interminable stretches in their faces, a kind of wild content came to her. She would be so happy here with Barret. Having him she had all. The weird glamour of the hour, the strangeness of the scene, the dear, protecting presence beside her, all thrilled her with delicious enthusiasm. She could have cried out with him who felt the fierce rapture of the "Last Ride": "Who knows but the world may end to-night?" Long hedges, like black, wavy ribbons, went running by; ragged bushes that skirted the creek; silent and unlighted farm-houses; little, dull, purplish pools, dimly discernible; "bunches" of cattle, motionless, as if cut from granite; and now and then a light in the window, more brilliant than the distant stars; fields, where the stacked cornstalks looked like huddled dwarfs; and, over all, that brooding sky closing down on the plains, until only that cold, strong, surging wind seemed to keep earth and sky asunder.

They had been driving for more than an hour when she became aware that they had left the road, and that the wheels of the buggy were crunching over the rough prairie. A square house, uncompromisingly bare of porches or bay-windows, loomed up before them. Landroth lifted her out.

"Welcome home, my Margaret!" he said softly.

Tired and dazed as she was, the loverly words thrilled her with an exquisite sense of satisfaction. She could feel her cheeks grow hot in the dark. She slipped her hand under his arm, and they went in the house together. To her surprise he led her by an uneven path, around to the rear of the building.

"Mother doesn't use the parlor often," he explained.

He pushed open the back door. Margaret found herself in a large, low-ceilinged kitchen. The stove glistened like a black mirror. The table, covered with a red-checked table-cloth, was already set for the morning meal. Near the door hung a cracked looking-glass, and under it, on a backless chair, was a tin basin and a piece of soap. A woman came from an inner room at the sound of the opening door. She was gowned in an ill-fitting black-and-white print, which revealed all the angles of her spare and slightly-stooped form. Her face reminded Margaret of those grotesque images the Chinese cut from ivory. It was thin, of a pale yellow, and covered from brow to chin with a spider web of minute wrinkles. Her eyes were black and piercing.

"Oh," she ejaculated, addressing Barret, "you've got back!"

"This is my wife, mother," Landroth said.

She extended a bony hand and gave a quick shake to the slim, gloved fingers, but vouchsafed no word of greeting to the stranger. Instead she turned to her son:

" 'Twas a bad time of the year for you to be away so long. The men that's been huskin' have needed some one to drive them. They're a shiftless set. Most hard work they do is at meal times."

Landroth had never seen "The Lady of Lyons." On his rare visits to the city he used to take in the cycloramas and the burlesque shows. He had never heard of Pauline Deschapelles. But the similarity of their positions struck Margaret. But Pauline had been deceived; she had not. When she married Barret Landroth, she knew she was not marrying a man of wealth, of position, not even of common culture. Still she had loved him for himself, and had been quite willing his life should be her life—only, she had not exactly comprehended what his life was.

"It is right," she told herself silently over and over. "This indifference of manner is like the snow that covers mountains in which fire smolders; there is a volcano of affection under it. I have been accustomed to color, to intensity. I am selfish and hypercritical."

So she strove; so she dissimulated. Solecisms which startled her she affected to regard as eminently natural and proper. She permitted no brusquerie of speech or action to astonish her. When her mother-in-law declared she must get print dresses "to save washin'," she obediently consented. The first day she sat down to the dinner of coarsely-cooked food, at which the huskers gathered. Her husband watched her furtively. With an indrawn breath of relief he noticed that she did not court attention by the manner of one unaccustomed to such fare or surroundings. She would make a good farmer's wife when broken in. He had not made a mistake. Singularly enough, it was not borne in upon his consciousness that she might have made one.

The scant knowledge of life which was hers had come to her through books. She had read how the affections of men were alienated by fault-finding on the part of their wives. She had also read pathetic stories of old people who were thrust out of the homes and hearts of their children by those whom marriage had brought into propinquity with them. In her heart she vowed she would endure any annoyance in silence rather than be the aggressor in domestic disturbance. There was a good deal to endure. Much of it, while existing, was not tangible. There were slights she could not openly resent, did she desire to do so.

The winter set in bleak and bitter. Margaret had imagined she would be glad when the husking was over, and the men for whom such incessant frying of pork and baking of pies was in progress had departed. But the sweet sanctity of isolation she had seen from afar proved to be but a mere taunting mirage, for Barret's mother seemed to be omnipresent. The young wife likened her sometimes to a malevolent old fairy who never slept. Always alert were those sharp black eyes of hers; always curved in a sneering smile her thin white lips. She was not to be won over or conciliated. In Barret's presence she was suavity itself to Margaret; only when he had gone back to the endless labor stock and granaries entailed did she vent her spleen and jealousy in smooth, purring words of insult. With a heroism there was no one to appreciate, Margaret kept dumb under the fire; she had given up venturing protest or denial. The few times she had dared to offer either, she had been confronted with the lachrymose reproach: "That is right! Make me the victim of your temper. I am only a helpless old woman. If Barret knew! He would never permit me to be abused."

One day a package of magazines came for Margaret. A neighbor who had called for her mail at the office handed them in as he passed. The dishes were washed, the cream skimmed, the rooms set in order, so she felt free to enjoy her treasure. A sibilant voice sounded in her ear.

"Wasting your time, of course. I thought perhaps you'd help me a little."

Margaret dropped her books guiltily and sprang to her feet.

"I shall, gladly," she assented with eagerness. "What can I do?"

"Put them away first," commanded Mrs. Landroth, pointing to the magazines and speaking much as she might have spoken to a disorderly child. Margaret obeyed. Then she followed the old woman into the kitchen. The back door stood ajar. Pointing to it, Mrs. Landroth handed her a tin pan.

"Go to the shed. They're stickin' hogs for winter picklin'. Hold this pan after they hang 'em up, and get it full of blood to make black sausage."

Margaret was not obtuse, but for a couple of minutes she actually failed to comprehend the command. Suddenly she dropped the pan with a clatter. She grew taller, whiter. All the lightnings of an angry heaven blazed in the stormy eyes she turned on her tormentor.

"I!" she panted hoarsely. "I!" In a lower voice she declared: "I would—will die first!"

And she went back to her magazines.

That evening, while the three were seated at supper, the elder woman made her antagonism openly manifest.

"You must look out for a housekeeper, my son," she began. "The work is too heavy for me."

"Too much?" glancing up stupidly. "Now? When you have Margaret to help you?"

"Margaret? Oh, she is a lady! She refused to help me to-day."

"Impossible!" And he looked angrily toward his wife. She did not speak; the meal was finished in silence. After that Margaret knew she need no longer look to her husband for faith or sympathy. Like the gourd of the prophet, the seed of disunion grew. There was no outbreak, no open warfare, but there was the awful, creeping paralysis of estrangement, the grinning ghastliness of disillusion.

Then the baby came. That was a day of horror never to be blotted out. Barret was in the pasture, not a quarter of a mile off, and his mother refused to send for him.

"He's gettin' in the last of that late hay," she grimly responded to every agonized appeal. "He can't be put about for whimsies."

So the supreme crisis of a woman's life found Margaret exiled and practically alone.

She got around after awhile—not nearly so soon as Mrs. Landroth urged. Barret took a deal of interest in his daughter. Margaret found a wan kind of pleasure in that. Only once did a single smoldering ember of spirit flare up in a fierce flame. That was when Barret suggested calling the child Rebecca, after his mother.

"No," she answered, in a tense voice. "After any one else. Never after her!"

He stood aghast. He had always feared his mother too much to condemn her even in thought. From that [*sic*] on he took less notice of the child. He had gradually omitted toward Margaret all tenderness. He now failed in common civility. He even began to echo his mother's carping remarks. Once he said a farmer had no right to marry a woman who considered herself above him.

Margaret had lived on the Kansas farm, proudly deaf to all voices from her old home, for two long years. Occasionally women came in "to set awhile." Some of them had young babies; but they all looked so sallow, so haggard, so old. They had a hunted look in their eyes, the look that is begotten of crushing, monotonous work, and the possible failure of crops. Their hair was almost always dry and scanty; their teeth out, or dark with decay. The knobby, nail-worn hands, the petty tyranny shown to the children, the fretful complaints as to their un-accomplished labor, the paltriness of their ambitions, the treadmill whirl of their mildly-malicious gossip all hurt her with a queer, pre-scient pang of pain.

"My God!" she used to murmur passionately to herself, "shall I grow to be like those women? Oh, my God!" For she felt the hideous con-viction crawling up on her that she would be as one of these. The knowledge forced itself in upon her one day when she found herself laughing aloud at a tale of vicious slander. She was fairly startled. She formed a desperate resolve; she would not have all the energy, vitality, individuality, all love for the lofty and the beautiful, filched from her, stamped out of her! She must keep them for her child. She went straight to Barret. She was quite calm, but very pale.

"Let me go home for awhile," she pleaded. "I—I am not well."

He turned and looked at her. Her slender figure, gowned in ging-ham, was outlined against the young greenness of osage-orange hedge. Her sun-bonnet had fallen back on her neck; her hands were clasped. He had just learned his latest shipment of steers had brought a poor price. He was not in the mood to be besought.

"You look well enough," he declared. "Wait awhile. My mother hasn't been off this farm for twenty years." And he walked away.

That night she found herself talking aloud, repeating his words over and over. A heavy fall interrupted her. She left the cradle, and ran to the steep stairway to the room of her mother-in-law. Prone on the floor lay a stark form. With a great effort Margaret lifted it, bore it to the bed.

"No—no!" came the querulous protest. "The chair. I'm—all right. Don't try—to put me to—bed. Don't make me—out sick—when—I ain't."

Margaret fled downstairs.

"Barret!" she screamed. "Barret!"

He came running in. They hastened upstairs. The old woman sat straight up in her chair; her stiff fingers were clenched convulsively; her thin gray hair straggled over her ashy countenance; the glazed eyes were wide open. She was dead.

When Margaret had the house to herself she began to think she

could live, to a certain extent, her own life after all. She did her best—
but vainly. From downright indifference Barret passed to a less endurable mood, that of facetious brutality. He expected the service of
a slave, not the dutiful homage of a wife. He spoke continually of how
other men prospered—men whose wives worked and saved. He became controlled by a penury so extreme, he denied, as unattainable,
many mere necessaries of life. And yet people on market days said to
Margaret: "A fine man, yours—smart, my! He'll make his mark. There
ain't many as doubts he kin go to the Legislatur' ef he wants to."

Mrs. Landroth had been dead more than a year, and life had rolled
on and on in the same unbroken routine. Season succeeded season,
and, working or tossing, too tired to sleep, Margaret kept her finger
upon the pulse of nature. This cold meant hail, this cloud foreboded
rain, the droop of this flower presaged lightning, the shrill cry of that
bird was a prelude to winter. The maddening monotony of it all! Then
it was that she first began to dread the silence, began to think she
could bear anything rather than that.

It was not so bad when the child was around, although she was a
quiet little girl at all times. It was in the hours of early morning, in the
afternoon while the baby slept, chiefly in the night. Many a day Margaret stood at the door and stared straight ahead. Corn, corn, corn!
Corn, short and green in spring, higher and greener in summer, still
higher and yellow in fall. Springing, growing and stacked. Nothing but
corn and that low-lying sky. A fear of it came upon her. She felt that
she was hemmed in by corn, prisoned by it. Sometimes it seemed an
impenetrable forest that shut her in, again a tawny, turbulent ocean,
through which she could not battle.

When little Lillian was three years old a letter came to Margaret.
Enclosed was a check for a legacy which had fallen to her, a check for
five hundred dollars. She made it payable to Barret. She had never
valued money till now. Now she prized it as a possible means of escape.
Not of escape in the actual, outer world. She could not bear that those
who had known her therein should look with pity upon her, but as a
final hope of losing sight and sound of corn. For, since its terrible voices
had begun to haunt her, she wondered why she had ever hated the
silence. A few days after the receipt of the letter she spoke to Barret

concerning it. He had just come from town, and was pulling off his wet boots by the kitchen stove.

"Barret, I wish to get a piano out of that money, and some books. I fancy I would not feel—as I do, if I had those."

"A piano—books!" he repeated with a harsh laugh. "If you keep the calves fed and the soap made, you won't have time to fool away on such things. When my mother got an hour to herself she used to sew rags again the spring house-cleaning. Besides, I paid off the mortgage on the new pasture with half that money, and made a payment on a thrasher with the other half. Don't," irritably, "look as if you'd seen a ghost!" And he flung his boots behind the stove.

The following week the thrashers were at the house. She had a woman to help her cook for them, but still the work was savagely hard. More frequently now she found herself talking aloud, always repeating some senseless words. She got in the habit of putting up her hand to cover her mouth, there was such a spasmodic twitching at one corner.

"I wish you'd brush my clothes, Margaret," Barret said one night. "I'm going to the county-seat to-morrow to pay my taxes." She did as bidden. The clothes were the ones he had worn on his wedding-day, and which he had only since donned when he went from home. As she brushed the coat she felt something hard in the inner pocket. She drew out a photograph. A young, radiant face, with soft curls clustering around the forehead, and lovely, eager eyes, smiling up at her. She was still looking at it when Barret came in. He glanced over her shoulder.

"Lord!" he exclaimed. "Have I been carrying that around all this time? You were a good-looking girl, Margaret!"

Later the child found the picture where she had laid it down, and brought it to her. "Who's ze pitty lady?" she cooed.

"That is mamma," Margaret answered.

The little one laughed merrily in disbelief.

"Oh, zis lady is pitty!" she averred, with charming cruelty.

Margaret took the picture from the child, looked at it again for several minutes, and then, still with it in her hand, walked to the glass. The face that glared back at her was of a chalky hue. The features were sharpened. The hair, brushed straight back, was dull and rough.

There were heavy, dark veins around the throat and temples. The mouth every few moments twitched nervously.

That night the voice of the corn roared louder than ever. It was like the surge of a hungry sea. There was something menacing in it. Ever nearer it sounded, and louder. Those frightful, relentless yellow waves. Were they closing in on her?

Shrieking, she sprang from her bed.

"What is the matter?" Barret cried.

"The corn!" she screamed, frantically. "Don't let it close in on me! Can't you hear what it is saying? 'Forever, ever, ever!' "

He leaped out of bed, caught her by the arm. The moonlight was streaming into the room.

"Margaret!" he gasped in fear.

Her eyes were quite vacant, but her mouth was smiling. "I—I must go downstairs," she muttered. "There's the washing—and the soap-grease to be boiled, and the—the carpet rags, and—"

There were those who said when Margaret's people took her and the child home that it was too bad such trouble should have come upon such a fine man as Barret Landroth—a man who was almost certain to go to the Legislature. There had been nothing in her life to cause insanity. It must have been hereditary.

A Prairie Sketch

Resembling the dark tone of "The Sculptor's Funeral," by Willa Cather, this sketch, published in the Chicago Tribune *on 7 July 1895, draws on Cleary's suffering over the loss of two of her daughters, who died three months apart. As in all small western communities in the late nineteenth century, isolated from adequate medical care, Cleary shared in her neighbors' sorrow over the deaths of their children. The naturalistic tone of this work, with its biological and environmental determinism, saves it from sentimentality and pathos.*

"Like a caged bird, escaping suddenly."
—Tennyson

THE WOMAN SAT in a rocking chair, drawn close to the sitting-room stove. She held a great shapeless roll of blankets in her arms. These inclosed the naked body of a child and formed a hood over the little quiet, brown head.

"You think there is no hope this time?" the woman asked in a controlled voice.

The doctor sitting near shook his head. He was thin, undersized, haggard from over-work, irregular meals, and scant sleep.

With eyes that ached the woman looked down on the wan, blue-lipped little face lying against her shoulder. She was conscious of a throbbing of the soft body. She felt the twitching of an arm.

"There is another spasm beginning," she said. The doctor rose, poured hot water into that already in the bathtub, prepared to combat a third attack. The mother kept looking down on the child's face, such a pretty, gentle face, so spiritualized by suffering. As she gazed a queer, short cry came from between the child's lips, a faint, wavering cry. Over its face swept the mysterious change which once seen is ever after recognized. "Look!" breathed the mother, "it is the end!"

The doctor took the slim little wrist between his fingers and held it for an instant. "Yes," he said gently, and turned away. The woman cuddled the child closer in the warm blankets, held it more tightly, bent her head over it. The doctor went away. Five, ten, fifteen minutes passed. Still the woman did not move. The hired girl peeped in at the door and tip-toed away. Three children rushed into the kitchen from school. They were rugged youngsters, wearing carefully patched clothes and clumsy boots. They ceased their clamor, crept into the front room, and, huddling open mouthed together, looked at the woman in the chair, thinking of the three words the girl had spoken. Heavy steps sounded on the walk without. A man turned the handle of the front door, which led into the sitting-room. He paused on the threshold, sending an angry glance around. The half-filled bathtub, the syringe, the rigid, blanketed figure, the medicine bottles on the table, told their own tale. The tale was familiar.

"Hallo!" he cried. "Has the bastard been having fits again?"

His tone was brutal.

The woman looked up at him but did not speak. She was not weeping.

"Dinner not ready, I s'pose," he went on, dropping into a chair and stretching out his legs. "That young one's allus makin' trouble. My children are healthy. She's 6 year old, an' no bigger'n our John that's 1. She don't get her rickettiness [*sic*] from you. Wish when you was pickin' out her father you'd have got a better physiceel kind—seein' I have to support her. Can't you put her down?"

For answer the woman rose, carried the body to a lounge in the corner, laid it gently thereon, and tucked in the dragging blankets. The man stared moodily out of the window. The Nebraska sky was densely gray, but here and there the grayness was penetrated by a yellowish glare. Snowdrifts flashed in the southwest. A dull rumble of thunder

sounded afar off. There were feeble flurries of lightning. The snow
ball bushes in the yard were bare. The lilac boughs were bursting at
the tips into clusters of tiny green leaves. Through last year's withered
grass spires of green were pushing upward.

The woman went to her work-basket, cut off a strip of muslin, and
approached her husband.

"Will you give me two nickels?" she asked.

"You're allus wanting money," he said, sullenly. He put his hand in
his pocket, drew out a lot of change, gave her the coins requested. He
watched her as she crossed to the lounge, turned the wrappings back
a little. Something in the way the children craned forward aroused
him. He sprang up, joined the group. His wife had just passed the strip
of muslin under the chin of her dead eldest child and secured it over
the brown curls.

"God, Mary!" he exclaimed. "Is she dead?"

She did not answer. She pressed tenderly down the white lids, laid
the nickels he had given her upon them, spread a handkerchief over
the peaceful face, then stood there motionless.

"Hadn't—hadn't I better go see the undertaker, Mary?" he questioned.

"I can go."

"No. I'll go, Mary." He put on his hat. "I'll get her a nice coffin—
and a plate. The plate will have a name on it—Elsie Worden."

She caught her breath, flared round upon him, the calm of her face
broken for the first time. "No!" she cried fiercely. "Not your name—
and you never knew her father's. She was mine for a year before I ever
saw you, mine all the wretched years since, more than ever mine now!
You have called her the bastard too often. Elsie—that alone shall be
on her coffin-lid!"

He looked at her dumbly. She had never spoken so before. The
children began to whimper.

"Come," she said, "mother will get you some dinner."

And when she had done so, and the man had walked off down the
one street of the little Western town, she went to the closet where the
children's best clothes were hanging.

She picked out the warmest underwear, and sat down to mend a tiny rent in a stocking. It was very cold, she told herself, where Elsie was going. She chose the daintiest gown, plain enough, to be sure, except for all the fancy stitching. She sewed a little bow of ribbon at the neck—the child had always loved pretty clothes!

The Stepmother

*Cleary's most controversial short story, "The Stepmother" por-
trays the harsh side of the homesteading experience.* McClure's
*published it as the lead story in its September 1901 issue, and
Nebraskans condemned it as a false representation of life in
their progressive and Edenic state, while easterners praised it
for its verisimilitude. Much like Hamlin Garland's stories in*
Main-Travelled Roads *in subject and tone, it echoes his depiction of the toll exacted from people who struggled to settle the
West and portrays a son's sorrow and guilt for the suffering
imposed upon his mother.*

"YOU ARE GOING IN TOWN to the memorial services, Dan?" questioned the woman. Her voice was appealing.

The young fellow standing in the doorway shifted his position im-
patiently. He was twenty-three, tall and brawny. Years of labor on the
farm had developed his limbs and toughened his muscles. Later in life
he would be stooped and shambling, as are those who follow the plow
and guide the harrow after the days of youthful manhood have passed.
Now he was straight and stately, and the colossal symmetry of his frame
was good to look upon. His cotton shirt, falling loose at the neck,
revealed a triangle of sunburnt skin. His low-browed, strong-featured
face was copper-red also. The jaw was heavy—the chin square. The
blue eyes he turned on the woman had the sullenness of one who
expects opposition.

"Yes. I'm a-goin'."

"In the new buggy?"

He nodded. There was a silence which she waited wistfully for him to break. As he said nothing, she picked up the sewing which lay in her lap.

"I was hoping I could get to go," she said, speaking in the plaintive monotone produced by colorless years of self-repression and self-denial. "I've been every time when I could take or leave the children. It's a year since I've been to town." Her needle was suspended. She looked afar over the boundless expanse of prairie with weary eyes. "My father and brother are buried on the hill there. Little Ruby—she's there, too. She died when she wasn't but eight. She was the greatest child for flowers! The weeds even were flowers to her. I guess she'd know if there were some put on her grave."

Again there was silence, she sending him eager, furtive glances; he staring out where an ocean of oats tossed turbulently in the glaring sunshine.

"Even if the celebration brings sad thoughts," she went on, "it's kind of cheerful, too. There's so many folks in town. There's the flags—and the music. The girls have new hats and dresses. It's sociable-like. There hasn't been a soul to this house since Christmas. Then it was only some campers whose wagon broke down. But it seemed good to see them, even."

"Look here, mother," he broke out. "I know you ain't got much pleasure. I'd like you could fix to go. But as for me drivin' you in—well, I promised to take Chastina Marks."

She said nothing, but the look that quivered out of her face made him set his teeth hard for an instant. Then, with a scarlet blotch burning on either thin cheek, she took up her sewing again, and went on stitching—stitching.

The home of the Carneys was a forlorn place. There was no timber in that region. The small, shabby house perched upon the bluff was exposed to the bitter winds of winter and to the almost more malignant furnace blasts of summer. It was nineteen years since Oliver Carney had married for the second time. Then, he and his two sturdy boys had sadly needed the ministration of a woman. The girl he married was young and romantic. She pitied him. She mistook her exquisite sympathy for the divine passion itself. When he traded his business in the East for a rocky Nebraska farm, and went to live where his lack of experience and the capricious climatic conditions together conspired against him, the outcome was despondency and futile regret. He not only failed to do one thing well; he succeeded in doing many things ill. He credited Fate with peculiar perversity toward himself—with an almost personal antagonism. Dyspepsia, that grim demon evoked by farm-house viands, became a constant torment. Insomnia duly followed. Pessimism, the prompt hand-maid of these, waited upon them. So he became gloomy and unreasonable, except when his depression was temporarily merged in the maudlin amiability of liquor.

It was upon the woman, however, that the burdens of failure pressed most heavily. She had been a brave and gallant young creature, but the cowardice and shirking selfishness of the man she married ate into the core of her being like an acid.

None knew better than she that work from long before light on winter morns, and from the first streak of pearl in summer skies, was hard. She knew that poverty was a rabid, a relentless thing. She knew that it made petty those who would be great and generous; that it fettered hands which would fain be extended in royal generosity; that none might scale its ramparts which barred out possible ambitions— pleasures—joys! But these she accepted—the poverty and the toil. At the melancholy of inertia surrounding her she rebelled. She dreaded its contagion. She refused to have her heritage of hope wrested from her. She would not live in an atmosphere of rayless foreboding. She denied the right of one man to condemn her to profound and enduring discontent. She was not one of those who succumb to adversity willingly. So she made a hard fight. Occasionally, she conquered—less frequently as the years went by. The struggle told on her. She lost expectancy of expression and elasticity of step. Child-bearing and child-rearing were part of her handicapped existence.

Now a fresh fear had arisen. What if Dan were to marry—Dan, upon whom they all depended, rather than upon the moping, misanthropic father!

"Dan!" Her voice sounded strange to herself, and she waited until she could speak as usual. "Dan, what would we all do without you?"

She had been a school teacher in her youth, and she spoke with a correctness and precision which, although marred by occasional idioms, still distinguished her speech from the lingual slovenliness of the Western farm woman.

"Oh, I guess you'd git along!" A dull, slow color had crept into his face. "It's goin' to be a good year. Dick could take my place."

Dick—take—his place! He was thinking, then—he was going to—

"We—we can't depend on Dick!" she murmured. A vision of Dick rose before her—gay, pleasure-loving, inconsiderate Dick! She smiled—a sad smile. "I didn't think Chastina was the kind of girl you'd take a fancy to, Dan."

He swung around.

"What," he demanded, "have you got agin her?"

Her work fell on her lap. She clasped her thin, knobby-jointed hands upon it, and looked up at her stepson. She was a frail little body, gowned in the everlasting print wrapper of the prairie housekeeper. Her large hazel eyes were bright—too bright. She breathed quickly. She had lost two of her front teeth. To have them replaced would be an extravagance not to be considered. Frequently when speaking she lifted her hand with a nervous gesture and covered her mouth.

"She's frivolous, Dan. She likes admiration—and pretty clothes—"

"Is that all? What girl don't, mother?"

"It seems to me," she went on hurriedly, "that your—your marriage to her would be a—a mistake! Think it over a bit—"

"Think it over!" he burst out. "Mother, you didn't use to want to stand in my way! Don't you s'pose I have thought it over? Do you think I'm goin' to be dray horse for all's here—two of 'em as well able to work as me—all the born days of my hull life?"

The hot May sun streamed down on him. She could see his great chest rising and falling, and the muscles of his arms working under the worn sleeves of his shirt.

"You have more than your share of the work!" she admitted. Her voice failed her again. A stray sunbeam glinted on her needle—an idle needle just then. "And—I don't want to stand in your way, Dan. Only—you've always seemed like my boy—the only boy I ever had! Maybe

I'm saying this to you about Tina because—because I want to keep you." Her hungry eyes never left his face. "Perhaps I'm—I'm just making excuses. Perhaps—"

The scarlet blotches faded in her cheeks. She picked up her sewing again, but the hands trembled over the coarse cotton cloth. She could not ply the glittering little implement she held. Suddenly she went deathly pale. She lay back, drawing her breath in short, soft gasps.

"Mother!" cried the young fellow. "Mother!"

"It's nothing," she panted. "Nothing."

But her lips took on a bluish tinge, and after a faint shiver she lay quite still. He dashed out to the well for water, brought it to her, forced her to swallow it. He watched her anxiously, all his sullenness gone, as she shuddered back to consciousness.

"I didn't mean to rile you, mother," he said. "But seems like I couldn't bear to have you comin' between Chastina an' me."

He had dropped on one knee beside her chair in a bewilderment of dumb and clumsy penitence.

"I know it's hard for you," she murmured. "You are young—and it's hard for you."

The tired tears were slipping down her cheeks.

"It ain't dead easy for you, mother."

"Oh, don't think of me."

"We don't. We've got out of the way of thinking of you."

Her little skinny arm lay near him. It never occurred to him to give it a gentle touch. They are chary of caresses—the prairie people. Perfunctory kisses are given at the marriage feast or before the burial— but even these are few and far between. He stumbled to his feet, ashamed of the compassionate impulse which had temporarily mastered him. The woman rose, too.

"It's time to get supper," she said. "They'll be in soon."

But as she crossed the kitchen to set her work aside she suddenly put her hand to her breast—stood still.

One stride and Dan was beside her.

"You're not forgittin' what the doctor said?" he questioned. "That if you got scairt—or—or hurt, an' had another heart spell you was like—like to—"

She flashed around on him. Suddenly her face was young, yearning, eager.

"Oh," she cried breathlessly, "oh, I *was* forgetting! Do you think—" But as suddenly as it had come the brilliance waned. She shook her head. "No—I shall not die—not soon," she said.

She went on filling the little rust-red stove with cobs. Dan did not offer to assist her. The attitude of a young Western farmer to his mother is that of an Indian to his squaw. All domestic drudgery properly pertains to her.

"I'll go out an' take a look at the young peach trees," he said. "They're comin' on fine. This'll be the second year of bearin'. There ought be enough made out'n 'em to pay dad for the hogs the cholery got."

"What you talkin' about?" rasped a dolorous voice. "Them peaches? They'll be some, maybe. But the nursery man fooled me on the settin's. He didn't give me the Baltimore beauties I bought off'n him—on'y the common kind. An' the common kind is dreadful plenty. It's best that fetches the price. Every one's again me. Every one cheats me. I allus had the worst luck of anyone I ever knowed."

He sank into the only comfortable chair the room afforded, a limp heap of inactive humanity. He watched the woman preparing supper.

"There's them," he announced placidly, arousing himself from a trance of indolent content.

"Them" came tumbling in, a riotous, roystering, healthy brood. They laughed, and mocked, and fought, and burst into peals of laughter. The head of the house regarded them with bland interest.

"Seems like," he remarked, "I ain't never so happy as when I a-sittin', so to speak, in the bosom of my fambly."

His conciliatory manner was one to incite distrust. His wife sent him a swift glance.

"Have you been to town?" she asked.

He declared that he had not been to town. That even if he had she knew better than to suppose that he would go into the Owl-King—or near the Owl-King, or—

Dick, perfumed, pomaded and in his Sunday best, came clattering down the ladder-like stairway.

"Hurry up, mother. I'm goin' in town to a strawberry festival at the

Methodist Church. Here, Dolly, you got your supper. You let me set there."

Dolly protested with a howl. Dick picked her up and deposited her on the floor, where she appeared to shrink together like a collapsible drinking cup.

When Dan came in from his aimless tramp through the orchard the owner of the farm was sunk in stertorous oblivion. The last child had been tucked in bed. The last utensil had been washed and set aside. And the woman, sitting by the kitchen table, in the dull light of the kerosene lamp, was sewing, stitching into Dan's denim shirt rebellion, regret, resentment—love. That one unselfish love of all loves!

Chastina Marks was waiting for Dan when he drove up. She was a slender, brown-haired girl, clad in the inevitable white lawn and fluttering ribbons of the prairie belle. She was not pretty, but she was charming. There was a fresh wholesomeness about her as pleasant as the scent of wild-plum blossoms. Her quiet eyes held a look of reserve. They were eyes which might, indeed,

> *Keep back a daring lover,*
> *Or comfort a grieving child.*

"I'm late." He had jumped down and was helping her into the buggy. "It's a fine morning, but I'm afraid it's going to blow up a bit."

She looked away to the horizon with the keen and prescient vision of those who are prairie-born.

"It will be a dust storm, I think."

The little town presented its usual Memorial Day appearance, which was that of festivity—festivity, however, the most seemly and decorous. But—as Dan's stepmother had remarked—the flags, flowers, music, the groups promenading in their finest attire, the uniforms of the band of bent veterans, the gold-lettered badges of the Women's Relief Corps, the importance and celerity of the few officials on horseback, the forming of the parade, the deliberate progress to the church, the singing, the speeches, even the bulging baskets in the back of the wagons, were "sociable-like."

Dan enjoyed neither the day nor the propinquity of the girl he loved. His brow was contracted. He spoke seldom. His companion wondered—silently. She was wise enough to know that to question a secretive man is to invoke a lie.

The dust storm she had prophesied did come. At first there was only the most infantile—the most ineffectual little breeze. Then tiny spirals of dust rose in the country roads. Suddenly the tawny spirals were as tall as waterspouts. The increasing wind, bellowing up from Kansas, blew the dust in a curtain—a wall—an encompassing, enveloping fog. Dan, urging his horses homeward, tried to protect Chastina. He pulled up the buggy top. He drew the linen robe over her lap. He gave her his silk handkerchief to tie over her eyes. But the man does not live who can combat a Nebraska dust storm. The yellowish powder sifted in through the joints of the canopy. It stung the flesh like the bites of myriad infinitesimal insects. It grimed the lap-robe and the girl's white gown. It maddened the old farm horses until they were mettlesome as pastured colts. It pierced, and penetrated, and choked, and blinded. And all the time the wind sent the buggy careening, screeched in the ears of its occupants, and howled in its fury after each rare pause to take breath. All the time, too, the sun blazed down—a great blotch of deep orange seen through saffron clouds.

"I shan't let you out at your house," Dan shouted. "I'll take the short cut to our place. There is something I want to tell you."

The violence of the storm was spent when they turned into the narrow road that zig-zagged towards the desolate house on the bluff. Dan slackened rein. At last he could make himself heard.

"Tina," he blurted out, "I asked you to marry me. I didn't know then—anyways I didn't think. But I s'posed we could git married this fall. Now—well, now we can't. I've thought it over good an' hard—an' we can't. I got to stick by my mother awhile longer. Maybe this year— maybe all next, too. I don't s'pose now you'll want to keep comp'ny with me no longer. But," doggedly, "I got to stick by mother."

She turned her grave eyes on him. The illimitable love in them dazzled him. His heart plunged.

"I wouldn't think much of you," she said, "if you didn't stick by your mother after all she's done for you. My mother often told me before she died how strong and pretty Mis' Carney was when she first come out to Nebraska. She said how nice she kep' you an' Dick—always

good clothes an' the best of everything for you, when she didn't have
a stuff dress to her back. I'll wait for you, Dan."

"Tina!" he cried. "Tina!" he ventured again. But the pain in his
throat precluded speech. He yelled to the horses. They forged ahead.
Suddenly Tina leaned forward—clutched his arm.

"Look, Dan, look! What's wrong? The children are running down
the bluff. They're comin' this way. An' your father—he's beckonin'!
There's Mis' Harrowsby—I know her cape—an' Mis' Peterson.
Hurry—hurry!"

"Oh, my God!" muttered Dan.

The world seemed to reel away from him. Tina's hand steadied him.
Tina's voice recalled him. All at once he was standing up—was lashing
the horses.

"I wish I'd taken her!" the girl heard him cry. "I wish to God I'd
taken her! She wanted so to go to this Memorial Day!"

"Hush, Dan! Hush, dear! It will be all right!"

Some one was at the horses' heads. He hurled himself out of the
buggy—was in the house.

"We don't know just how it happened," one of the whispering group
in the kitchen was saying. "She was alone when the storm came up."

"She went out to drive the young calves under the shelter," inter-
posed another.

"A loose scantlin' struck her in the side," volunteered a third. "She
ain't been real strong of late anyhow. That heart trouble's awful onre-
liable. The doctor? Can't git him. He's over in Kansas. Mis' Peterson
knows well as him, though. She 'lows there ain't anything to be done."

Dan pushed by them into the little poor best bedroom. His stepmother lay in the pine bedstead. The patchwork quilt was drawn to
her chin. He fell on his knees beside her. His head drooped on his
clenched hands. His shoulders were heaving. She lifted one weak arm
and laid it around his neck.

"Look at—me—Dan."

He lifted his haggard eyes to hers, which were sweet and luminous.

"Dan," went on the voice, which seemed to come from a distance.
"I'm—I'm sorry for what I said—about Tina. She *is* dear—she *is*
good—like her mother before her."

"Mother—she is here."

"Yes—I can see her now. I am glad—very glad. But—Dan."

A woman came in, insisting the sufferer should not speak. The work-worn hand was imperious then as any which ever swayed a scepter. At its light motion the intruder left the room.

"Dan—where are you? Listen!"

"I am listening, mother."

"Don't make Tina's life—too hard! Women are not fitted—to bear—as much as—men. They—must—bear—more. Men love women, only—they don't understand. This is Memorial Day." Her hand found his rough head and rested there. "I hope you'll remember—every Memorial Day—about Tina. And that a woman isn't always—well—or happy—just because she keeps on her—feet—and doesn't—complain. And let her know—you—"

Grayness swept over her face like an obliterating billow.

"Mother!" he sobbed hoarsely. "Mother!"

The bed shook to the beat of his breast.

"Little Dan," she was saying softly. "No—I can't think he's my stepson. He's my boy." The hand on his head moved caressingly. "Such pretty—pretty curls! My boy—the only boy I ever had."

Then she was whispering about Ruby, the little sister who had died when she wasn't but eight. The little child who had loved all flowers—to whom the weeds were flowers.

A Vigil

Poetry fulfilled many purposes for Cleary. With rhythm and rhyme coming easily for her, she often penned verses that she could easily sell. However, many times her poems were deeply personal and served as loving gifts for her family, as memorial tributes, and as a means of releasing her emotions. The following, published in Poems, *embodies all of these functions.*

Dear Christ, in dark Gethsemane
I wept the hours away with Thee,
And wildly prayed that God would let
    One cup most bitter pass from me.

He pressed it to my lips that shrank
Rebellious from its rim. I sank
Despairing—then submissive, drank!
Up the steep heights of Calvary
How gladly now I'd climb with Thee,
And take a thief's place on the tree,
If, crucifixion done, I'd see
A child's face loving, tender, sweet,
    Turned trustingly once more to me!

An Old Fashioned Mother and Wife

This narrative essay affords modern readers a glimpse into the daily life of a young homemaker in the late nineteenth century. Probably written around 1890, just after Cleary's son Gerald was born, it was published posthumously in the September 1912 issue of Extension *magazine. The narrative depicts both Cleary's domestic satisfaction as a mother and wife and her desire and ability to enter the public spotlight through publication. These two desires caused conflicts both in Cleary's mind and in her life, as they did for many other nineteenth-century women, who were expected to be fully committed to their families yet wanted the independence and personal recognition accessible primarily to men. Cleary's later comment "If I had done more writing and less housework I would be better off in every way today" attests to this conflict.*

LIGHT! Is it moonlight or daylight that peers in at the window? She closes her eyes for a few minutes. When she again opens them she notices that the penetrating light is broader, so she rises, dresses, prays, goes down the stairs, through the little parlor, untidy from the children's last night frolic, and into the kitchen which looks chill and cheerless in the grayness of the dawn. She touches a match to the "laid" fire in the stove, and the wood flares up with a gay cackle. Then she takes the pail, and unhasping the kitchen door, goes out to the well for water. Nearby a bird is tilting on a twig and trying his voice in a series of murmurous and ecstatic little trills—the prelude to a song of bravest rapture. A smile comes into her eyes, and she is humming as she goes about her work. She fills the kettle and puts it on, "straightens" the sitting-room, and, drawing out the kitchen table from the wall, lays on the cloth and sets it with the mechanical precision born of habit. She does not fail to put Dick's rubber bib beside his mug, or the baby's little lettered plate on the shelf of her high chair. Then she makes the biscuits, boils the coffee and skims the milk. Young feet come clattering down the stairs, and she dresses the children while Will attends to the chores. Breakfast over, the elder children hurry off to school, the dishes are washed, Robbie sent out to play, the baby bathed and sung to sleep, and the pot-pie for dinner put on to cook. Then she half pauses for a minute, deliberating what is most important to do next. The house plants must be watered, the bedrooms aired and beds made up, lamps filled and cleaned, the pantry shelves washed down, and the strawberries, standing since last evening under their juice-crimson cap of sugar, preserved. When all of this is done it is time to pare the potatoes and make the dumplings for the pot-pie. Eleven! and the baby awakes cooing and rosy. Twelve! and the other children come scampering in. "Mother, mother! Is dinner ready? Dick didn't know his lesson. I tore my dress. My, this is good!"

The husband has come in also and the wife and mother waits on all, hastily eating her own dinner while the others are attended to. In the middle of the meal she leaves the table to see that Dick washes thoroughly the little hands that grow so grimy, and to brush out afresh Mary's tangled curls. They rush off; then Will goes, and she finishes her now cold dinner with the baby for company. Again are the dishes washed and put away. Again is the kitchen swept. The baby again grows fretful. Mindful of the afternoon's work awaiting her, the baby's mother puts the irons on the stove and then soothes the wee one to slumber. Without, the June day lies steeped in calm splendor. The sky is just the shade of a robin's egg and is dappled with little fleecy, harborless clouds. By the fence the red roses hang heavy with fragrance. A butterfly floats by, a thing of tropical tints and superb indolence. In the air hangs a faint silvery haze which seems to pulse and palpitate. The intense beauty of the summer afternoon sinks into the heart of the worker, and now and then she glances wistfully through the casement as she irons the clothes crowded over from yesterday. She begins singing softly old ballads about "Cruel Barbara Allan," and "Bonnie Doon" and other songs she heard her mother sing.

"Good-day, Mis' Hervey," says a lachrymose voice, as a lank, worn woman steps across the threshold. "I come to see ef you couldn't bake us a batch of light bread for the supper of the Ladies Social Club that's to be held at the town-hall on next Friday? Say, Mis' Hervey, I never knowed as you could sing."

"I can not," she answers, briefly. "I only try to when alone—or for the baby." By the time the visitor takes her departure the baby is again awake, and is committed to the care of the elder children in the sweet-scented garden.

The mother draws a breath of pleasure at the thought that it will be a whole hour before it will be necessary to prepare supper. So she secures the magazine her sister in the city sent her, and which has lain for a week with leaves uncut in the bureau drawer of the spare room. As she sinks into the cushioned rocker, Dick's shrill voice comes in at the window.

"Mamma, mamma! There's a man at the back [door and he would like something to eat!"]¹

Laying down her book, she goes out to confront the latest applicant for aid, for it is contrary to her creed to turn one hungry from her door. When the tramp has eaten and the empty dishes are washed and replaced, twenty of her precious sixty minutes are gone.

"Mamma," cries a chorus of young voices, "here is Ruthie Field. She can stay till her aunt hollers to her over the back fence. And you know you said when next she came we could have a White Pudding Party with the doll dishes on the back porch."

"Yes, dear!" she answers, rising, and wishing vaguely that children possessed memories less mercilessly retentive. Fifteen minutes later she again takes up the magazine. She commences reading a delightful sketch. The style is fresh. The incident is rapid. She is conscious that

---

1. The bracketed words are hard to read on the only copy of this story that I had access to, but I believe the words here are accurate.

her body is chained in a tired trance, of which mental exhilaration renders her half oblivious. This is rest indeed. Hark!

"The baby!" gasps Mary, putting in a scared, freckled face at the door. "She ketched hold of a bee, an' she's a-screechin' awful!" The mother flies to the relief, draws out the sting, kisses the wee palm "to make it well," and binds it up in a bandage spread with wet blue clay. Half-past five! She brightens the fire, sets the table, brings berries and cream from the spring-house, fries some home-cured ham, and makes the tea. It is a trifle hard to keep amiable during supper, for the children are fractious, and the head of the house, with whom business has been contradictory, is disposed to resent their absurd little altercations. But under the benign influence of a tempting meal mutual tolerance is restored, and they rise with gay words and laughter.

When the kitchen is again restored to order, the milk strained and the lamp lighted, the mother goes to the door to call the children. Will is walking up and down between the borders of phlox smoking his pipe. She undresses the little ones, bathes hot hands and faces, slips on the nighties, hears them say their prayers, gives them a final drink of foam-fresh milk, kisses them and tucks them in bed—all but the baby, whom she croons to sleep on her bosom. Outside the dew-wet flower stalks are wands of ivory in the lustre of the moonlight. She drinks the air blowing in at the open window with a pleasure in its purity and perfume so intense as to be almost pain. In the town-hall the band is practicing. Mellowed and magicized by distance, the music floats to her. Fireflies—those lantern-bearers of the fairies—go flashing by, their flame, like love, most luminous in the shadows. She sits down near the lamp and puts new pockets in Dick's pants, and darns Mary's stockings, and mends Robbie's apron, and repairs the rent in Will's Sunday coat, and sews buttons on the baby's little dumpling shoes.

Ten! The day is done. A monotonous day—a dull, tiresome, dreary day. Ah, no! A beautiful day, because of a duty done; a bright day, because of love's own compensations; more than all a dear and happy day because at its close the one voice in all the world for her, whispers, "How I love you!"

A Trip Postponed

In this sketch published in the 5 October 1892 issue of Puck *magazine, Cleary continued to develop one of her favorite characters, whom she would later name Mrs. McLelland. This humorous character also appears in "The Mildewed Pocketbook," published in* Puck *on 30 December 1891, and in her novel* Like a Gallant Lady. *Cleary's satire on farmers and their reactions to capricious and fluctuating market prices remains accurate today.*

"IT'S COOKIN' HOT, AIN'T IT?" she queried. "An' it ain't a-goin' to rain either, though it looks some like rain, an' my corns is a-hintin' continooal that we're goin' to hev a shower. What?"

As I had not attempted a remark, it rather startled me when she straightened up, pushed back her sun-bonnet, and fired the interrogation at me.

"It does look like rain," I assented, with the cordial sincerity of Polonius, when he agreed: "Very like a whale!"

She scrutinized me closely, as if doubtful of my proving a sympathetic confidant. Then she sighed profoundly.

"How does it happen you are still at home?" I ventured to question; "you told me a week ago you were to leave on Tuesday for a trip to Colorado."

"So I did," she acquiesced, mournfully; "an' I'd a been gone ef 't was n't fur a loss Pa had—a heavy money loss!" Again she breathed a dismal sigh.

Interested, I inquired: "How was that? I thought you told me you got a splendid price for your hogs at Kansas City."

The trip referred to had been the desire of her dreams, the reward of her penury, the hope of her dumbly-rebellious heart for many a year.

"We was n't expectin' but three-an'-a-half cents an' we got four—which counts on a carload. An' I can't say but what we was satisfied, an' felt we could afford the tower of pleasure which we had amalagated. But what happens the very next week do you think—just as I was denudin' a chicking to fry for the journey?"

I did not know—and I said so.

She leaned her elephantine proportions over the fence, balancing a clumsily-clad foot on the lowest rail. Her shrewd eyes blinked rapidly, and she spoke in sepulchral tones as she explained the cruel occurrence which had caused the postponement of her trip.

"Hogs riz!"

"Ye-es!" There was more uncertainty than comprehension in the affirmative.

"That's all!" she declared, with some asperity. "Hogs riz. Sech a dilemmer we never had suspicioned. After we shipped, hogs riz to five cents. Ef we'd a waited we'd ha' made money like the Dobbs's did. Ez 't was, we lost. So we had to posterior our tower."

"But," I returned, puzzled, "you have made money. You were satisfied. Why are you not satisfied?"

She looked at me keenly as if she fancied somewhere in my head there was a screw loose.

"We got to stay home," she said slowly, as if she were trying to pound conviction into the brain of a stupid child, "because we did n't make ez much money ez we might ha' made! We must economize. Sposin' four cents paid Pa an' me—would n't five ha' paid us better? You people ez lived in the city hez no comprehensibility of the losses the farmer hez to stand fur not bein' able to prevaricate ahead of the contrariety—(Pa said the cussed contrariety, but I repudiated him fur that, him bein' a deaking an' a passer of Plate)—of the markets which is bein' controlled by the corpulent of the country. Well, I got to go an' knock off them pesky potato bugs. Half-pas' seven! Most bedtime, anyhow!"

The Rebellion of Mrs. McLelland

By the 1890s, the demise of the genteel Victorian woman had begun, accelerated by women's increasing impact in politics, education, and business. Although Mrs. McLelland, a well-drawn and recurring character in Cleary's fiction, would never have considered herself a "New Woman," a subject avidly discussed in the late nineteenth century, her rebellion from her submissive role would certainly have been cause for Mr. McLelland to consider her a part of the also-much-debated "Woman Problem." Cleary employed humor to soften the conflict with established norms that her ideas on women's unequal status and need for empowerment might have provoked. In this story, the irony of the physically strong Maria bending to the will of her frail husband serves as a comic device for Cleary's social criticism. The Chicago Tribune *published this story on 2 April 1899.*

"I GOT FOUR YEARS' WEAR OUT'N IT," explained Mrs. Mc-Lelland. "It's been turned twice, an' the moths have got into it some. I b'lieve it had better go into the carpet, Mis' Har'rot."

She laid down her shears and doubtfully surveyed the faded garment on her knee. Mrs. Harriot, a bent, slender, toothless old woman, with a peaked chin and pointed nose, put her sleek gray head on one side, and discriminatingly scrutinized the skirt under discussion.

"I don't expect you could get the hull of another winter out'n it, Mis' McLelland, though I do say it seems a shame to cut up wool

Hubbell, NE.

goods, even when it is clean wore out. Seems like it could be made to do for linin' somethin'."

"Linin' costs most as much as goods, Mis' Har'rot. You remember the dress I got last winter—the one that looked like a flannel, but of course, 't wasn't, only cotton. It cost 10 cents a yard in Bubble. When Mis' Chastina Gibbs come here to cut it out she allowed it ought to be lined. I ast pa about it, but pa he said as how he didn't see no sense in slappin' one gownd on top of another, so to speak. 'Linin's only six cents a yard,' says I, 'an' I won't want but ten or twelve yards.' But pa—"

She sighed, and lapsed into mournful silence. There was no sound save the slashing of her shears along the checked print on her lap, an old shirt of her husband. She removed the sleeve with a deftness suggestive of amputation and surgical skill. Mrs. Harriot sighed, too. She hitched her chair nearer to that of her hostess, and sniffed sympathetically.

"He's close, ain't he?" she ventured.

"Close!" Mrs. McLelland's grim brow wrinkled over her glasses. "He's closer'n bees a-swarmin', an' them's the closest thing I know."

"But you did git the linin', Mis' McLelland. Leastways, Chastina give out she'd cut a lined dress for you."

Mrs. McLelland laid down the shirt with the neckband half cut off. She rose with an effort. She strode across the farmhouse kitchen. She lifted the lid of a little old horsehair trunk that stood under a deal shelf in the corner. From this she took a shapeless mass of material. This material was of a sage green, arabesqued by a vine of brilliant orange. She carried the garment over to Mrs. Harriot.

"This here's the dress, Mis' Har'rot," she said, "an' this here's the linin'."

She turned the garment inside out. The lining was of coarse muslin of a pale biscuit color. It was stamped and penciled with blue markings. These, however, had been partially obliterated. Mrs. Harriot, however, managed to make out: "—ller M—ls—est—n—t—r——eat."

"For the land's sake, Mis' McLelland! I never see no dress linin' like that."

Mrs. McLelland compressed her lips. She whisked the gown into shape, folded it, straightened its bulkiness into comparative symmetry with divers tugs and pats, and restored it to its place in the horsehair trunk. It was not until she was again seated and snipping savagely at the collar of Mr. McLelland's discarded shirt that her neighbor's patience was rewarded.

"No more did any one else, Mis' Har'rot. That linin's flour sacks. I saved 'em. I washed 'em, an' bleached 'em, an biled 'em, an' ironed 'em. It seemed like I couldn't git the letters out, though I used most enough lye to scald every bit o' skin off'n a body's hands. There was 'Bubble Roller Mills Best Winter Wheat' on every one."

"Seems like that's a lot of work when new linin' is only six cents a yard," put in Mrs. Harriot. "Mr. McLelland that rich, too!"

Mrs. McLelland's face softened.

"We ain't on the road to the poorhouse, I'll admit. We got this farm, an' one in Illinois, an' a half section over in Thayer County, an' 6,000 bushel of cribbed corn, not to talk of the cattle an' the hogs—" She broke off, smiling complacently.

"Then there's the farm you give Tommy, Mrs. McLelland. I'm sure you've treated him like he was your own son."

Instantly the old face was grim and wrathful again.

"Didn't I? An' see all that pa ever done for my daughter! It's fifteen year since I seen her even. Her little girl weren't but 3 years old then. An' I've been beg—who's that?"

She had lowered her head and was peering over her spectacles through the one little window down the yellow strip of wagon way which stretched across the prairie to the road. "That" was a masculine figure which had dropped from a white horse and was shambling toward the farmhouse. He was an ill-hung youth, who had run to legs and arms in a manner quite disproportionate to his body. His denim overalls were too short by five inches. A tattered straw hat which had endured the successive suns of three Western summers surmounted his brick-red head.

"Ain't it Plunkett's Joe?" queried Mrs. Harriot.

She had risen, a reel of cut rags over her left arm, and was peering over the shoulders of her portly hostess.

"It's him. I can see his red face now. What's bringin' him here?"

"He's got a letter in his hand."

"He ain't never brung our mail. Besides, it come yistiday. It—it—"
The shears clattered down on the floor. She leaned forward, shaking,
breathless. "Look you, Mis' Har'rot! The—the envelope—it's yaller.
Isn't it yaller, Mis' Har'rot? Isn't it—let me go—he's nigh the door
now—isn't it a—a telegram?"

It was a telegram. The rose colored youth offered it to her with a
word of explanation. The agent had asked him—he'd been in town to
get spavin cure for the bay mare—if he'd bring out the message, seein'
he'd be passin' the McLelland farm on his way home. He'd said he
would, and here it was.

Now the bulk of Mrs. McLelland was that of three ordinary women.
The mind of Mrs. McLelland was a marvel of piercing penetration and
crystalline comprehension. And the nerve of Mrs. McLelland was a
thing before which tramps fled, cattle were conquered, and the sac-
erdotal mountebanks who scoured the prairies retreated humiliated
and aghast.

But Mrs. McLelland could no more have put out her hand and
taken that telegram from the rose colored boy on the threshold of her
home than she could have asked her spouse for a dollar to spend
precisely as she pleased.

"What's in it?" she gasped.

She tore her cotton gown loose at the throat and stood leaning
against the door.

The rose colored boy grinned.

"I dunno," he answered.

Little Mrs. Harriot pushed forward.

"Set down, do, Mrs. McLelland. I'll break it to you. Likes as not it's
business. Once my husband got a telegraph an' 'twas only about the
price of corn. You give it to me—you're Plunkett's Joe, ain't you?"

"Ya-as," returned the rose colored boy, doubtfully. "But this here's
for Mrs. Mc., you see. Here, Mrs. Mc."

He thrust the yellow envelope into her hand, turned on his heel,
and disappeared in the swirling dust of the June afternoon.

Mrs. McLelland attempted to open the envelope. Her fingers
shook. Mrs. Harriot snipped off the end of the envelope with the

shears. She pulled Mrs. McLelland's spectacles from her forehead to her nose.

"There, now!" she said.

In the burning hush of the midsummer noon the two women stood in the doorway and Mrs. McLelland picked out the words one by one.

"My Maria is sick. Can't you come, ma? Your daughter,
ELIZA LOUISE."

Mrs. McLelland sank down trembling.

"There! It's just as I was beginnin' to tell you when he come, Mis' Har'rot. I've been beggin' an' beggin' these years back to see Eliza Louise. Her little girl has growed up an' got married since I seen either one of 'em. Pa, he'd allus put me off. One year it 'ud be the drought. The next year it 'ud be the grasshoppers. The year after there was something to be done for Tommy—his boy, you know. There was Tommy's schoolin', an' Tommy's courtin', an' Tommy's farmin', an' Tommy's marryin', an' the mortgidge on the new farm, an' so between it all I never got to go. Fifteen year—an' now her little girl's like to die, no doubt—she was married a year ago, Mis' Har'rot—an' I'll never set eyes on them again!"

She fell to sobbing. The sound was horribly harsh on the hot silence. The powerful frame was quivering. The old gray head was bent.

"Don't take on—now, don't!" Mrs. Harriot entreated. "I knowed a woman once that the doctors give up, an' she lived to be a hundred an' five. Leastways she said she was a hundred an' five when she died, and that once the doctors had give her up. She'll git better—your granddaughter will."

"But I want to see them—my own Eliza Louise an' her sick girl."

Mrs. Harriot thought of the three farms beside the one which had been given to Tommy. She thought of the fat cattle, the two hundred hogs, the six thousand bushels of cribbed corn, and her bent old back straightened.

"Why don't you go an' see 'em?" she demanded.

The strangling sobs ceased. Mrs. McLelland lifted a tear-blotched face.

"If I was to ask pa for the money to go he'd have a duck fit."

"Let him!" decided Mrs. Harriot.

Somewhere back of her bowed old body, somewhere back of her shrunken frame, must have been a dash of warlike blood, a fine streak of defiance. A look of awe came into the face of Mrs. McLelland. "What do you mean?" she asked in a strained voice. "Do you mean I ought to—ought to stand up again pa?"

There was a hush in the world just then—their world. The oceans of corn which hid the little farmhouse in the hollow from sight were stirless in the steeping sunshine. Not a cloud moved overhead; not a bird wing cleaved the blue air.

"Yes," returned Mrs. Harriot, "that's what I mean."

Again there was silence. The tempter sat breathlessly eyeing the tempted. The attenuated little creature regarded the majestic matron opposite her much as a tiny spider might regard an enmeshed and struggling blue-bottle fly.

"Stand up—again pa!" whispered Mrs. McLelland at length. "O, I—I dasn't! We been married thirty year, Mrs. Har'rot, an' we never had a quarrel—so to speak. Of course we had spats off an' on when I got worried wantin' to go see Eliza Louise—she's the only child I ever had, Mis' Har'rot. She was a big girl when I married pa. But we never had no conjuglar rows. Pa, he'd say, 'Wait till after killin'.' I'd wait. Then 't would be the thrashin', or the hay, or else pa would predicate that there'd be a cheap rate, soon, an' I'd better wait for that! Fifteen years have gone that away, Mis' Har'rot. And the things I've done for his sons—'specially Tommy. You ask me to tell you sometimes about the things I done for Tommy—an' when he was a-sparkin'. It's no use talkin'." She read the message over and again her eyes filled. "If I wanted to ever so I couldn't git the money out of pa. The fare to Illinois is all of $17."

"I know where you kin borrow $17," cried Mrs. Harriot. Her old eyes kindled with the excitement of the occasion. "My niece in Bubble has saved $21. When she has all of twenty-five she's goin' to buy a plush parlor set at the county seat. But she won't raise the other $4 soon. She's been two years savin' this. You'd likely be takin' the night train from Bubble anyhow. She'd be proud to let you have the loan of the money. Say you'll go, Mis' McLelland."

Mrs. McLelland rose. A great resolve thrilled her—transfigured her. A flush came into her tanned old face—a color and a light. Determination of self-assertion was a revivifying draft, stimulating as rare old wine.

"I will!" she cried. "I'll go!"

Mrs. Harriot bounced up.

"That's right! Now we'll git to packin'." She ran across the room and jerked the horsehair trunk forward.

"You'll gather up the carpet rags—an' tell Sam to save the eggs an' let pa trade 'em when he goes to town—pa'll have to see about the churnin' himself—an'—there! it's on at last—I usn't to weigh but a hundred an' eighty, though you wouldn't think it. Hand me the net fichu—an' the brooch. Eliza Louise's father give it to me when we were married. There's a pair of kid gloves in the bureau drawer next to pa's necktie. I ain't ever wore them, though it's six year since I got 'em for Tommy's weddin'. It seems sinful to put real kid gloves on. It wears 'em out. Carryin' them shows you've got 'em, an' keeps 'em lookin' nice. Well, I'm going. I'm under complications for your help, Mis' Har'rot. I'll send you a postal card after I git there. Wait! I'll put some of them sody biscuits an' a bit of the spice cake in my valise. They'll stay my stomach till I git to Eliza Louise's house. It's terrible rapacious buyin' food on trains, an' I won't be more'n twenty-two hours on the way. Well, goodby, Mis' Har'rot!"

"Goodby!"

The mistress of the house lumbered out into the dust and glare, a ponderous and portly figure in all the glory of the green gown with the orange vine, a bonnet on the top of which three ostrich tips which once had perhaps possessed the grace to curl, stood stiff as grenadiers on sentry duty, a pair of gloves clutched tightly in one hand and an apoplectic old valise in the other.

The wagon way to the road was rough and dusty. The road was dusty, but not so rough. It was a main traveled road. Mrs. McLelland turned westward and plodded on. At first she held herself erect and walked briskly. But after awhile her steps flagged and her progress was less rapid. As she had remarked to Mrs. Harriot it was a good three miles to Bubble. That was the time when the McLellands lived on their farm across the State line in Kansas, before Mr. McLelland had attained the dearest desire of his heart and become an undertaker in a town having the actual population of 500 bodies—souls were not considered much in Bubble in those days.

"Sakes!" she panted, "but it's hot! Seems like some Joshua's been commandin' that there sun to stand still an' it's obeyin' him."

A couple of wagons coming home from town or mill jolted by her. The drivers, lurching forward on their seats, gave her a stolid nod. There was no chance of a lift. No one was going into town at that hour. Dipping and twisting, blurred, yellow, and apparently interminable, the road stretched away into the vivid, copper-colored sky. A flock of birds whirred overhead and settled in a cottonwood by the roadside; beautiful, jet black, shining things, with breasts of gleaming scarlet just dashed with gold. On she plodded, now past a lonely farmhouse, now by recumbent cattle, now under walls of sunflowers, now over a bridge spanning the dry bed of a creek in which swine huddled, black and unsightly—on and on.

"I'm beat!" groaned Mrs. McLelland. "I'm beat! An' I ain't more'n half way, if I'm that."

She sank down on a grass ridge at the side of the road. Her bonnet was awry. The perspiration poured down her flushed face. She was breathing heavily. A boy came skipping along the road—a little, skinny, freckled, bare-legged boy. He stopped before the traveler.

"Hallo, Mrs. Mc. Goin' away?"

"Yes—into Bubble. Then on the train."

"I'll give you a lift with that bag." He picked it up and started off. She lumbered up and after him.

"You're reel commodious, Dicky Peters," she declared, gratefully. Relieved of the bag, her journey was less wearisome. The sun was going down at last, and here, between the high hedges of osage orange, was shade and comparative coolness.

"O, that's nothin'!" he trotted beside her, bending sideways under the weight of the bag. "When my step-pa was shinglin' your barn you give me three cookies."

"Eh?"

"An' when I let your white cow into the cornstalks you didn't tell him. He'd ha' licked the hide off'n me."

"Yes."

"An' you let me git two hull pocketfuls of cherries off'n your tree before you sicked the dog on me."

"Did I?" She felt cheered. She began to think there was gratitude in the world. The two went on, she pleased by the companionship, he proud of his prowess with the bag, which bumped and thudded against his bare little legs. They went out on the highroad again. The sun had set. Purple shadows lurked along the creek. The air was palpitant and shimmering in its transition from amber to amethyst. Suddenly Mrs. McLelland stood still. From afar down the dim stretch ahead came to her keen old ears a familiar sound.

"Hark!" She clutched her companion's arm. "Ain't that a hoss—Tommy's bay hoss?"

Distinctly to the listeners came on the still evening air the sound of hoofbeats on the hard road.

On the rise of the hill ahead three things came simultaneously into sight—a spring wagon, a horse, and a man.

"It's Tommy!" she said, "pa's Tommy. Like as not pa ast him to go out to our place till he got back. What'll I tell him? Here he is now, and—O, Lordy!"

The man on the wagon seat heard the despairing cry—saw the massive, motionless form.

"Maria!" he cried.

"Pa!" she wailed.

He clambered down—confronted her. His head barely reached her shoulder. He was a spare, lame, white-headed, white-bearded, stern-eyed, little old farmer. To his trembling wife he represented just then all that was most mighty in existence, most inexorable in fate, and most inevitable in destiny.

"Where are you a-goin'? What's that bag for?"

"I'm a-goin' to see Eliza Louise," answered Mrs. McLelland.

"You—You're a-goin'—" He broke off stammering.

"I'm a-goin' to see the only child an' grandchild I got. You got a heap of 'em, pa. I ain't got but the two. An one of 'em's sick—dyin', maybe. O!" she burst out piteously, "I ain't never stood up again you before, pa—never!"

Silence. He tries to speak, once—twice, but in vain. Thirty years of obedience, sacrifice, submission, and now insubordination—now rebellion! A General, struck in the face by a private, could not feel more outraged—more aghast.

"It's—it's a—a put up job!" he squeaked. "You planned it—an' then waited till I should go to Lincoln. But I only went far as Tommy's, an'—"

"No—no, pa. You'll see the telegram on the table to home. It come while Mis' Har'rot an' me was a-cuttin' carpet rags. It's a real telegram."

He took a step nearer her.

"Where'd you git the money to go?" he cried, his thin voice rising shrilly.

She shut her lips hard. She would not get her friends into trouble.

The legs and arms of Mr. McLelland jiggled like those parts of a jumping jack when the string is pulled.

"I know—I know," he declared, dancing around in ankle deep dust, to the delight of Dicky Peters, who was watching him with an irreverent grin. "You found the $20 I got hid in my winter mitts in the old stove in the barn!"

"I never!" protested Mrs. McLelland. "I never knowed there was a cent there, pa!"

A short, incredulous laugh answered her. Mr. McLelland climbed to his perch on the spring wagon and drove off without a word. Mrs. McLelland stood immovable until the sound of hoof-beats and wagon wheels became inaudible. Twenty dollars lying there! And she was going to try to borrow her railroad fare in town. She had told the truth when she said she had neither known of it nor touched it, but—

"I can and I will!" she cried aloud.

Dicky Peters jumped.

"Will what, Mrs. Mc.?"

"Dicky, you set right down there beside that bag," she directed tremulously. "I got to go back, but I won't be long. I'll drive back. You kin open the bag, Dicky. There's some sody biscuits in it, an' some spice cake. You kin eat it all, Dicky— if you can hold it all."

Dicky gurgled ecstatically, promptly took her at her word, and fell to work. She turned and hastened back the way she had come. She felt stronger than when she had left home. Excitement upheld her. She felt surprised at the swiftness with which she found herself walking. She was not conscious of fatigue when she reached the rear of the barn, which she had approached by making a detour around the sorghum patch back of the house. There was no light about the place, nor any sound. The chores were done long before. A lamp was never lit in the McLelland home in summer. The inmates went to bed at dark. Kerosene cost money. Five minutes later a bulky shadow moved among the stirless shadows in the barn. There was the click of iron. Then the barn doors were softly set wide. A huge thing hurled itself around the corner of the house—into the barn, a warm and shaggy thing.

"Sh—s—sh, Rover!"

Rover poked his nose into the hand of his mistress and waved his plume-like tail in mute but joyous greeting. It was not for nothing Mrs. McLelland had helped her spouse in the hard and active labor to be performed on a farm when they were both younger and less rheumatic. With feverish rapidity but accurate precision the trappings of the bay horse were adjusted, the animal backed between the shafts of the spring wagon, and all made ready for flight. Then Rover saw the horse led around the barn, a heavy old figure climb with many trippings and ineffectual efforts to the seat, and all disappear around the patch of sorghum in the direction of the main road.

Mr. McLelland as a rule slept soundly and rose early. On that particular night he slept badly and rose earlier than usual. He missed Marie. Something was wrong. He felt a sense of loss, of disturbance.

"It's the heat," he assured himself. "An' the musquitoes was bad last night—a body couldn't sleep with 'em. I'll feel all right when I git some coffee."

When he had lighted the fire and put on the kettle he went out in the yard.

"Sam!" he called. "You, Sam!"

There was no reply. Sam must be up, because the barn doors stood wide. He had likely gone into the field. But Sam usually did the chores and then had his breakfast before he began the main work of the day. His master hobbled down to the barn, Rover frisking before him. "Eh—what?" he began, and stood there rubbing his eyes. The bay horse was gone. The spring wagon was gone. Tommy's bay horse and spring wagon! Thieves—robbers! A terrifying thought convulsed his weather-beaten face. The twenty dollars—in the mittens—in the oven of the old stove! A minute later he had wrenched the door open—was peering in. The oven was empty. Neither to sight nor to groping touch were mittens or money revealed.

Mr. McLelland, staggering into Harriot's house just at "sunup," was a pitiable figure. Ten years in ten minutes appeared to have been added to his burden of age.

"Robbed!" he burst forth. "Robbed, an' by that scoundrel Sam, I'm sure! Twenty dollars! 'Twas where I put it when I got home last night, for I went a-purpose to look—had a reason for lookin'. Now it's gone— Tommy's horse an' spring wagon's gone, too—an' there ain't no sign of Sam. We must git the marshal out an' a posse—quick!"

Mrs. Harriot pushed him into a chair.

"I dunno whether Sam took your money or not, but he wouldn't be such a fool as to take a horse an' wagon that every one knows for miles around. When Sam come back last night an' I told him your wife had gone East on a visit, he swore. He said he wasn't goin' to stay alone of you—said he'd be clean starved. Said if 't wasn't for what Mrs. Mc. give him to eat unbeknownst to you he never could stand up to his work. 'Mis' Har'rot,' he says to me, 'if I have to depend on the old man, I'll git that lean that when I got a pain I won't know whether it's backache or stomachache that ails me,' he says. 'So I'm goin' to quit in the mornin',' he says. Look there! Who's drivin' up here?"

They crowded to the door.

"It's Tommy's horse an' spring wagon!" cried McLelland. The town marshal jumped down, came towards them.

"How do, McLelland? This is your son's rig. I seen you drive out home with it yesterday. We found it hitched just outside town early this morning. Don't know who left it there."

Mr. McLelland poured the story of his misfortunes into the officer's attentive ear, with the result that a warrant was speedily secured for one Sam Brown. Before noon that individual was taken from his mother's house into town, where he sat in the drug store until the Justice of the Peace had finished playing pool across the street. Then Sam Brown was bound over to the County Court for the theft of $20 from Mr. McLelland, "one of our most prosperous and respected farmers," as the local paper stated.

One week passed—two weeks. It was known that Mrs. McLelland had walked into Bubble, dusty and fatigued, on the night of the disappearance of Sam Brown. It was also known that she had bought a ticket for Illinois, and had taken the 11 o'clock train. Mrs. Harriot had not seen her niece, but felt convinced she had loaned Mrs. McLelland the money for her trip East. The only ones having guilty knowledge of the actual proceedings were Dicky Peters and Rover, and neither of these offered evidence.

Those were hard days for Mr. McLelland. His loneliness weighed on him. He missed the ponderous presence, the well-cooked meals, and the unceasing chatter of his spouse. He took to sitting up until 9 o'clock, and even occasionally lighting a lamp in the evening. He called regularly at the postoffice for mail, but no letter came for him. The feeling of remorse he would not admit even to himself rendered him irritable. "She allus set store by that wuthless Sam," he declared. "I'll let her see the kind of a serpent she's been warmin' in her buzzum."

So he folded up the town and county papers and sent them to her. She duly received them. Sitting by the chair of her convalescent granddaughter she read them.

"Eliza Louise," she called, "you tell Lemuel to hitch the team. There's a train this afternoon. I'm goin' home."

Eliza Louise thought instantly of her stepfather.

"Is pa sick?" she asked.

"No, not that I know. But I'm a deceiver. I'm a retrograde. I'm as bad as a common conjurer."

"Perjurer, you mean. Why, ma!"

"It's all the same. I'm as wicked as one. Poor Sam Brown a-sufferin' for my voraciousness! I'm a absconder, Eliza Louise—that's what I am. And I'm goin' straight home. I've had a fine visit, an' I feel all of ten year younger. It's been worth standin' up again pa for—though I don't know as I'll ever do it again."

It was the day set for the trial of Sam Brown at the county seat. Mr. McLelland, supported by the presence of his son Tommy, Tommy's wife, Tommy's children, and several interested and sympathetic friends, was donning his black coat and necktie preparatory to his drive to court, when the door opened and Mrs. McLelland walked in.

"Maria!"

He stood staring at her, his coat half on.

"Pa, Sam Brown never took your money."

"Didn't! Who did, then?"

"I did."

"You! Mrs. Harriot told me you borryed the money to go from her niece."

"I was projectin' to do that same when I started. But when you told me where you had $20 layin' ubiquitous, so to speak, I thought as how I had some right to it. I've worked hard for you, pa, for thirty year— for you an' your other wife's prodigy. An' I never stood up again you before."

"But the—the horse an' wagon?"

Mrs. McLelland removed her bonnet and sat down.

"I reckoned," dryly, "that I was compensated to a ride in Tommy's wagon, after all I done for Tommy sense he wasn't but 4 year old— even to makin' his courtin' neckties out'n the strings of the bunnit I got when I married Eliza Louise's father."

Tom McLelland turned red. She giggled.

"We'll be goin'," they said.

And they went. So did the neighbors. Mrs. McLelland told of her trip while she got dinner. The two sat down.

" 'Taint but 11, pa. You got time enough to git there an' have the case dismissed. An' bring Sam back with you. I'll make a chicking potpie for supper. I bet you ain't had any chicking potpie sense I been gone, pa, an' you've got such a affinity for it, pa. Why, pa, you're stranglin'! You'll scald yourself a-gulpin' down that tea!"

He blinked at her across the cup.

"Dry fur corn!" he said.

Gold

Allusions to works of Shakespeare abound in Cleary's works, and the humorous poem "Gold" comments on this quotation from Othello:

> *Good name in man and woman, dear my lord,*
> *Is the immediate jewel of their souls:*
> *Who steals my purse steals trash; 'tis something, nothing;*
> *'Twas mine, 'tis his, and has been slave to thousands;*
> *But he that filches from me my good name*
> *Robs me of that which not enriches him,*
> *And makes me poor indeed. (3.3.155)*

Cleary spoke to the bard in his own language here, heroic couplets, as she questioned the wisdom of his lines.

In this poem Cleary referred also to the biblical story of Elijah, who, upon ascending to heaven in a chariot of fire, dropped his mantle down to Elisha, conferring its gifts upon him (2 Kings 2:13). Cleary wanted Shakespeare to bequeath his literary abilities to her, but she also realized the necessity of making a living.

Immortal Shakespeare! Were you not too rash
In saying, "He who steals my purse, steals—trash!"
Such trash forsooth, as the whole world desires,
Whose golden hue each human hope inspires:
" 'Twas mine! 'tis his!" that line at least is true,
It melts away sometimes like morning dew;

And, slave to thousands it may once have been,
But now those thousands are its slaves, I ween!
I must confess I thought in sunny youth
Your sentiments sublime, and full of truth, —
And looked with pity or derisive laugh
On those who worshipped that old golden calf!
Nor felt I ease, until I saw unfurled
The flag that flings defiance to the world!

Oh, shade of Shakespeare! hear my humble call
And let, Elisha like, your mantle fall,
About this inefficient, quaking pen —
Or else 't will tell the toiling sons of men
In spite of me, — that purses filled with cash,
Are indispensable — by no means — trash!

Jim Peterson's Pension

This short story embodies Thorstein Veblen's economic theories of the leisure class and its conspicuous consumption. In addition, the physical decline of Mrs. Peterson, the main character, mocks the frail condition expected of the upper-middle-class Victorian woman by delineating the reasons for her incapacity, as well as the cure—less idleness and dependence on others and more common sense. Again, Cleary mocked the pretension of the culture, not of Mrs. Peterson, in this story published on 19 February 1899 in the Chicago Tribune.

The idea for this story may have come from local news. On 26 June 1896 the Hebron Journal *announced: "There is much rejoicing among the neighbors over Mr. Keiser's pension. His utter helplessness and the enduring patience of his faithful wife have aroused the sympathies of everybody for a number of years."*

IT WAS A MODEST LITTLE HOUSE at the door of which Nannie Blake knocked. The room into which she stepped was unassuming also, but it was cozy, and immaculately clean. There was a rag carpet on the floor; crisp muslin curtains were on the windows; a jolly red fire burned in a well polished mite of a stove; and a stand of plants stood between the two wooden rockers.

"Well, if it isn't Miss Blake!" cried the cheery voice of the mistress of the house. "Come in, Miss Blake. Take this rocker with the cushion. It was only yesterday I was asking Dolly how you was. She's learning awful good with you. She thinks you're the nicest teacher she ever had, and so does Willie. Is that a bundle of sewing you've got for me?"

"Yes; I wonder if you will have time to do it."

"Time!" echoed the little woman. "Oceans of time when it's work you want done. I'm glad to get it, too. Every cent counts in this house since Jim hurt his arm, and had to quit working."

Nannie Blake looked approvingly at the bright little body who was briskly unrolling the package of ginghams, and inspecting the tissue paper pattern inclosed. Bright is the word that best described Mrs. Peterson. She had bright pink cheeks, and bright brown hair, and bright blue eyes that sparkled mirthfully. She gave one the impression of perfect health, a sunny disposition, and a sanguine spirit. Gayety radiated from her as unconsciously as the warmth from the fire or the pleasant pungence from the winter-bound plants, and was quite as enjoyable as were those.

"I should think so, with the children to clothe and feed. I notice, too, that since Mr. Peterson was injured you have had the outdoor work to attend to. Mother had begun to make these aprons for Nell and Neddie, but when I came home from school and saw what she was attempting I bundled up the whole lot of stuff and brought it over to you. Mother isn't strong enough to give her little leisure to sewing when she ought to be resting, or reading, or out in the air."

"That's right. What with having a house that's got all of ten rooms in it to oversee, not to mention having a hired girl to look after, and her being more or less delicate—your mother, I mean, not the hired girl—it's all she ought to do. It must be a chore to see that a hired girl does the work she's paid for—not that I ever had one. This is the biggest house we ever lived in, and it ain't got but four rooms, but, bless you, it's lots big enough for us." Having paused to take a breath Mrs. Peterson proceeded to spread the gingham on the table, lay the tissue paper pattern smoothly upon it, and fill her mouth with pins.

"Your days must be well filled," the girl remarked. "I don't know how you manage to help others so much and keep the children looking so nice."

Mrs. Peterson, rapidly removing the pins from her mouth, and inserting them with much precision in the work upon which [she] was intent, shook her head.

"They don't look as nice as they would if I could buy new stuff. I've just got to patch and turn what they have got. I keep hoping, though, that one of these days Jim will get his back pension money. It was in 1880 that he applied for it. That was fifteen years ago. If he gets it at all, he will get it from that time."

"It would amount to quite a sum by now."

"Dear, dear!" cried the little woman, "wouldn't it, though? Twenty-one hundred and sixty dollars up to the end of last month! We never lose count of it. We've been adding on that $12 a month regular every month for the whole fifteen years. When the day comes we say, 'It's time for that letter.' Then we make believe we get it. We try to think we've put the money in [the] bank, and that one of these days we'll draw it for the children's education—or maybe to help us out when we're getting old. It's a heap of comfort to keep on talking that way. Then, when it don't come, we're not so badly disappointed as if we hadn't been having some pleasure out of believing it did, you see!"

"I see," said Nannie gently.

"I'm right thankful we've got on so well these months. Jim couldn't earn a dollar," she avowed, her shears flashing along the folded gingham. "Having a hog salted down was a help. I clean the Methodist church every Saturday. That, and helping your mother's hired girl days when there's extra work or company is expected, let alone the fact that Mrs. McLelland lets me have a chicken once in awhile for sewing up her carpet rags, we keep real comfortable, and I'm not complaining."

"There is Mrs. McLelland now," the girl remarked.

The door was unceremoniously opened. Mrs. McLelland, her immense bulk enveloped in a shapeless garment of faded calico dotted with brown lozenges, her head covered with an "ice-wool" veil, resting one hand on the sawed-off broomstick that served her as a cane, stood on the threshold.

"Pa," she panted, "has got a funeral tomorrow. It's that crippled child of Dow that's dead. They want a white coffing—the best pa's got—an' the hearse. Think of that, will you? Gittin' the hearse for a child that ain't never walked a step in its life. An' pa ain't got a white shirt made up. I want you should come over this afternoon an' starch him one. Will you?"

"Certainly. I'll be over."

The undertaker's wife let herself heavily down on the chair set for her.

"What I want to know now," she said, "is where's that other black rooster belongin' to Mis' Jones?"

Mrs. Peterson looked up from her snipping. "The other black rooster?"

"Yes. She had two of 'em. She ain't got but one now. What happened [to] the other?"

"I'm sure I don't know."

Mrs. McLelland turned sharply to Nannie. "Do you?"

"No," Nannie answered, trying hard not to smile.

"I want to know if they killed it an' ett it or if they give it away. They don't sell their chickings. Her aunt was to the house Friday. Mebbe they give it to her. I says to pa this mornin': 'Do you see that other black rooster of Mis' Jones around?' Pa says: 'I ain't seen it in a hull day.' 'Well,' I commensurates, 'the other one is around with the hens, but he ain't.' I'd have sent over to ask Mis' Jones what she done with it, but she ain't to home. The blinds was shut all mornin', so I made up my mind she was washin' in the back, but when it came to noon an' there was no smoke I says to pa that she must have gone out to her mother's, an' now I won't know what happened [to] that rooster till she gits back. Like as not she cooked it into soup an' ett the soup without absorbin' any of the soup meat. She's fearful extravagant."

"I did not think so," ventured Nannie.

The bright old eyes snapped.

"You didn't? Let me tell you what she's got. She's got a hat that cost six dollars! Six—dollars! I never seen the day that I'd dispose a bunnit on my head that cost six dollars—not, in particular, when corn is only fourteen cents a bushel. At that price what she's a-carryin' on her head is two hull wagonloads of corn! Six dollars!" And she rose in her righteous indignation and hobbled away.

Nannie stood up, laughing. "I must be going," she said. "Hark! Who is that running?"

Mrs. Peterson dropped her shears. "It's Jim!" she cried. "What's wrong?"

Suddenly the door was flung wide. A big man, breathless and shaking, lurched forward into the room. The little woman sprang up aghast.

"Mother!" he roared, "we've got it!"

He threw a letter towards her. Then he sank down on a chair and began to sob. His wife, white now as the walls of her humble home, could only grasp the envelope and mutter over and over: "The back pension—the back pension!"

Nannie Blake slipped out and hurried home.

"Mother," she cried, "just think! Jim Peterson has got his back pension. He brought the letter up while I was there."

"I'm so glad! But she won't make the aprons now, Nannie."

"O, I think she will. She is such a sensible little woman. She has been so contented in her poverty I believe she will be wise in her prosperity."

"I hope so, dear."

The next morning Willie Peterson brought back the blue-checked gingham, in which not a stitch had been set.

"My ma ain't going to do plain sewing no more," he announced.

Not long after Mrs. McLelland, wrath written on every line of her shrewd old face, came lumbering in.

"You heerd Mrs. Peterson promise to come to my house yesterday and do up a shirt for pa, so he could present the precarious appearance suited to his profession at the funeral—didn't you? Well, she never come. An' pa had to go off this mornin' with his coat buttoned clean up to his chin."

"I suppose she was so excited by hearing of their receiving their back pension that she forgot," ventured Nannie.

"Forgot nothin'! She's just got money-proud! That's all. I declare, between not havin' a white shirt on such a perspicuous occasion an' not bein' yet able to find out what happened [to] that other black rooster of Mis' Jones I'm near sick. You jest watch Mis' Peterson— that's all," she recommended darkly.

Nannie Blake, teaching her Sunday-school class a week later, recalled the advice of the undertaker's wife when she saw approaching her a dazzling apparition. It was a girl of 12, attired in a bright blue cashmere gown, trimmed with cotton velvet and gold braid, a scarlet jacket banded with white fur, and a hat on which yellow feathers and green aigrettes struggled for supremacy.

"You are late, Mary," Miss Blake gently reproved her.

Mrs. Peterson's elder daughter tossed her head.

"Ma says that I'm to be called Marie after this," she declared.

Nannie spoke of the incident to the young lumberman who walked home with her after church.

"I'm not surprised," he said in an amused tone. "Jim was figuring a bill with me yesterday. He says his wife wants a parlor and two extra bedrooms—one for possible guests, the other for the hired girl."

"Gracious!" gasped Nannie.

The parlor and bedrooms were duly built and the house painted. The local furniture dealer of the little Nebraska town grumbled because the articles deemed necessary for the new apartments were hauled from the county seat. Mrs. Peterson actually made a trip to Chicago, from which city she returned with various purchases of pictures, chiefly valuable for the width of their gilt frames, and enough cheap laces, silks, and embroideries to have furnished a small dry goods store. When these materials had been wrought up into many astonishing garments she made frantic attempts to enter the exclusive circle which every town, no matter how small, boasts.

On Sunday morning she went to the Methodist Church. In the evening she attended services at the Presbyterian. She sat with her family in the triple row of reserved seats at the opera-house whenever "a show" came to town. But finding that all these pretensions to social distinction did not avail, she resolved to give a reception, and to this end took Jim into her confidence.

"You see," she explained, "there's folks we'd like to ask that maybe wouldn't come if they knowed other folks we've got to ask—else they'd say we was stuck up—was coming. I've been studying how to do it so as to have pretty near all the people we know in town, and yet not offend any of them. It all come to me sudden how we could do it. We'll send to Lincoln for the cake and ice." Jim looked stupidly at the beaming face of his spouse.

"Ice! Land, what do you want to send for ice for? There's heaps of it lying around. Or you might put out a tub of water to freeze over night."

"O, Jim, I didn't mean that, but water ice. I got some when I was to Chicago. I don't suppose any one in Bubble ever tasted it. It's made of sugar and lemon juice froze together till it's like ice cream. It will be something new to have. Here's how we'll manage the invitations. We'll ask the Liningers, Jikses, Salsburs, and Wattses, say, from 2 to 3. The Kellys, O'Briens, McCarthys, and Flanagans from 3 to 4. Then the Cheropskys, Chotts, Solinskis, and Saprinskis from 4 to 5. After them could come the Robinsons, Whites, Hills, and Smiths. Going and coming that way, there wouldn't be too many to bother about at the time, and folks that didn't want to meet the other folks wouldn't have to." She paused—breathless, triumphant.

Jim gritted his stub pipe between his teeth. "It would take a heap of money, Mollie."

"Money!" she echoed resentfully. "What's money?"

"Well," deliberated Jim, who was slow of speech, "there may be other names for it, but to me it's jest money—and that's something you and me had been hoping hard and long to get."

"Yes, and we got it. Now the children are growin' up, we got to have a position in sassiety. We'll give the reception, Jim."

So cards, glorious with gilt script and inclosed in envelopes of the stiffest of cardboard, pinked at the edges with symmetrical accuracy, were duly issued. The town attended the reception; the voracious town, the curious town, the predatory town, the deprecatory town, the supercilious town. Some of the mothers brought their babies. It was on a bitter March afternoon that the social function was held. The Blakes did not attend. Mrs. McLelland did. The next day, more enraged than she had been at the defection of her laundress, she blundered into the home of her neighbors.

"Was you," she panted, "was you to the reception?"

"No," replied Nannie.

"Then," she decided, "you ain't missed as much as would blind you. I went."

"Did you, really?"

"I did that. My legs bein' bad I couldn't walk the hull way, so pa he hired the chair of that crippled cobbler that supports his family on one leg, down to the elevator, an' he propelled me, so to speak. You mind how cold it was—snowin' from every pint of the probuscis [*sic*]—at least the wind made it seem thataway. But I says: 'Pa, you bein' a prominent citizen an' a church member in good standin', we got a deputation to support. We must fulfill our sassiety obligations. One of them is to go to the reception. An' apart from the fried chickings they're most sure to have—though onless they're fall chickings they won't be fit for fryin' without first steamin',' says I, 'they'll have hot coffee most likely, not to mention pickles, an' we'll be recuperated by attendin'.' The idea of chickings jest set pa's mouth waterin'. 'As you say, Maria,' he secedes, so to speak."

"I was dressed for the occasion. I had on my black wrapper with the gimp and bead trimming—for, being of a large frame, I don't wear tight-fitting waists, they havin' not sufficient corsage to them—and my niece frizzed my hair a bit. I hunted up my teeth an' put 'em in. I didn't have no perfumery, so I put a dab of vaniller on my handkerchief. Then, I says to pa: 'I'm ready, exceptioning the coverin' which you an' Eleolanda must adjucate.' When they got done adjucatin' I had on my knit hood, my bunnit on top of that, an' my ice-wool fascinator over both of 'em. Pa's cardigan jacket was next my dress, a good thick jacket that used to belong to my sister back East that died of paralysis over that, an' on the two of 'em a new style cape that pa paid all of six forty-five for down to Saprinski's store. Besides them things, I've circum-scribed to you, I had on pa's fur mitts that he never wore but onct, then only when the County Clerk died, an' he was called on to do the derilictions. They was drawed on over the wool mittens with the stripe down the back, that my niece knitted for me a year ago come last Christmas. I had on overshoes, an' hosiery pulled up over them, an' I took my Paisley shawl, thinkin' I might need it."

"You must have been warm," Mrs. Blake hazarded.

"Warm!" grunted Mrs. McLelland. "I never was so froze in my life—but I ain't sayin' the weather did all of the freezin'. I got to the house. I got up the slippery steps. I rang their new-fangled bell, an' was let in."

"And had a delightful visit?" Nannie prompted.

Their guest snorted. "I was met," she continued, "by Mollie Peterson in a blue silk gown, with gloves on. Gloves—mind that! She said she was awful glad to see me. Then she shoved me into a room. There was folks with their things on, movin' out, an' more comin' in behind me. A young woman—I expect 't was Mary, but she was that fixed up I couldn't be sure, says: 'O, I'm so happy to see you!' an' shoved a plate into my hand. 'Have some cake and a ice,' says she. I looked at the plate. There was a bit of cake on it, an' a dab of stuff that might have been egg whipped up, an' colored with beet juice. I couldn't eat it, havin' only hands that was attired in wool gloves an' fur mitts to do it with, so I set it down reel careful on a table. Then I stood an' waited for some one to come an' ask me to take off my things. No one come."

"I'm of pretty fair propositions, anyhow, but jest then, with all the coverin's, was about as big as a hipporhinocerous or a reel born goriller. After awhile I got one hand free, an' I looked around for the refreshment, that wasn't fried chicking an' pickles by no means. It was gone. I don't know who got it, but I suspect 't was that young one of Kavish's, that was a'snoopin' around as I come in. Pa didn't come in when he seen there was only ladies attendin'. Well, there I stood. Along come Mollie Peterson, jest as the clock struck. 'Good-by,' she says, awful pleasant. 'So cha-r-m-ed to have seen you!' Then she put her hand on my shoulder an' shoved me out pretty much the same way that she shoved me in. Pa seen me from Tom Myers' house across the street, so he come with the vehicle. The Bohemians was approachin' as I left. It was thirty-five minutes from the time we left our house—slow propulsion an' all, until I was agin articulated into my abode!"

"Mercy me!" cried Mrs. Blake.

"Well, indeed!" ejaculated Nannie.

Mrs. McLelland, her broomstick cane clutched firmly in her sinewy grasp, and looking more than ever like a possibly malevolent but decidedly substantial witch, nodded rapidly.

"O, that ain't all! Across the room from me was Mary Snider, whose son married one of the Eurichs that hates the hull brood of Sniders. Well, there was three Eurichs, an' they all glared on to poor Mis' Snider like she had made Sophy, which was her daughter, marry into their fambly. Then in come Katie Choipsky—a nice little girl, but she'd jilted one of the Eurich boys for a brother of Mary Snider's, an' the Sniders didn't like the match either, so they all scrowled [*sic*] at her like she was p'ison ivy. I guess Mis' Peterson must have got her people mixed or she never would have so transmogrified us visitors. I couldn't understand how she come to give that sort of a entertainment till, after I got back last night, I got to tellin' Eleolanda about it, an' says I, 'It makes me think of what she seen in the big stores when she was back to Chicago.' 'One to two,' says she, 'they got silks that is worth two dollars a yard marked down to $1.68. Then, from two to three they got reel French kid gloves—actual $1.50 value, for only 79 cents. An' perhaps from three to four they sell off silk-lined suits for four-fifty that has been sold earlier in the season for $23.' 'That's where she got her idee, pa,' I gesticulates, 'jest there! What she's give to the ladies of Bubble was a bargain reception—an' don't you forgit it, neither!' says I."

A few days later Mrs. Peterson called on Mrs. Blake. Nannie answered the bell. At first she hardly recognized her caller. The latter was gowned in green satin, lavishly ornamented with iridescent trimming. She wore an elaborate bonnet, white kid gloves, and carried a lace-covered parasol. The warmth of the capricious Nebraska weather authorized the airiness of garb which in another climate might have been deemed premature. But, in spite of all of her finery, the caller looked neither well nor happy. Her cheeks were pale. Her eyes no longer sparkled.

"Why, it is you, Mrs. Peterson!"

Mrs. Peterson deliberately extracted a card from the case she carried. A pink rose blossomed on the card. Under the rose, adorned with many flourishes, ran in Roman type the name: "Mrs. James Worthington Peterson."

"Please give that to your mother," directed the visitor.

"Certainly," faltered Nannie. "Mother is out at present, but won't you come in? I'm afraid," she added, smiling, "I must ask you to come out to the kitchen with me. I'm cooking over into jam the fruit we put up green last year. We have got out of jam and jelly and the children are aghast at the domestic condition of affairs."

"O, yes, I'll come," agreed Mrs. Peterson, condescendingly. She added, as she sank into the comfortable chair Nannie brought to her, "you know I ain't proud."

Nannie turned her head away a little as she stirred the bubbling green mass in the granite kettle. "I hope," she said, "the children are well."

"No," sighed Mrs. Peterson, "they ain't. Seems like their victuals don't set well on their stomachs. They eat such a heap of butcher's meat and canned goods now. Don't you keep a hired girl any more?"

"Yes, but Annie is at home this week."

"Do you do all the work when she's away?"

"Not all, but a good deal of it. Mrs. Rogers comes to do the heavier part of it every day. She does a great deal in an hour or two. There she is now."

The kitchen door opened. A pleasant faced woman, wearing a calico dress, and with a red shawl over her head, came in. "Well, here I am, Miss Nannie," she said. "What's to be done first? O, excuse me! I didn't notice that you had company." Then she burst out laughing. "Why, I declare to goodness, if I knowed you, Mollie Peterson! How's Jim and the children?"

Mrs. Peterson looked at the presumptuous newcomer in stony silence. She rose stiffly.

"I must be going now," she said, addressing Nannie.

There was an instant of embarrassed silence. Then Mrs. Rogers drew nearer the woman in the silken gown. The smile had faded from her honest red face. There was contempt in the eyes which a minute before had been so friendly.

"So you won't speak to a body, Mollie Peterson, because Jim has got his back pension! And to think—it ain't so long ago but that Miss Nannie here can remember it—that you and me has took turns at comin' to scrub this same kitchen floor we're both a-standin' on, and was glad enough to get our 75 cents a day when it come 5 o'clock, not to talk of the skim milk and broke meat. I've heerd tell of beggars on horseback, but you're the first one I ever seen." And Mrs. Rogers strode wrathfully into the buttery, and closed the door with unnecessary force and emphasis.

Nannie meekly followed her visitor to the front door. "I'm so sorry,

Mrs. Peterson," she said. Mrs. Peterson only swallowed hard, nodded, and walked away, quite forgetting to unfurl her lace-trimmed parasol. The Nebraska summer came on, even more hot and exasperating than usual. Skies of glowing metal stretched over white roads that cracked apart with heat, and fields where the shriveled corn kept up a sound like the rattling of dry bones in the surging dust storms. Bubble was quiet. Women tried to be patient, and kept their children indoors until evening. They ate cold meals, and the few who were fortunate enough to have ice were envied. But at the Petersons' was much excitement and gayety. Mrs. Peterson kept a servant. She also had her washing and ironing "done out." So she was at liberty to entertain her relatives and those of her husband who, attracted by the back pension money, flocked from afar, as well as such of the townsfolk as accepted her invitations. The potato patch at one side of the house was converted into a croquet ground. Ice cream frequently came from Wymore for the Petersons, and fresh vegetables from Kansas City. John Henry sported white linen and ties of rainbow hues. The other boy became the possessor of an expensive bicycle. The services of the town physician were in frequent requisition at the Peterson residence. The rich and unaccustomed fare disagreed with the children. The new cares and duties of social life told on their mother. And so the scorching months wore away and fall came. The guests had vanished from the Petersons' before the first frost. The hired girl was discharged. Mrs. Peterson no longer gave out her washing. It was rumored that for the future she would do it herself. When winter set in the children still wore their tawdry summer finery. One morning, when Willie came to school, his teacher took his blue, stiff fingers in her own and rubbed them.

"Dear child," she asked, "why did your mother let you come to school without your mittens?"

"I ain't got any mittens. But then she didn't know," he went on, indifferently. "She's sick abed."

"How long has she been sick?"

"O, she's sick off an' on all the time now."

Miss Blake went to the Peterson home that afternoon. Mary, in a gown that had once been considered gorgeous in Bubble, but now was deplorably dirty, opened the door. It was with a certain dismay the caller looked around the parlor. The cream-colored velvet carpet, sprawled all over with mammoth pink roses; the "set" upholstered in brocade and plush; the hanging lamp with its fringe of prisms; the massively framed chromos; the profusion of ugly and worthless ornaments and photograph frames offended her artistic eye and her cultivated taste. But she forgot all about these at sight of the wan and haggard little woman who came feebly out of the bedroom and sank limply down in a chair.

"You're real good to come, Miss Nannie," she began. Nannie did not know what else she was trying to say, because she was crying so hard.

"There—never mind! It will help you. Only tell me what I can do."

When Mrs. Peterson could speak for sobbing, she begged: "You will listen."

She burst forth with her confession. "Jim don't say a word," she concluded. "If he was like other men and would swear some, maybe I wouldn't feel so bad. He trusted me to spend the back pension wise for the children, and me, and I spent it foolish—wicked foolish. It's gone now—all gone. There was three hundred I lent to a lady that was stopping at the hotel. She said she'd take Mary into society in St. Joe. She's in jail at Omaha now for stealing. The rest—well, I guess you seen about as well as other folks how the rest went. And I've been tired to death trying to keep it all up. The girl I hired knew more'n I did, because she had lived with people that was used to money and knowed how to spend it. She told me that pretty plain. Then the clothes that was done out never suited me. They always had too much bluing, or they wasn't suddled enough. Then the style—and the parties! And the things the people I'd done the most for, said behind my back. It all got me down flat. Miss Nannie, whatever will I do?"

"You'll be the brave little woman you used to be," Miss Nannie decided heartily. "You'll hurry and get strong, and put new courage into your husband, and take the best care of your home and children."

Mrs. Peterson straightened up and looked at her with shining eyes.

"Do you think I could make up for it? Have you any plain sewin', Miss Nannie?"

"Loads of it! Enough to keep you busy every spare hour you may have for four months, for—" There she broke off, blushing.

"Is it the young lumberman? I'm glad of that. Every one has a good word for him. I know what a kind husband he is. There's Jim that's hard hit, but he ain't blaming me in word. O', I'd just like to let him see—"

"Who see—what?" cried Jim, blustering in. "Good day, Miss Blake. What's this, Mollie? Crying and laughing all at once!" The big fellow sat down beside her, took her hand in his and lightly patted it. "This has been a hard summer on her, Miss Blake. I'm sorry for society people. They've got no end of hard work. We tried it this summer and it didn't pay. Now that I've got a job on the section and the $12 a month regular, we'll get on all right. For we don' have to pretend any more we're getting a pension. We do get it—eh, Mollie? There—there, little woman! Going, Miss Blake?"

To Nebraska

"To Nebraska" prefaces Cleary's novel Like a Gallant Lady *and depicts her love/hate relationship with the frontier. Cleary realized that harsh and unremitting toil was required of pioneers and of herself, yet she saw the inherent beauty of the land and understood the allure of a better day to come. The two contrasting stanzas of the poem heighten its ironic ambiguity, according to critic Jean Keezer-Clayton, who also points out that Cleary's metaphors of "bride, and slave and guest" describe the roles of all frontier women.*

To the village and the plain
   Of a land of toil and pain,
Of a land where drouth devoureth
   Making labor void and vain;
Where ambitions cease to glow,
   Where high hopes are buried low,
And the mad mirage of other
   Lands, the sweetest thing we know.

To a land that yet shall be
   Fair and fertile, proud and free,
Golden grain and happy homesteads,
   'Twixt the east and western sea—
From a woman whom the west
   Harbored bride, and slave and guest,
Has been kind to—has been cruel—
   And has given worst—and best!

A Dust Storm in Nebraska

The pioneers of the 1890s suffered through a drought and depression as bad as that of the "dirty thirties." In this sketch, published as part of a trilogy of stories entitled "Some Prairie Sketches" in the Chicago Tribune *on 16 June 1895, the promise of May is broken by Nature. Cleary piled detail upon detail in her sentences just as the dust collected in higher and higher drifts on her furniture and on her windowsills, and her rich verbs heighten the intensity of her prose.*

A SWEET, BREEZY MAY MORNING, so crisp and cool as to be autumnal in suggestion. A sky intensely blue, with just the fugitive sail of a cloud showing once in a while on its sapphirine expanse. A wind blows up, a wind that is warm—caressingly so. Soon it stings. The eyelids tingle. One goes indoors, contemplates the weather from a comparative point of vantage. But it is necessary to keep the windows shut, else the dust, that is like pumice stone, would choke, suffocate one. As it is it blows in through closed shutters and secured windows. It furs the carpet. It dims the velours of the best chairs. It ridges the woodwork of the furniture. It makes gritty to touch the cup you drink from, the paper you write on, the page of the book you read. It grimes the baby's white gown. Everywhere it lies, on chair and bookcase, on shelf and stair, on window ledge and picture frame, thick and soft as pale brown velvet.

As the sun goes up it grows hot—hotter. The wind from Kansas, blowing up scorchingly, is a fierce fever of kisses—kisses that, like a courtesan's, burn, blight, and disenchant.

The sky has darkened. Is it going to rain—by any blessed mischance? No, the darkness is that of dust. Dust in little, long, wave-like currents on the country roads; dust rising in whirls, the spirals of which are shaped like water-spouts; dust which surges up with a sullen roar; which hangs a thick, dun pall between earth and heaven; which makes darkness at 5 o'clock in May; which sifts in on your pillow all night long to the tune of a vagrant and accursed wind; which dries your throat, grits between your teeth, and colors your dreams; which lies upon your garments in the morning and shows on your haggard face. You rise, bathe, dress. You are deceived by an abrupt, a sudden, a delightful lull, which lasts perhaps two or three hours. But before noon it begins all over again.

Repetition! Revenge! Resignation! the clock seems to tick. The first is inevitable. The second is impossible. The third—they say St. Lawrence suggested a turn on the gridiron during his martyrdom. Those who endure the torture of a summer in a small Western town, where a sprinkling cart is an unknown institution, never make a similar demand. For the heat is enveloping, and they are roasted in the most prompt, uniform, and impartial manner imaginable.

A November Day in Nebraska:
An Impressionist Picture in the Country
Where Leaves Have Turned

*Painting a landscape of the Nebraska prairies with words,
Cleary displayed here not only her artistic background but
also her love of language. This sketch, full of sensory delight,
depicts the natural beauty she admired in her ambiguous relationship with the West. It was published in the* Chicago Tribune *in the mid-1890s.*

A SKY, SWIRLED WITH FLEECY CLOUDS, that holds the silvery
blueness of polished steel, that towards the horizon pales to translucent
pearl, and turns to tawny gold where it blurs with the brown grass of
the billowing prairies. Such myriad tints as that grass holds! Gray that
fades into fawn; fawn that deepens into bronze; bronze that glimmers
into green; green that gleams into gold.

By the roadside tower tall sunflowers, their dun stalks just dashed
with burnt sienna. From a dwarf oak down in the creek flutter some
stubborn leaves of crimson and gold.

A squirrel darts across the road.

The "stripped" corn rustles mournfully. Or is that queer, faint whispering a murmur of exaltation that, because it has grown, and borne,
and given, many little children are fed? Crisp is the air. A blue haze
drifts across the bluffs. On the white road lies the tangled tracery of

bare branches. Comes a cold wind. The skeleton shadows dance fantastically.

The barberry bushes by the farmhouse hedges have a thousand tints of reddish gold. The few leaves on the catalpas are scrolls of copper. The grape vines are cut from dull bronze. The rose leaves are of shriveled saffron. In the straggly country gardens not a flower dares to blow. Not an aster, not a dahlia, flaunts its poor bright banner of defiance.

Keener grows the air. The sun sinks redly. Here and there a light outgleams: "A beacon of home to hurrying feet." Drift forth fugitive scents—of warm milk, of savory meat—of coffee.

Sounds the bark of a watchdog.

Some stars steal out.

And the frost has a kiss that stings.

Bleakness, barrenness, isolation? No; although the winter be at hand. Peace, plenty, solitude that is not loneliness, being sweet and sacred—these, and the laughter of children!

A Western Wooing

The settling of the frontier involved the postponement of many marriages, often when a man went ahead west to establish a home or strike it rich in the new, free lands while a woman waited in the East. Once his homestead was claimed, he sent for his bride, and they were duly married. Cleary's husband did just that, and her wait was only a matter of months. In this story, Cleary humorously caricatured the patient western woman and the land-hungry western man in order to satirize human folly. This story appeared in the Chicago Tribune *on 16 June 1895 in a trio of stories entitled "Some Prairie Sketches."*

PEOPLE HAD BECOME RATHER TIRED of the romance. Perhaps in part because it had ceased to be romantic. When first Andulasia Stebbins had come out from Illinois to live with her mother and stepfather on the Nebraska prairie it was considered by the neighboring farmer folk quite proper, probable, and desirable that Ira Harris, whose half-section joined that of her relatives, should fall in love with her—which he promptly did.

Ira was 30, stout, stolid, loutish, methodical. He was a successful man. This is hardly to be explained of a person with the characteristics mentioned unless one includes selfishness. To be supremely selfish is so frequently to be successful. At the time of their meeting Andulasia was 27. There are women of *twenty*-seven and women of twenty-*seven*. She was one of the latter. With her square figure, her unequivocal complexion, her dull brown hair, and her calculating eyes she looked her years. One would never excuse her mistakes on the ground of immaturity. One could never condone them on that of impulse. Indeed, to attribute to her certain errors would be subtle flattery. She was not the kind of woman who is ordinarily subjected to temptation.

Harris, however, accepted her propinquity and her affection much as he accepted the drought or the price of hogs. He was willing she should decline the company of other men on his account. He reasoned that if her stepfather, old man Solveriny, were to clear off the mortgage on his place and die, and if the two sickly young Solverinys died also, she would be wealthy in her own right, as wealth is estimated in the Philistine West. Consequently it might prove a prudent proceeding to wait for Andulasia.

So he waited.

A year after their acquaintance began he gave her an inkling of his sentiments. Her concurrence with his views was almost pathetic. It was alert, reciprocal, conclusive. Matrimony at some indefinite date they might look forward to. Such an indiscretion at the present time would be a tremendous mistake.

"Of course, Ira," she said, "land's land. And if my stepfather and your mother—who is mighty feeble, I notice—and the twins don't die there won't be any land for us worth mentioning, much less a-marryin' on."

Nevertheless she felt as the years, two, three, four passed, that her acceptance of his suggestion had been a trifle overemphatic and unconsidered. Fate, she could not in justice rail against. One of the twins succumbed to ivy poisoning. The other, a few months later, was run down by the train. Andulasia's stepfather went the way of the apoplectic, and Ira's mother, with utter disregard for the sensation she might have caused, slipped from life in the most meek, genteel, and unimpressive manner imaginable. Then there was only Ira on one farm, and Andulasia and her mother on the other. No apparent obstacle intervened. Still Ira did not speak, and it was seven years since Andulasia had come from Illinois. He frequently visited her, helped her, and deferred to her. He carried her butter and eggs into town and "traded" them; when the circus was at the county seat, he drove her there; he took her into the side show where the fat woman was on exhibition; he bought her pink lemonade, and peanuts, and hot candy made on the grounds. He escorted her to the merry-go-round at Mahaska and rode side by side with her on the spotted ponies. He drove her into town twice a week. They attended prayer meeting together. They both professed religion at the revival. He bought eleven tickets for her crazy quilt raffle. He was in all things her constant and dependable cavalier, but he never once mentioned marriage—never once.

In this manner eight more years passed. She was 42. He was 45. He was stouter, more stolid. She had some wrinkles, gold fillings in her teeth, a reputation for irascibility—also a comfortable bank account.

The two continued to drive across the majestic prairies in all kinds of marvelous nights and days. But the prose of life had so eaten into their hearts they saw nothing of the beauty surrounding them, heard none of Nature's music. For them there was no charm in the blossoming miracle of dawn, the yellow sweep of the ripe corn, the translucence of the moonlight, the blue infinity of space, the meadowlark's gay vest, the fugitive radiance on the bluffs, the restless shiver of the cottonwoods, the ocean shadows of the wheat, the swiftness of the gopher, the snow of wild plum blooms by the creek, the rank and file of goldenrod flanking the dusty roads. And they never heard the pattering flight of the quail, nor the swallow's swerving wing, nor the scurry of the rabbit, nor the murmur of the maples, nor the rustle of the sunflowers, nor the first crackle of the frost, nor the breaking of the ice, nor the gossip of the wild grass, never—never.

Theirs were the years the majority of prairie people know. Always vague, unrestful, apprehensive, material. Never gay, never educational. If hopeful, elated; if despairing, sullen; if contented, bovine. It is rather hard to be philosophical in a country the conditions of which one day promise prosperity and leisure, and after the next hail or wind storm express starvation.

One day Ira brought Andulasia a letter. It was from her mother's brother who lived in Iowa. He was dying. He wished to see her. She handed Ira the letter.

"Shall I go?" she asked.

Harris deliberated. "Has he money?" he questioned.

"Yes."

"Then go."

He saw her off the next day. She wore a new dress that didn't fit in the back. The skirt was too short at the sides. Her shoes were dusty. The heat had taken the curl out of her bangs. She had forgotten to bring the piece of chamois skin with the powder on it, which she was in the habit of using surreptitiously. Her nose shone as if polished. She wore kid gloves which were too large.

The train was late. As they walked up and down the platform she talked to Ira steadily and monotonously. She warned him about the brindle cow, and advised him concerning a piece of his fence which needed repairing.

He heard her, but all the time he was watching a girl who played with the agent's children in a green patch near the station. She was a little blonde sprite who had come from Omaha to visit the agent's wife.

"Of course," he said.

"And you won't forget about the chopped feed?"

He gave her an intense glance. "How could I?"

"You'll see that Star gets well watered?"

"I'll attend to it."

"You'll have Alvy Marknam pull pursley for the young pigs?"

"I will."

"And—O, yes! If mother seems to feel another fit coming on you'll get her a bottle of Indian relief cure at the drug store."

He assured her he would. And all the time he was thinking what a wonderful way her hair curled about her temples—not Andulasia's. And how slim her waist was—not Andulasia's. And how pretty were the twinkling feet in the tan slippers—not Andulasia's. How fluffy and blue her gown was—and how deliciously merry her laugh rang out. And neither gown nor laugh was Andulasia's.

The train steamed in. Andulasia went away. Ira did not kiss her. She was relieved—and disappointed. The conductor and the train boy might have laughed. But then he should have cared enough to risk that.

When the train had pulled out and was well around the bend Harris, who had lingered on the platform, asked the agent to introduce him to his visitor. The agent did so.

Harris joined in the games of the children. He made himself clumsily delightful. Soda water was unknown in that particular small town, but Ira did the next best thing. He bought bananas and chocolate drops with a reckless liberality which would have made the absent Andulasia doubt his sanity could she have been aware of his behavior.

He came to the depot the next day, the next, and the next. The little visitor with the flax-flower eyes and yellow hair smiled divinely.

"The children," she confided to the agent's wife, "are having such a good time. It is all great fun."

She even thought it was great fun when she went buggy-riding with Mr. Harris.

"Take me past your farm," she commanded.

He grew red with ecstasy at the request. He explained apologetically many conditions of his property as they drove by.

"When I'm married," he announced with much determination, "I intend to live in town."

"I have heard," she ventured innocently, "that there is no house vacant in town."

"I shall build one," he declared.

Three weeks passed—four. Harris had several letters from Iowa. The contents of the letters were chiefly relative to hogs, and pasturage, and baled hay, and discounts. Ira did not actually dread Andulasia's return, but he would have preferred to postpone it indefinitely. To be sure they had considered the possibility of an engagement once, but he had never been really engaged to her. He never could be now. It was only right she should understand that. She was a sensible woman. She would understand that in such a matter a man had a right to please himself.

As for Alys, was there ever such an eye, such a hand, such a voice, such a foot, such a smile? To be sure he had once met Alys walking home from church with the lumberman. But then the lumberman was only young and good-looking. It was well known he was conducting the yard for an Eastern firm on a salary. To compare Vail to him—Harris—who was so "well fixed"! There could be no comparison.

One evening in late summer, when Ira was jogging into town, he settled mentally all the minor matters to his satisfaction. He decided to whom he would rent his farm, the kind of a house he would build in town, the direction his wedding journey would take, the brotherly letter he would leave for Andulasia, and the invitation he would send the lumberman to be present at his wedding.

"Poor devil!" he concluded commiseratingly, "it will be tough, but he will have to stand it."

He dismounted at the postoffice, which was also the general store and tin shop. There was a letter for him—a letter from Andulasia.

> Dear Ira: Things is all upset. Uncle Jake died a week ago. They can't find no will, and I'm tired waiting for dead men's stockins. Meet me night after tomorrer. Your
>
> Andulasia Stebbins.

Harris smiled curiously as he stuffed the letter in his pocket. He was thinking of the little Omaha girl. The next night Andulasia arrived. She was fatter than ever. Her Eton suit was crumpled. She wore a shirt waist. It was voluminous and not immaculate.

"Well, it's you, Ira. I'm clean beat. Put them things in the buggy while I get some sody and yeast up-town."

"Up-town" Miss Stebbins learned several things, chief of which was that Ira Harris had transferred his affections to Miss Alys Lane.

Half way home Andulasia said quietly: "I hear you reckon to marry Miss Lane."

Her composure, the loss of her expected fortune, the witchery of Alys, all gave Harris courage.

"I—I was figgerin' some on it," he avowed.

He drove Andulasia to her home, but she did not again broach the subject.

He went back to town that evening. He met Alys at an ice cream sociable. He gained grace of heart and proposed.

She laughed gently.

"I am honored, Mr. Harris, of course," she said. "But I always supposed you were engaged to Miss Stebbins. I am to marry Mr. Vail at Christmas."

The following evening, Ira, feeling exceedingly depressed, went to call on Andulasia. He found her talking with a brother farmer, a widower with three children. He asked to speak to her a moment alone.

"Fact is, Andulasia," he said, "it's you I want. I fancied for awhile I'd like that silly little thing. I must have been kind of hypternized. I'm sure now it's you I want."

Andulasia smiled—a peculiar smile.

"I've just promised to marry Mr. Muggs. He asked me last night before he found out what you know."

"What I know? Andulasia!"

"Yes. The news that come in on the noon train about the will bein' found, and me getting $7,000, and—"

"Andulasia!"

What a fine woman she was! Why had he never noticed that fact before?

"It's true!" she declared triumphantly.

"But," he fairly howled, "I've been meaning for fifteen years to marry you, Andulasia."

"Then, why didn't you?" inquired Andulasia.

He remembered some lines he had once read. It would be quite safe to repeat them as original, for Andulasia never read any thing.

"I feared my fate too much," he protested, striking his breast dramatically, "and my deserts was too small!"

He did not impress Andulasia. She turned scornfully away to where Mr. Muggs waited.

"Go back," she counseled, "to that yeller-haired girl at the depot."

He did go back, but not to the depot.

"Eh?" said the saloonkeeper. "We don't often see you, Mr. Harris."

"No. But I feel tonight as if I'd got a chill. I'll take some straight."

Sent to Syringa

According to eighteenth-century Swedish theologian Emanuel Swedenborg, who claimed to have communicated with angels, a spiritual kingdom exists between heaven and hell that human beings pass into after death and where direct mystical communication with friends and family can take place. Many Americans, eager to establish contact with the spirits of the dead, contacted mediums and clairvoyants, whose advertisements for spirit boards, séances, and rappings filled whole columns in the newspapers. Cleary saw the possibilities for spiritualism in her plots and the opportunity to poke fun at her neighbors' gullibility while promoting compassion and understanding between the sexes. This story was published in the Chicago Tribune *on 29 January 1899.*

"TRAIN'S LATE," announced Peter Pollock.

He said it apologetically. But, for the matter of that, he always spoke in a humble manner to Mrs. Pollock—to this Mrs. Pollock. He had been domineering enough with poor little, gentle, dove-eyed Syringa, who just two years ago had been laid to rest on the rocky slope of a desolate Nebraska prairie. The neighbors said she needed a rest if ever a body did. Even the preacher said something in his sermon about her having earned repose. People wondered how Peter had ever let her take time to die. Peter was a hard man and an unsympathetic husband, but there were those who decided he appreciated her when she was gone. He had asked the minister several questions as to reunion after death, and when he went down to Kansas City with a car of cattle it became rumored that he had visited a spiritualist, in the hope of establishing communication with the little creature he had worked to death, as he would never dream of working a valuable horse. But when, six months before the particular train he especially desired to catch happened to be late, he married Miss Regina Jenks, his fellow-farmers grinned and rubbed their beards and said he had met his match.

"Late!" echoed Mrs. Pollock in a deep voice. "How late?"

"I—I didn't think to ask, Regina."

His spouse bestowed a withering look upon him. She sat on the high spring seat of the farm wagon, holding the reins over a spruce pair of horses. He stood on the platform. She was looking down upon him, so she had the advantage. It is easier to wither with a look when one is higher than the person to be withered.

"Go and ask!" she commanded in the same deep tones.

He went as fast as his shambling feet, accustomed to plodding behind plow and harrow, would carry the spare frame, prematurely bent by labor and penurious self-denial. Mrs. Pollock, sitting stiff as a ramrod, glanced contemptuously after him. She was a big-boned, rigid, flat-chested woman, with a firm-hewn face of Indian outline. Indeed, many said confidently that she came rightfully by her bold hawk nose, straight, black hair, and striding walk. Her skirt was brown as a catalpa leaf in November, and the town drayman had been heard to remark that her gimlet eyes would "bore a hole in a feller's back."

Peter came back, followed by the agent, a friendly fellow, with his hat on the back of his head and a quid of tobacco in his mouth.

"Morning, Mrs. Pollock! Fine day. Train's four hours late. Washout at Red Cloud."

"What time does the Rock Island train leave?"

"In an hour and a half."

"Then we got time to drive over to Narky and catch that. Climb in, Peter."

Peter climbed in. She tooled the horses skillfully out of the depot inclosure and turned their heads west on a level road, which presently, turning south and crossing the railroad track, brought them to the base of the hill which marked the State line and divided Nebraska from Kansas.

It was a glorious midwinter day—the kind of a day one finds only on the plains. Around, the rolling prairie stretched, measureless, magnificent. The air was so clear one could see the wind, quivering like a fluttered ribbon along the bluffs many miles away. There were fields of tawny cornstalks and fields where winter wheat gleamed emerald green—a verdant prophecy. A pond where the wild ducks came to float was brimming and purple. And overhead was a sky of infinite beauty, blue and foam-fleeced as a sky of June.

"What," demanded Mrs. Pollock so suddenly that Peter jumped, "what did you sigh for?"

"Did I sigh?"

"You did. What's more, I often catch you a-sighing. And I don't like it. You used to be as jolly a man as there was in Thayer County. Now when you ain't sighing you're groaning. You make me think of our old windmill that keeps a-creaking and a-creaking. I've heard tell of that fool trick you done last time you was down in Kansas City." She turned in the seat and looked sternly down upon him. "I don't want none of that done now, Peter Pollock."

"What fool trick?" demanded Peter faintly.

"You know right well. Going to see them spiritualists to try to see Syringy. I ain't going to jaw about that, though I will say that a man with as much sense as a settin' hen has got ought to know better. But now it's me that's your lawful wife, and I won't have you philandering after another woman, dead or alive."

"Very well, Regina."

"You promise you won't go a-hunting her ghost around?"

"I promise."

"And you can let the live ones be, too. I don't hold that it helps a man's character to go to the places they call theayters, where shameless hussies plays, and sings, and dances worse'n that wicked girl did before King Herod. When you've seen about the mortgidge, and got me a dress pattern, and attended to them other little things I told you of, you come straight home. This here's Monday. You could make it to get back tomorrow night, but I'll look for you Wednesday at the latest.

You've got $10 over and above your ticket. You can tell me what you done with every quarter of it when you get back. There's no call for you to have your hair cut at a barber's. I can do it, and save the price. And you don't need to buy peanuts. It's awful wasteful to chaw up a quarter of a bushel of corn in five cents' worth of peanuts. You hear?"

"O, yes, I hear."

"And you'll let the women alone—both kinds? Say 'So help me.' "

"I will," panted Peter. "I will—so—so—so help me!"

It was Mrs. Pollock now who sighed—a sigh of satisfaction. Her grim mouth relaxed at the corners. As near an approach to a smile as she ever permitted herself flitted over her stern countenance. She held him out the reins.

"Here, you may drive a bit," she said.

Peter meekly and joyfully grasped the extended leathern lines. It was good to feel his grip on the leather, good to find the answering concession or resistance of the brutes ahead, good to be able to curb or urge as the fancy of the moment possessed him.

If Regina had the face of an Indian she also had the hearing.

"Train's coming," she declared. "I heerd it. It's a long way off—a good twelve mile it must be to that station west, but I heerd it. You'd better push them a bit. We don't want to miss two trains in one day."

Peter pushed them. A gratitude for the permission swept him like a vibrant joy. He loosened the reins. He leaned forward. He shouted at the animals.

"Git up, Gyp! Git up, Nannie!"

The road was high, level, hard as iron. The farm horses sped over it at a fine rate, the clumsy wagon rocking at their heels. In the distance, against the azure expanse, a faint trail of smoke became visible. Faster—and faster. Then they were rumbling up the street of the little, new, ugly Kansas town, and the express was sweeping down the glittering rails away to the west. Peter jumped down as they reached the platform.

"Don't trouble to git down, Regina. It ain't worth while."

"I never thought of doing so, Peter."

"Look out the team don't scare."

"Don't be afraid, Peter, when I got the lines."

"Well, good by, Regina."

"Good by. You'd better hustle for your ticket. And don't forget what I told you."

Peter wasn't likely to forget. He found himself in a serious and unpleasant situation as the train bore him eastward. He had told Regina a lie about the necessity of going to Kansas City. There was no particular need to attend to the mortgage just then. He had made out that his presence in the chief city of Missouri on a certain day was important and imperative. He had cherished a sneaking determination to have another "spirit" interview with Syringa, to tell her—but that was Peter's secret. Anyhow, when he found himself in a position from which he could not recede, and in which his mendacity had placed him, he had been pledged to abstain from the one enthralling enticement which was drawing him to a larger town than that of Bubble. Not that his wife's strictures upon the theater annoyed him. The footlights held no fascination for a man tortured by self-scorn and hounded by remorse. To be shut out from the audacious charms of sirens was no deprivation, but to have spooks also denied to him was a sad blow.

He pulled at his stubby beard and stared out of the window as the train flew along. He was a man of his word. He had never broken his word. He would not do it now. But how, apart from Regina's few commissions, should he spend his time in the big place to which he was speeding? And then the needless expense of this wholly unnecessary journey!

He spent the night in a cheap lodging-house opposite the depot. The next morning he went up into the town, executed Regina's commissions, and hung around the window wherein the clairvoyant's sign was displayed until it was time to catch his train. He went straight back to Bubble, and alighted in the clear yellow light of a wonderful January sunset—the only passenger from the East.

"Caught your train on the Rock Island, did you?" asked the agent, shouldering the mail bags. "Had a pleasant trip? That's good. Cheers one up to get away from home and see the sights once in a while. News? No; none I've heard unless about Mrs. Cicero Morrison. She's had a turn for the worse, and Eldridge has given her up. Says she can't live the night out. Your team ain't here, I see. Guess Mrs. Pollock wasn't looking for you so soon."

He gave the heavy sacks an extra hunch on his shoulder, and walked off, bending under their weight, up the main street of the town. Trembling and open-mouthed the prosperous farmer stood looking after him. His face was ashen with agitation. A queer expression, several expressions, indeed, of hope, daring, doubt, quivered like sheet lightning across his countenance.

Dying! Mrs. Morrison—commonly called Mrs. Cicero to distinguish her from her sister-in-law, Mrs. Sam Morrison—was dying. Why not send by her a message to Syringa? He had heard of such things being done. He felt confident the message would be delivered. He felt jubilant that he had not delayed in Kansas City. Some merciful power must have impelled him to hasten homeward before it would be too late to deliver to the living a message for the dead. And Regina had not expected him, or she would either have come herself or have sent the chore boy with the team. It was all arranged beautifully. He felt he could not have settled matters more satisfactorily himself than some remote and beneficent power had done.

"I'll hire a livery rig, by gum!" he decided, in the first flush of enthusiasm. "I'll drive out there—no, that wouldn't do. They'd wonder, and ask questions, and Regina might get word of it. No, I'll walk out. I'll go in real careless like, and say Mrs. Pollock had me come over to inquire for Mrs. Cicero. I'll fling in something easy and natural about Mrs. Pollock and Mrs. Cicero having been such friends. They was, I believe, before Mrs. Cicero's jelly cake took the prize over Regina's at the county fair. Well, here goes!"

He started out, walking up the main street, but at the first turning he branched off to the left, and followed the road that ran east beside the tracks. He walked rapidly, if somewhat stealthily. Pleasurable excitement thrilled him. Occasionally he stopped to glance back over his shoulder. But the apprehension which now and then seemed to still his heart in his bosom was each time succeeded by a stronger sensation of satisfaction—of mysterious and spiritual exaltation which the object of his pilgrimage engendered.

About a mile from town he turned north, and, crossing a little bridge, struck out along a road bordered with huddled brown trees—poor, naked things shivering against a steel gray sky. In the distance ahead he could see a pair of tawny horses approaching.

"It's Eldridge's buggy!" he exclaimed. "She ain't dead yet, thank God!"

He hastened his steps, but was not in time to intercept the physician, who shortly after came out of the house, got into the vehicle, and, turning the team, drove away in an opposite direction from that in which Pollock approached. It was a somber old frame building, set back from the road in a bare and treeless yard. Cicero Morrison, in his shirt sleeves, and carrying a pail in each hand, was turning towards the rear of the house as Peter came to the door.

"I believe I'll go in a bit," said Peter, "if you don't mind."

"O, I don't mind," returned Cicero. "Go on in."

Peter was about to knock when the door was opened and Mrs. Sam Morrison appeared. She was a toothless woman, clad in a faded blue cotton gown, with a bow of soiled pink ribbon at her scraggy throat.

"I don't like to be presumin', Mrs. Sam," said Peter, timidly, "but I've a reason for wanting to see her alone a few minutes if I might make so bold."

"To be sure—why not?" said Mrs. Sam. "You naturally would just coming back from a journey and all that. She's in there to the right. The other folks are eating supper in the kitchen. I wouldn't talk long, though, if I was you. She's pretty well tuckered out."

"I won't," Peter assured her gratefully.

He tiptoed forward, his old felt hat clutched in his nervous fingers, his heart beating hard. He turned the handle of the door indicated. From a room in the back of the house came the rattle of crockery, the clatter of knives and forks, and sound of voices. The blinds were down in the apartment Peter entered. A lamp, its feeble glare banished from the bed by a coat hung on the back of a rocker, stood on a table in a corner of the room. The bedclothes outlined a motionless form. The face of the woman in the bed was buried in the pillows. A hand on the coverlet and a tangle of dark hair were all Peter could see as he sat softly down beside the bed.

"Mrs. Cicero," he began in an excited whisper, "you don't need to answer back. Just move your hand if you understand and mean 'yes.' I know how weak you are. I won't stay but a minute. I felt I couldn't let you go without asking if you'd take a message where you're going—a message from me to Syringy?"

Then there was silence in the room.

"I'd take it a great favor," went on Peter, tremulously, "if you'd only say when you meet her: 'Syringy, Peter come to see me before I left my mortal sphere, and he wanted I should say to you that he loved you, dear, all the ten year he drove you so hard, though he never let on. Now, he wishes he had. He wishes you'd got the stuff gown you wanted to wear to Mary Luken's wedding. He wishes he'd got a girl to help you during the thrashing. He wishes he'd done more of the milkin' himself, and had let you have the butter and egg money. He's a-thinkin' all the time of how sweet you was when you married him, and come out from the millinery shop on to the farm. He remembers how white your hands was, and what pretty clothes you had—ribbons, and such like. And he keeps remembering, too, how you got to look so thin, and sad, and stooped—and O, how awful hard-worked your pretty hands looked when they was crossed on your breast in the coffin. And—and,' " his voice broke, and he gulped, " 'he'd like you to know that he's sorry—sorry—and that, if he could only live them ten year over again things would be different—O, so different!' "

Again there was silence in the room.

"Do you understand all I said, Mrs. Cicero? If you do, move your hand."

The fingers on the coverlet moved restlessly.

"That's right. I'm that thankful to you, Mrs. Cicero. I must hurry and get through before the folks come. You'll tell her that, I know, and if she seems hurt about my—about my gettin' married again, why just tell her she can't feel any worse about that than I do."

The hand on the bed opened and shut.

"Tell her I wanted some one to look after the young calves, and the milk, and all the rest of it. I didn't think I was gettin' one that wouldn't let me call my soul my own, but that's just what happened to me—and served me right for an old fool. Tell her I caught a Tartar, Mrs. Cicero—a brown-skinned old maid that—did you speak, Mrs. Cicero?

No? I thought you said something. Well I'm gettin' my punishment good and hard. Tell her an angel out of heaven couldn't live peaceable with the kind of a wife I got now, nagging, cantankerous, small as ground spice, and bitter as green gooseberries."

The hand on the bed opened and clutched convulsively. Peter Pollock rose with a sigh of relief.

"You're awful good to take these messages for me, Mrs. Cicero. Tell her, too, that I'm goin' to sell a lot of hogs that I got in partnership with Dick Howard. She—that pison ivy I married—don't know a thing about them, and she'll never guess where the money come from when the finest tumestone that ever was planted in the Bubble Cemetery goes up over Syringy's grave. I'm going now, and my heart's best thanks to you. I wish I could do something in return. There ain't much I can do. I'll go to your funeral in a carriage, Mrs. Cicero, and I'll send in some of the cuttin's off'n my lilac bushes to be set out in your lot. Good-by, and my dear love to Syringy."

He met no one as he stole out, escaped from the vicinity of the house, and started to walk home. He had to pass through town to reach his farm in the north. As he walked up the main street he noticed that the door of the furniture shop was open and that the drayman and Mr. McLelland, the undertaker, were lifting a pine box into a wagon.

"Hallo," he said. "Who's dead?"

Mr. McLelland, hobbling around as briskly as his stiff leg would permit, turned his shrewd, white-bearded old face over his shoulder.

"Mrs. Morrison—Mrs. Cicero."

"Wh—at!" gasped Peter.

He fell back, staring wildly at the two men.

"Yes, she died this afternoon. Doc Eldridge didn't know, and he went out there. She was dead when he got there, so Eldridge come back. Sam Morrison has been here and made all arrangements. He did pick out a pretty casket, if I do say it—quite as fashionable a one as has ever been brought to Bubble."

Peter stood riveted to the sidewalk.

"What's the matter with you, Pollock?" the drayman questioned. "Ain't you feeling good?"

"She—she moved her hand!" blurted Peter.

McLelland turned from his congenial task to peer at the speaker. The drayman grinned as he lifted the hitching weight into the wagon. "Aw, he's been to Kansas City, and he's come home rocky. They allus git full when they go there."

"But he's a prohibitionist!" protested the undertaker in a shocked undertone.

"Prohibitionist nawthin'! They all git full when they go to Kansas City, I tell you. Hi, there, you Jenny!"

Peter Pollock made his way home—how, he never precisely knew. He remembered afterward thinking that the road was rough and he staggered several times, as if indeed there had been some foundation for the suspicion of the drayman. All he could think of was the terribly quiet figure on the bed—all he could see was the hand that had moved, not once but several times. There was no light in his house when he reached it. He reached the kitchen and lit a lamp. Evidently the chore boy had got his own supper, and afterward gone to bed. Pollock sat down in the cold, bare room, and leaned his head on his hands. A house wasn't of much account without a woman in it, and Regina was as clean and thorough and capable a housekeeper as there was in the whole State of Nebraska, if she had her faults.

The feeling of light-headedness wore off after awhile, and despite his uncanny experience Mr. Pollock became aware that he was hungry. If Regina were there she would fry him a slice of ham and make him a cup of coffee that would cause him to feel like giving a whole dollar to the collection for the missionary society. Syringa was sweet—sweet, but there never was a better cook than Regina. It was 9 o'clock—it was 10 o'clock. The hungrier Mr. Pollock grew the more he appreciated the domestic virtues and culinary acquirements of his wife. By the way, where was his wife? Where was Regina?

At 11 buggy wheels stopped before the door. Peter heard voices without. Then there were steps around the side of the house, and Regina came into the kitchen.

"Where have you been?" asked Peter.

She was taking off her bonnet and cloak. She looked broken and weak—as if she had been ill a long time.

"They sent for me when Mary Morrison was taken bad yesterday. I had just got back from seeing you off. I went over there. Mrs. Giles and Carl said they would see to things about here. I didn't like to come back until it was all over. Mrs. Sam is no account to manage, you know, and there wasn't anybody else to get the heft of things. I'd come away quick as she died this afternoon if it wasn't that one of my bad headaches come on. I lay down a while to see if I could rest it off. Mrs. Sam said she wouldn't let any one in to bother me, but I said if you should get home from Kansas City tonight, and come after me, you'd be anxious, and she'd better let you in a spell."

She took the front lids off the stove, shook down the ashes, and began piling in cobs from a bushel basket. Peter sat motionless watching her. His face was gray and strained in the lamplight, and a strange look was deepening upon it—a look of mystification, that was merging in one of alarm—of horror. This horror was only held in check by the calmness of the woman who was filling the kettle, and who now swung it on the blazing fire.

"I'll make you a cup of coffee, Peter," she remarked. "You look clean beat."

He did not reply. The fearful fascination of his conjecture was still strong upon him. She tied on an apron and ground the coffee, all the time maintaining a silence that was meekly stubborn. She did not speak while she cut and fried the ham of which he had dreamed, poached a couple of eggs, and sliced the light, home-made loaf, nor even when she poured the rich cream into his coffee, and set the delicious meal before him. He ate and drank. Refreshed and stimulated he looked pleadingly up at the second Mrs. Pollock.

"Regina," he asked, "was you layin' down in the room to the right?"

"I was."

"And—and was it you I gave the—the—" He faltered, broke down.

"The message to Syringy. Yes—it was."

Then there wasn't a sound in the kitchen save the ticking of the clock and the purring of the cat behind the stove.

"Regina," he faltered at length.

"Well?" The voice was hard, and his heart sank. But the coffee had put pluck into him. So he said resolutely, "I'm dreadful sorry."

The second Mrs. Pollock wheeled around, and stood leaning against the kitchen table, both hands gripping it behind her back.

"So am I. Syringy was as sweet a little soul as ever drew breath. She was the only body that come and nursed me when I had diphtheria, and there wasn't another person would come nigh me. I seen how you misused her, and I was sorry for her—like other folks was. I married you when you asked because I wanted a home of my own, and I allus had a thought that I'd like to have 'Mrs.' cut on my gravestone. It looks more respectful, and as if some man had wanted you. But I hadn't got the sorrow for that poor little thing out of my heart, and, not having any particular love for you, I made up my mind I'd see who was the tyrant this time. I was. I don't think I was as bad as you made out this afternoon, but a body can't see theirself, so maybe I was. And if I was, I'm sorry for it. If you'll call it quits, and begin again, I'll be as good a wife to you as I know how to be, Peter Pollock."

He rose, touched, changed, entreating. In his hard old eyes was "something that felt like tears."

"O, I will, Regina, I will! You call it quits, too, and I will!"

So it is safe to infer that the message sent to Syringa was never delivered in the celestial world.

Teddie

Perhaps the last poem that Cleary wrote, "Teddie" was to be a gift to her youngest son. When she ascended the steps of her apartment for the last time, hand in hand with Teddie, she may have wanted to show him what she had just written for him. It was fitting that her last poem revealed not only her enduring love for her children, but her all-encompassing love of life. The text that was reprinted in Poems, *published by her children, differs from the version published in the* Record Herald *in her death notice. The newspaper did not print the third through seventh stanzas, and the book version did not include stanza eight. The following includes all of the stanzas.*

I love the world with all its brave endeavor,
  I love its winds and floods, and suns and sands,
But oh, I love—most deeply and forever—
  The clinging touch of timid little hands.

I love the dawn all pearl and primrose glowing,
  Or that which covert comes—all wet and grey;
Or the blue gleam through frosty windows showing,
  That ushers in the day.

All these I love as I love mountain places,
  And sloping sea sands golden in the sun,
As I love too the old familiar faces,
  And great deeds that are done.

And as I love the rank, dry prairie grasses,
  And as I love the crumbling crimson rose,
And leaping streamlets in the forest passes,
  And music crashing to supreme repose.

I love all flowers in fragrant beauty blowing,
  Laces like sea foam, delicate and white,
The splintered splendor of rare jewels glowing
  To opalescent light.

And I love pictures, statues, books eternal,
  Slaves and conquerors of we who wait,
Content to ask their aid—divine—fraternal—
  Within their city's gate!

I love the autumn wind that comes—one only
  Remonstrant vagrant at my window pane,
And I do love dull reaches of the lonely
  Flagellant wind and rain!

And love of man—the love that's worth the winning,
  (Not always worth the keeping, sad to say)—
Because of all the sorrow and the sinning,
  Like his—who did betray!

But oh, above all love for man or story,
  Above all friendship for the human race,
Above all Nature's passionate great glory,
  Give me the sunlight of a little face!

Give me the head against my shoulder lying,
  The feel of one soft body close to mine,
The strength to face the world for him—defying
  All power—the rest be thine!

But ever still afar the laddie lingers,
  And ever still alone do I repine,
While longing for the touch of trusting fingers,
  And a little loving hand in mine!

Bibliography

I compiled the following Cleary bibliography from clippings of stories in the family scrapbooks as well as other stories I discovered while attempting to fill in sketchy publication data and verify it. Because of the myriad of newspapers and magazines in which Cleary published, often with no byline, and the lack of indexes in most of the publications, this list is incomplete and should be considered as ongoing.

NOVELS

The Lady of Lynhurst [Mrs. Kate Chrystal, pseud.]. Street & Smith's Leading Novel Series, no. 8. Chicago: Street & Smith, 1884.

Vella Vernel, or An Amazing Marriage [Mrs. Sumner Hayden, pseud.]. Street & Smith's Select Series, no. 3. Chicago: Street & Smith, 1887.

Like a Gallant Lady. Chicago: Way & Williams, 1897, 1900.

COLLECTED WORKS

Poems, by Margaret Kelly McPhelim, Kate McPhelim Cleary, and Edward Joseph McPhelim. N.p.: Published by Vera Valentine Cleary, Gerald Vernon Cleary, and James Mansfield Cleary, May 1922.

The Nebraska of Kate McPhelim Cleary. Ed. James M. Cleary. Lake Bluff IL: United Educators, 1958.

CRITICAL REVIEWS

On *Like a Gallant Lady*

New York Post Exchange, 31 August 1897.
Chicago Tribune, 11 November 1897, 8.
Westfield (Mass.) Times and Newsletter, 13 November 1897.
Nebraska State Journal, 22 November 1897.
Omaha World-Herald, 28 November 1897.
Cincinnati Tribune, 5 December 1897.

Seattle Post Intelligencer, 5 December 1897.
Kansas City Star, 8 December 1897.
Omaha Bee, 8 December 1897.
Baltimore Sun, 10 December 1897.
Hartford (Conn.) Post, 29 December 1897.
Rochester (N.Y.) Post Express, 15 January 1898.
Superior (Nebr.) Daily Journal, 26 February 1898.
Land of Sunshine (Calif.), February 1898.
Boston Herald, 8 March 1898.
Munsey's Magazine, March 1898.
Baltimore American, 23 April 1898.

On "The Stepmother"

Omaha World-Herald, 28 August 1901.
Chicago Times, 29 August 1901.
Chicago Tribune, 29 August 1901.
Interlocutor, 31 August 1901.
Rochester (N.Y.) Post Express, 31 August 1901.
San Francisco Chronicle, 1 September 1901.

On "The Mission of Kitty Malone"

Westfield (Mass.) Times and Newsletter, 13 November 1901.
Boston Pilot, 23 November 1901.

ARTICLES ON KATE M. CLEARY

A Woman of the Century, ed. Frances E. Willard and Mary A. Livermore, pp. 180–81. Buffalo: Charles Wells Moulton, 1892. Reprinted in *Portraits and Biographies of Prominent American Women* (1901).
"A Bohemian in Nebraska," by Elia Peattie, *Omaha World-Herald,* 23 April 1893, 7. Reprinted in *Nebraska of KMC,* 13–15.
"Kate McPhelim Cleary," by Charles Wells Moulton, *Magazine of Poetry: A Quarterly Review* 5, no. 2 (April 1893): 144–46.
"Woman and Her Ways." *Chicago Evening Post,* 8 November 1897.
"Women Who Have Humor." *Chicago Chronicle,* 21 July 1898.
"Writers of the Day." *Writer* 14, no. 10 (October 1901): 154.
Poets of Ireland: A Biographical and Bibliographical Dictionary of

Irish Writers of English Verse, by D. J. O'Donoghue, p. 70.
    London: Henry Froude Oxford University Press, 1912.
"The Literary Dimension," by Charles Fanning. In *The Irish in
    Chicago,* by Lawrence J. McCaffrey, Ellen Skerrett, Michael
    F. Funchion, and Charles Fanning, pp. 98, 112–16. Urbana:
    Univ. of Illinois Press, 1987.

STORIES, ARTICLES, AND SELECTED POEMS

1885

"Her Diamond Earrings." *Chicago Tribune,* 9 May 1885, 16.

1887

"A Nebraska Hired Girl." *Chicago Tribune,* 27 December 1887,
    6. Reprinted with the title "Hired Girls" in *Nebraska of
    KMC,* 27–36.
"Fresh Laid Eggs." Unpublished ms., ca. 1887, Cleary family
    collection.

1888

"Mrs. Cleary's Visitors: The Neighborly and Entertaining Ladies
    of Bubble, Neb." *Chicago Tribune,* 22 January 1888, 17–18.
    Reprinted with the title "Visitors" in *Nebraska of KMC,* 19–
    26.
"All a-Blowing" (poem). *St. Nicholas,* September 1888, 814.
    Reprinted in *Poems,* 90–91, and *Nebraska of KMC,* 149.
"A Rhyme for Little Folks" (poem). *St. Nicholas,* October 1888,
    949. Reprinted in *Poems,* 96–97.
"Drifting Down" (poem). *St. Nicholas,* ca. 1888. Reprinted in
    Poems, 123–25, and *Nebraska of KMC,* 13.
"Out on the Shelf" (poem). *St. Nicholas,* ca. 1888.

1889

"How Billy Blundered" (poem). *Fireside,* 11 May 1889.
Untitled Christmas story. *Chicago Tribune,* 22 December 1889,
    25.
"At the Play: To E. J. M." (poem). *Chicago Tribune,* 29
    December 1889, 25. Reprinted in *Poems,* 112–13.

1890

"Peter's Patriotism: How the Lamps Came Pretty Near Fooling the Little Man." *Chicago Tribune*, 4 July 1890, 25.
"A Mutual Misunderstanding." *Detroit Free Press*, 2 February 1890. Reprinted in *Chicago Daily News*, 26 October 1903, 9.
"A Prairie Prelude" (poem). *St. Nicholas*, April 1890, 537. Reprinted in *Poems*, 46–47, and *Nebraska of KMC*, 226.
"Caught by a Tartar." *New York Ledger*, 17 May 1890.
"Rocking the Baby to Sleep" (poem). *Good Housekeeping*, 24 May 1890, 55. Reprinted in *Poems*, 101.
"What Flossie Found Out." Clipping, ca. 1890, Cleary family scrapbooks.
"The Exposition Picture." Clipping, ca. 1890, Cleary family scrapbooks.
"Why Bessie Barrett Was So Happy." Clipping, ca. 1890, Cleary family scrapbooks.
"Good Times Coming" (poem). Unpublished ms., 1890, Cleary family collection.

1891

"Angel Food with Variations, a Foundation Recipe on Which a Half Dozen Other Recipes Are Builded." *Good Housekeeping*, July 1891, 26–28.
"Lost in a Cornfield." *St. Nicholas*, September 1891, 812–17. Reprinted in *Nebraska of KMC*, 50–57.
"Ten Tongues: And How to Cure Them, How to Cook Them, and How to Serve Them." *Good Housekeeping*, November 1891, 223–25.
"The Mildewed Pocketbook." *Puck*, 30 December 1891, 323.

1892

"Cooking Quail: With Fifteen Tested and Reliable Recipes." *Good Housekeeping*, February 1892, 63–65. Reprinted in *Nebraska of KMC*, 195–202, and *Nebraska Pioneer Cookbook*, comp. Kay Graber (Lincoln: Univ. of Nebraska Press, 1974), 130–38.
"A Bunch of Bananas, and Fifteen Ways of Serving Them."

Good Housekeeping, September 1892, 107–9. Reprinted in
   Nebraska of KMC, 203–12.
"A Trip Postponed." *Puck,* 5 October 1892, 102.
"The Storeroom: Its Convenience and Contents." *Good
   Housekeeping,* November 1892, 229–30. Reprinted in
   Nebraska of KMC, 213–17.
"On Thanksgiving Night" (poem). *Philadelphia Star,* 3
   December 1892.
"Identity" (poem). *Puck,* 7 December 1892, 244.
"Cleveland Once Again" (poem). Clipping, 1892, Cleary family
   scrapbooks.

1893

"Fall of an Apostle." *Chicago Tribune,* 14 January 1893, 40.
"Feet of Clay." *Belford's Monthly,* April 1893, 720–32. Reprinted
   in *Nebraska of KMC,* 59–68.
"The Fatal Test" (poem). *World's Fair Puck,* 15 May 1893, 45.
"Incognito" (poem). *World's Fair Puck,* 29 May 1893, 39.
"You Take Your Choice" (poem). *World's Fair Puck,* 29 May
   1893, 5.
"For the Housewife: Trifles That Make Perfection: Parts I and
   II." *Housewife,* June and July 1893.
"A Seasonable Bluff." *World's Fair Puck,* 10 June 1893, 9.
"The Sweet Girl Graduate" (poem). *Chicago Tribune,* 10 June
   1893, 10.
"The Pharisee Cry" (poem). *World's Fair Puck,* 12 June 1893,
   62.
"Kissick's Back" (poem). *Hubbell Times,* August 1893.
"The Tyrant Man" (poem). *World's Fair Puck,* 25 September
   1893, 250.
"Blavatsky Verified." *Puck,* 18 October 1893, 138.
"A Warning to Novelists" (poem). *Puck,* 13 December 1893, 294.
"The Bride's Prelude" (poem). *Puck,* 1893.
"Nebraska" (poem). Clipping, 1893, Cleary family scrapbooks.
"Told of a Prairie Schooner." *Chicago Tribune,* ca. 1893.
"World's Fair Visitors, or Steva Silverthorne's Abduction: A Story
   of the Columbian Exposition at Chicago." Clipping, ca.
   1893, Cleary family scrapbooks.

1894

"A Lesson in Spelling" (poem). *Chicago Tribune*, 14 June 1894,
34.

"The Little Rift" (poem). *Puck*, 27 June 1894, 294.

"When Mother's Cookin' Fer Company" (poem). *Puck*, 13 July
1894, 272. Reprinted in *Poems*, 102–3.

"He'd Been Looking at Diana" (poem). *Judge*, 1894.

"Heard Every Evening at Bedtime." *Chicago Tribune*, ca. 1894.

"A Lesson in Finance." *Puck*, ca. 1894.

"Romance of the Alley L." *Chicago Tribune*, ca. 1894.

1895

"How Many" (poem). *Puck*, 9 January 1895, 356.

"Some Prairie Pictures: 'The Camper,' 'A Man Out of Work,' and
'A Race Horse to the Plow.'" *Chicago Tribune*, 28 April
1895, 46.

"For the Rest of Her Life." *Chicago Tribune*, 2 June 1895, 41.
Reprinted in *Nebraska of KMC*, 150–63.

"Some Prairie Sketches: 'The Judas Tree,' 'A Western Wooing,'
and 'A Dust Storm in Nebraska.'" *Chicago Tribune*, 16 June
1895, 41. (The third sketch was reprinted with the title
"Dust Storm" in *Nebraska of KMC*, 15.)

"A Prairie Sketch." *Chicago Tribune*, 7 July 1895, 39.

"The New Man." *Puck*, 10 July 1895, 24.

"On the Hubbell Hill." *Chicago Tribune*, 4 August 1895, 34.
Reprinted as "Hubbell Hill" in *Nebraska of KMC*, 45–48.

"A Call on the Bride." *Chicago Tribune*, 11 August 1895, 39.
Reprinted in *Nebraska of KMC*, 37–40.

"A Bicycle Conundrum" (poem). *Puck*, 28 August 1895, 22.

"Leslie's Lucky Sixpence." *Youth's Companion*, 3 October 1895,
464–65.

"In Sympathy with Lions" (poem). *Puck*, 4 December 1895, 265.

"Then a Kiss before We Part: Waltz Song" (sheet music). New
York: John Church, 1895.

"About Cradles and Coffins." Unpublished ms., ca. 1895, Cleary
family collection.

"An Incident of the Prairie: A Board, a Saw, a Few Nails, and a
Mother's Hot Tears." *Chicago Tribune*, ca. 1895. Reprinted
with the title "On the Way West" in *Nebraska of KMC*, 49.

"The Lower Part: Being One of 'The Short and Simple Annals of the Poor.'" Unpublished ms., ca. 1895, Cleary family collection.

"A November Day in Nebraska: An Impressionist Picture in the Country Where Leaves Have Turned." *Chicago Tribune,* ca. 1895. Reprinted as "November Day" in *Nebraska of KMC,* 14.

1896

"Around the Bonfire" (poem). *Youth's Companion,* 2 January 1896, 10.

"A Pastel Portrait." *Chicago Tribune,* 27 April 1896, 3.

"Class of '96 to '98" (poem). *Hubbell Times,* 5 June 1896.

"Shouting for McKinley" (poem). 21 November 1896.

1897

"A Terrible Temper." *Chicago Tribune,* 20 April 1897, 12.

"Gems by a Dead Bard: Verse of Edward J. McPhelim Compiled by His Sister." *Chicago Tribune,* 27 June 1897.

"Golden Wedding Anniversary at Hubbell." *Hebron Journal,* 27 August 1897, 1.

"Ma and Mag" (poem). *Puck,* 27 October 1897, 14. Reprinted in *Poems,* 97–101, and *Nebraska of KMC,* 57–58.

"Like a Blooming Chump, or Snatched from the Jaws of the Sheriff." Clipping, 9 December 1897, Cleary family scrapbooks.

"To Nebraska," preface poem in *Like a Gallant Lady.* Chicago: Way & Williams, 1897.

"McPhelim's Poem on a Queen's Wooing." *Chicago Tribune,* ca. 1897.

"Phrases Devised by Irish Wit." *Chicago Tribune,* ca. 1897.

"Reveal a Poet's Soul: More Verse by Edward J. McPhelim Compiled by His Sister." *Chicago Tribune,* ca. 1897.

1898

"An Extraordinary Exception" (poem). *Puck,* 2 March 1898.

"War—with the Nero of Nations." *Nebraska State Journal,* 1 April 1898, 4.

"A Lady's View of War." *Havelock Times,* 2 April 1898.

"Burt's Men in the Van." *Chicago Tribune,* 9 April 1898, 10.

"Memorial Day—1861–1898" (poem). *Nebraska State Journal,* 30 May 1898, 1. Reprinted in the *Hubbell Times,* 3 June 1898, 1.

"Soldiers' Day in Kansas: Strewing Flowers on the Graves of the Nation's Heroes." Clipping, ca. May 1898, Cleary family scrapbooks.

"At the Omaha Fair." *Chicago Tribune,* 4 September 1898, 42. Reprinted in *Nebraska of KMC,* 41–43.

"Nothing Left but the Tale" (poem). *Puck,* 14 September 1898.

"Dedicating a Book." *Chicago Tribune,* 11 December 1898, 42.

"One of McPhelim's Gems." *Chicago Tribune,* 11 December 1898, 30.

"Lenten Regulations" (poem). *Chicago Tribune,* ca. 1898.

"Mrs. Brady's View" (poem). *Puck,* ca. 1898.

"St. Catherine's" (poem). *Puck,* ca. 1898.

"When the Sheep Come Marching Home" (poem). Unpublished ms., 1898, Cleary family collection.

1899

"Some Gems of Poetry." *Chicago Tribune,* 15 January 1899, 40.

"Sent to Syringa." *Chicago Tribune,* 29 January 1899, 40. Reprinted in *Nebraska of KMC,* 124–34.

" 'Tramp,' the True Story of a Brave Dog." *Chicago Tribune,* 5 February 1899, 39.

"A Vicarious Valentine." *Chicago Tribune,* 12 February 1899, 42.

"Jim Peterson's Pension." *Chicago Tribune,* 19 February 1899, 46. Reprinted in *Nebraska of KMC,* 84–96.

"Why We Didn't Hear Nilsson." *Chicago Tribune,* 19 March 1899, sec. V, p. 2.

"The Rebellion of Mrs. McLelland." *Chicago Tribune,* 2 April 1899, sec. V, p. 2. Reprinted in *Nebraska of KMC,* 173–86.

"An Ornament to Society." *Chicago Tribune,* 9 April 1899, sec. VI, p. 2. Reprinted in *Nebraska of KMC,* 97–109.

"The Story of Frances Dever." *Chicago Tribune,* 23 April 1899, sec. VI, p. 2.

"The Jilting of Jane Ann." *Chicago Tribune,* 7 May 1899, 53.

"The Road That Didn't Lead Anywhere." *Chicago Tribune,* 14 May 1899, 42. Reprinted in *Nebraska of KMC,* 135.

"Two Decoration Days and the Time Between." *Chicago Tribune*, 28 May 1899, 50.

"Old Man Kennedy's Daughter: A Story of the Last Fourth of July." *Chicago Tribune*, 2 July 1899, 43.

"The Agent at Magnolia." *Chicago Tribune*, 6 August 1899, 30.

"Some Deaths in Fiction." Clipping, 12 September 1899, Cleary family scrapbooks.

"How Jimmy Ran Away." *Chicago Tribune*, 5 November 1899, 46. Reprinted in *Nebraska of KMC*, 69–83.

Untitled Nebraska Christmas story. *Chicago Tribune*, 22 December 1899, 25.

"A Nebraska Idyl: The Story of a Christmas Conspiracy in the Town of Bubble." *Chicago Tribune*, 25 December 1899, 9.

"Getting Shet of Mary Mason: A Tale of Western Social Life." Ca. 1899. Reprinted in *Nebraska of KMC*, 187–92.

"His Onliest One." Ca. 1899. Reprinted in *Nebraska of KMC*, 110–23.

"The Course of True Love." Unpublished ms., ca. 1899, Cleary family collection.

"A Genuine Refellini." Unpublished ms., ca. 1899, Cleary family collection.

"Journeys End in Lovers Meeting." Unpublished ms., ca. 1899, Cleary family collection.

"The Man of the Hour." Unpublished ms., ca. 1899, Cleary family collection.

"The Story That Was Never Written." Unpublished ms., ca. 1899, Cleary family collection.

1900

"The Boy's Mother." *Chicago Tribune*, 8 February 1900, 7.

"Sister Margaret." *Chicago Tribune*, 9 February 1900, 7.

"A Penitent Pianist." *Chicago Tribune*, 24 March 1900, 16.

"Lenten Lilies." *Chicago Tribune*, 27 March 1900, 16.

"A Lenten Costume." *Chicago Tribune*, 31 March 1900, 16.

"This House for Rent." *Chicago Tribune*, 14 April 1900, 16.

"T. J. Smith." *Chicago Tribune*, 6 May 1900, 63.

"What the Winner's Hand Threw By." *Chicago Tribune*, 13 May 1900, 43.

"The End of the Rainbow." *Chicago Tribune*, 20 May 1900, 55.

"The Wisdom of a Woman." *Chicago Tribune,* 27 May 1900, 55.
"A Miniature." *Chicago Tribune,* 9 June 1900, 16.
"Mrs. Basset's Boarders." *Chicago Tribune,* 16 June 1900, 16.
"The Attractions of Gravity." *Chicago Tribune,* 23 June 1900, 16.
"The Romance of a Ring." *Chicago Tribune,* 27 June 1900, 16.
"The Truth about Tobias." *Chicago Tribune,* 28 June 1900, 16.
"The Portrait." *Chicago Tribune,* 1 July 1900, 34.
"At the Eleventh Hour." *Chicago Tribune,* 9 July 1900, 7.
"Married Eyes How Sweet They Be." *Chicago Tribune,* 14 July 1900, 16.
"A Race with Death." *Chicago Tribune,* 15 July 1900, 36.
"An Antique Treasure." *Chicago Tribune,* 16 July 1900, 7.
"The Absence of Agatha." *Chicago Tribune,* 28 July 1900, 10.
"A Precious Trust." *Chicago Tribune,* 1 August 1900, 10.
"The Jewels of Jane Jardine." *Chicago Tribune,* 10 August 1900, 7.
"Mrs. Ryder's Ruse." *Chicago Tribune,* 11 August 1900, 16.
"A Dollar of Destiny." *Chicago Tribune,* 18 August 1900, 16.
"A Country Cousin." *Chicago Tribune,* 25 August 1900, 16.
"The Tale of a Tinker." *Chicago Tribune,* 29 August 1900, 13.
"Incognito." *Chicago Tribune,* 8 September 1900, 16.
"The Man from Manila." *Chicago Tribune,* 18 September 1900, 16.
"The Portrait of Patricia." *Chicago Tribune,* 29 September 1900, 16.
"An Appropriate Wedding Gift." *Chicago Daily News,* 9 October 1900, 8.
"Frank's Football Fatality." *Chicago Tribune,* 10 October 1900, 16.
"An Unfair Advantage." *Chicago Tribune,* 11 October 1900, 7.
"McShane's Mother." *Chicago Tribune,* 13 October 1900, 16.
"The Winsome Widow." *Chicago Tribune,* 15 October 1900, 7.
"Two People and a Parrot." *Chicago Tribune,* 19 October 1900, 7.
"The Lovers of Lila." *Chicago Tribune,* 20 October 1900, 16.
"Edged Tools." *Chicago Tribune,* 23 October 1900, 7. Reprinted in the *Chicago Daily News,* 9 September 1903, 10.
"Dorothy's Dinner Dress." *Chicago Tribune,* 25 October 1900, 10.
"Chili Sauce." *Chicago Tribune,* 27 October 1900, 16.

"His Last Love." *Chicago Tribune,* 16 December 1900, 66.

"Cupid Cornered." *Chicago Daily News,* 21 December 1900, 18.

"How Blessings Brighten." Clipping, 1900, Cleary family scrapbooks.

"Love's Blunders." Clipping, 1900, Cleary family scrapbooks.

"A Pair of Plotters." Clipping, 1900, Cleary family scrapbooks.

"The Price Paulina Paid." Clipping, 1900, Cleary family scrapbooks.

"An Unpardonable Interruption." Clipping, 1900, Cleary family scrapbooks.

1901

"The Value of a Valentine." *Chicago Daily News,* 13 February 1901.

"The Feud of the Fergusons." *New York World,* 15 February 1901.

"The Mother of Men." *Boston Post,* 3 March 1901.

"A Summer Storm." *Chicago Tribune,* 18 March 1901, 7.

"The Predicament of Polly." *Chicago Tribune,* 19 March 1901, 7.

"The Story of Sedalia." *Chicago Tribune,* 22 March 1901, 7.

"The Siren of the Studio." *Chicago Tribune,* 25 March 1901, 7.

"A Batch of Biscuits." *Chicago Tribune,* 26 March 1901, 7.

"A Silent Service." *Chicago Tribune,* 21 April 1901, 70.

"The Martins' Masquerade." Clipping, 25 April 1901, Cleary family scrapbooks.

"A Modern Desdemona." *Chicago Tribune,* 23 May 1901, 16.

"In the Light of a Life." *Household* (Boston), May 1901.

"The Finale of a Flirtation." *Chicago Tribune,* 23 June 1901, 66.

"Devoted to David." *Chicago Chronicle,* 16 August 1901.

"The Stepmother." *McClure's,* September 1901, 436–42. Reprinted in *Nebraska of KMC,* 164–72.

"Mission of Kitty Malone." *McClure's,* November 1901, 88–96.

"The Destiny of Delores." Clipping, 1901, Cleary family scrapbooks.

1902

"Apropos of Story-Writing." *Writer,* 15, no. 1 (January 1902): 8. Reprinted as "Apropos of Story Writing" in *Nebraska of KMC,* 193–94.

"A Happy New-Year." *Home World,* February 1902.

"The Strange Lady." *American,* 24 March 1902.

"The Day's Disguise." *Leslie's* 53, no. 5 (March 1902): 518–23.

" 'And the Joy That Came at Last!': A Decoration Day Story."
Chicago Tribune, 30 May 1902, 13.

"Turn of the Tide." *Chicago Daily News,* 4 June 1902, 9.

"Under False Colors" [Vera Valentine, pseud.]. *Chicago Tribune*
(First Prize "Vacation Story"), 22 June 1902, 41.

"The Story behind a Personal Advertisement: 'A Personal.' "
Chicago Tribune, 31 August 1902, 43.

"The Children's Hour." Clipping from *Home World,* 1, Cleary
family scrapbooks.

"Cooking Over." Clipping from *Home World,* 25, Cleary family
scrapbooks.

"The Literary Mother." Clipping from *Home World,* Cleary
family scrapbooks.

"The New Furniture." Clipping from *Home World,* Cleary family
scrapbooks.

"Notes about House Decoration." Clipping from *Home World,*
1902, Cleary family scrapbooks.

"Plants." Clipping from *Home World,* Cleary family scrapbooks.

"Some Charming Interiors." Clipping from *Home World,* Cleary
family scrapbooks.

"The Uses of Denim." Clipping from *Home World,* 10, Cleary
family scrapbooks.

"Old English Cookery." Unpublished ms., ca. 1902, Cleary family
collection.

1903

"In Love and War." *New Orleans States,* 24 April 1903.

"The Statelier Mansion." *Cosmopolitan,* November 1903, 106–
12.

"As Ithers [*sic*] See Us: State Street Stories." Unpublished ms.,
ca. 1903, Cleary family collection.

"Contentment of a Kind: State Street Stories." Unpublished ms.,
ca. 1903, Cleary family collection.

"Wistful Wisteria." Unpublished ms., ca. 1903, Cleary family
collection.

1904

"The Vanreith's [*sic*] Visitor." Clipping, 8 April 1904, Cleary family scrapbooks.
"By the Merest Chance." *Chicago Daily News*, 18 April 1904, 11.
"A Leap Year Prerogative." *Chicago Daily News*, 23 April 1904, 12.
"A Receipt for Rugs." *Chicago Daily News*, 26 April 1904, 12.
"Aunt Miraldi's Ring." *Chicago Daily News*, 27 April 1904, 12.
"A Matinee Idol." *Chicago Daily News*, 29 April 1904, 12.
"A Little Luncheon." *Chicago Daily News*, 30 April 1904, 11.
"An Easter Escapade." Clipping, April 1904, Cleary family scrapbooks.
"Vivian's Valentine." *Chicago Daily News*, 2 May 1904, 13.
"Proof Positive." *Chicago Daily News*, 5 May 1904, 12.
"With Easter Lilies." *Chicago Daily News*, 12 May 1904, 12.
"Denniston's Dissolution [Disillusion]." *Chicago Daily News*, 14 May 1904, 9.
"Pity to Love Is Akin." *Chicago Daily News*, 18 May 1904, 11.
"An Apostle of Culture." *Chicago Daily News*, 20 May 1904, 12.
"A Going Away Gown." *Chicago Daily News*, 27 May 1904, 12.
"Price Pandora Paid." *Chicago Daily News*, 8 June 1904, 12.
"Her Graduating Gown." *Chicago Daily News*, 15 June 1904, 14.
"From Peril to Peace." *Chicago Daily News*, 24 June 1904, 12.
"The Rose of Romance." *The Red Book: A Short Story Magazine*, July 1904, 383–87.
"Is It Mornin'?" Clipping, 3 July 1904, Cleary family scrapbooks.
"Charlie." *Chicago Daily News*, 20 July 1904, 9.
"The Miracle That Happened." *Chicago Daily News*, 29 July 1904, 11.
"Impulse of the Moment." *Chicago Daily News*, 6 August 1904, 9.
"Being Good—For Something." *Chicago Record Herald*, 21 August 1904.
"Disciples of the Little." *Chicago Record Herald*, 21 August 1904.
"From Over the Sea." *Chicago Daily News*, 21 October 1904, 12.

"A Halloween Ghost." *Chicago Daily News,* 29 October 1904, 10.

"A Twentieth Century Cinderella." *Chicago Daily News,* 2 November 1904, 12.

"Buttercups and Daisies." *Chicago Daily News,* 3 November 1904, 12.

"A Forward Young Person." *Chicago Daily News,* 19 November 1904, 10.

"When the Mist Cleared." *Chicago Daily News,* 28 November 1904, 9.

"By Breezes Blown." *Chicago Daily News,* 29 November 1904, 12.

"A Willful Widow." *Chicago Daily News,* 9 December 1904, 12.

"Little Lovers." *Sunday Magazine,* 18 December 1904.

"Kitty's Christmas Box." *Chicago Daily News,* 22 December 1904, 12.

"At the Price of Pride." Unpublished ms., ca. 1904, Cleary family collection.

"Cophetua to Date." Clipping, 1904, Cleary family scrapbooks.

"Her Society Craze." Clipping, 1904, Cleary family scrapbooks.

"Magic Melody." Clipping, 1904, Cleary family scrapbooks.

1905

"Keziah." *Chicago Daily News,* 5 January 1905, 14.

"A House Built of Cards." *Sunday Magazine,* 22 January 1905, 13.

"The Double Stratagem." *Chicago Daily News,* 7 February 1905, 9.

"A Proposal to Twins." *Chicago Daily News,* 25 February 1905, 11.

"Her Fellow Traveler." *Chicago Daily News,* 8 March 1905, 11.

"A Midwinter Walk." *Chicago Daily News,* 9 March 1905, 12.

"An Automobile Accident." *Chicago Daily News,* 16 March 1905, 12.

"Bertie's Betrayal." *Chicago Daily News,* 18 March 1905, 10.

"How Judge Dunne Began Winning: Stern Jurist Is Fond Father." *Chicago Examiner,* 23 March 1905, 4.

"Suitors of Serena." *Chicago Daily News,* 24 March 1905, 10.

"Judge Dunne Ideal Husband and Father." *Chicago American*, 2
    April 1905.
"Mrs. Blayne's Blunder." *Chicago Daily News*, 4 April 1905, 12.
"Not Written on the List." *Chicago Tribune*, 16 April 1905.
"Easter Eggs." *Chicago Daily News*, 18 April 1905, 12.
"The Day Between" (poem). *Youth's Companion*, 20 April 1905,
    194.
"On the Highway." *Chicago Daily News*, 29 April 1905, 13.
"Patty's Pumpkin Pie." Clipping, 1905, Cleary family scrapbooks.
"The Unsolved Problem." Unpublished ms., ca. 1905, Cleary
    family collection.
"About Being Super-Sensitive." Unpublished manuscript, ca.
    1905, Cleary family collection.

1908

"My Castle in Spain" (poem). *Sunday Magazine*, 31 May 1908.

1909

"Midnight Mass under Three Flags." *Extension*, January 1909,
    13–14.
"As One of These" (poem). *Extension*, February 1909.
"The Belated Pension." *Extension*, February 1909, 13–14.
"The Rath of Garryvenus." *Extension*, April 1909.
"The Only Son of His Mother." Clipping, June 1909, Cleary
    family scrapbooks.
"A Witch of the Wild." *Extension*, June 1909.
"The Things We Eat." *Extension*, August 1909.

1910

"Culture and Cooking." *Extension*, February 1910.
"The Patience of Peter." *Extension*, February 1910, 8.
"Cooking an Exact Science." *Extension*, March 1910.
"A Woman's Privilege." *Extension*, March 1910, 7–8, 22–23.
"Compassion" (poem). *Extension*, August 1910.
"A Western Lullaby" (poem). *Extension*, August 1910.
"The Magic Circle" (poem). *Extension*, ca. 1910.
"The Singer" (poem). *Extension*, ca. 1910.
"A Thought in Failure" (poem). *Extension*, ca. 1910.

1912

"An Old Fashioned Mother and Wife." *Extension,* September 1912.

1914

"Not Found Wanting." *Chicago Post,* 17 February 1914.
"When Peter Helped." *Chicago Post,* 28 July 1914.

1935

"Kipling" (poem). *Kipling Journal,* December 1935, 126–30.

UNDOCUMENTED STORIES

The following stories found in the Cleary family scrapbooks are known to have been written by Cleary, but I have not been able to verify any publication data for them: "An Elevator Accident," "An Error of Judgment," "Apropos of Royalty," "As Others See Us," "A Beauty Born," "A Bit of a Blunder," "At Harvest," "At the Price of Pride: A Thanksgiving Story," "A Bag of Old Coins," "The Boy across the Street," "Brandon's Heiress," "A Desperate Dilemma," "Dotty Dimple's Diplomacy," "Edna Nelson's Thanksgiving," "For Rent," "The Gordon Girls' Great-Grandmother," "An Heiress to Millions," "His Last Love," "His Terrible Tests," "The Horse's Prayer," "A Lady of the Lake," "Leafarden," "Lennie Stafford's Valentine," "The Letter That Went," "Little Lovers," "Love's Blunders," "Maida's Music Master," "Mr. Granger," "Mrs. Belford's Boy," "Mrs. Meagher's Piano," "Mrs. Merton's Mirror," "One Bad Little Boy," "Patricia's Picnic," "A Rainy Day," "Reeva's Romance," "A Resurrected Romance," "Rita's Recompense," "Rosine's Romance," "The Secret of a Screen," "A Singular Situation," "A Successful Stratagem," "Sylvia's Storm Coat," "Their Christmas Guest," "Three Pretty Prisoners," "A Timely Discovery," "Told by Telephone," "An Unavoidable Delay," "Uncertain, Coy, and Hard to Please," and "The Valentine Tommy Sent."

Index